CALIFORNIA SERIES IN PUBLIC AN

MØØØØØ5962

The California Series in Public Anthropology en.,......... ... .
engaged intellectual. It continues anthropology's commitment to being an ethnographic
witness, to describing, in human terms, how life is lived beyond the borders of many readers' experiences. But it also adds a commitment, through ethnography, to reframing the
terms of public debate—transforming received, accepted understandings of social issues
with new insights, new framings.

Series Editor: Robert Borofsky (Hawaii Pacific University)

*Contributing Editors: Philippe Bourgois (University of Pennsylvania), Paul Farmer
(Partners in Health), Alex Hinton (Rutgers University), Carolyn Nordstrom (University
of Notre Dame), and Nancy Scheper-Hughes (UC Berkeley)*

University of California Press Editor: Naomi Schneider

I Did It to Save My Life

The publisher gratefully acknowledges the generous support of the Anne G. Lipow Endowment Fund for Social Justice and Human Rights of the University of California Press Foundation, which was established by Stephen M. Silberstein.

I Did It to Save My Life

Love and Survival in Sierra Leone

Catherine E. Bolten

UNIVERSITY OF CALIFORNIA PRESS

Berkeley · Los Angeles · London

University of California Press, one of the most distinguished university presses in the United States, enriches
lives around the world by advancing scholarship in the
humanities, social sciences, and natural sciences. Its activities are supported by the UC Press Foundation and by
philanthropic contributions from individuals and institu-
tions. For more information, visit www.ucpress.edu.

University of California Press
Berkeley and Los Angeles, California

University of California Press, Ltd.
London, England

Library of Congress Cataloging-in-Publication Data

A catalog record for this book is available from the
Library of Congress.

ISBN 978-0-520-27378-8 (cloth : alk. paper)
ISBN 978-0-520-27379-5 (pbk. : alk. paper)

Manufactured in the United States of America

21 20 19 18 17 16 15 14 13 12
10 9 8 7 6 5 4 3 2 1

In keeping with a commitment to support environmen-
tally responsible and sustainable printing practices, UC
Press has printed this book on Rolland Enviro100, a
100% post-consumer fiber paper that is FSC certified,
deinked, processed chlorine-free, and manufactured with
renewable biogas energy. It is acid-free and EcoLogo
certified.

For Mabinty Tenneh
1998–2012
The radiant smile next door

Contents

Illustrations

Acknowledgments

In a 1999 article reviewing ethnographic work on war in the twentieth century, Catherine Lutz states, "Ethnography in its modern form has lived through a century of wars, global and local, hot and cold. It has been at once an indifferent bystander, engaged witness, survivor and soldier in the battles and war preparations that have pockmarked the historical terrain that is being imaginatively reviewed and rearranged as the arbitrary date of the new millennium arrives." She notes that ethnography's "finer impulses" of truth and beauty seem mocked and fragmented by war; the ethnographic project has therefore left as its aim only a search to restore good. Over ten years later, I hope I am answering her challenge, specifically by giving survivors the space to narrate their memories, and highlighting the emotional framework and content of how people live—hopefully, courageously—through war and aftermath. What they narrate is *truth,* and the fearlessness of their defense of their social world is the essence of beauty.

This book would not have been possible without the contributions of many people, to all of whom I owe my unfailing gratitude. In Sierra Leone, I must begin with Khadija Bah, without whom this project would have never left the ground. For their assistance with my first trip to Makeni in 2003, I would like to thank Colin Nursey and Martin Bamin. To Martin I owe extra thanks for his unfailing support throughout the years of the project. In Freetown, I am grateful to John and Ernest Sisay, Ziad and Ione Haroun, Kapri Kargbo, and

Colonel Hugh Blackman for their friendship and assistance with logistics, and to Abu Koroma and Mr. Moore of the Fourah Bay College Archives. I would like to extend a special thank you to the members of IMATT SL in 2003–5 for medical support, transport, and friendship. In Makeni, my heartfelt gratitude goes out first to Mohamed Kallon and Idriss Conteh, to my Krio teacher Foday Mansaray, and to my first roommate, J. P. Kamara. I would also like to thank Paramount Chief Bai Shebora Kasanga, RSLAF Four Brigade Commander Colonel F. K. Kamara, and the members of the town council for their unwavering support. My research would not have been possible without the friendship and assistance of Father Daniel Samura at Our Lady of Fatima, Dr. Patrick Turay at Holy Spirit Hospital, and Father Joe Turay and his colleagues at the University of Makeni. May our ties grow ever stronger.

In the United States, my primary thanks goes to Carolyn Nordstrom, who bravely read and commented on the entire first draft. I must also thank my colleagues at the Joan B. Kroc Institute for International Peace Studies, especially Christian Davenport, for commenting on early draft chapters. My heartfelt thanks go out to my colleagues in the anthropology department at the University of Notre Dame, especially Susan Blum, for thoughtful advice and encouragement. I also extend my thanks to Rob Borofsky of the California Series in Public Anthropology and my editor Naomi Schneider at University of California Press for their fortitude and encouragement. It is because they saw potential in the book proposal that this project has reached fruition. The patience and helpful comments of Catherine Besteman, Melissa Caldwell, and an anonymous reviewer for University of California Press helped sharpen the focus and analysis. I also extend my gratitude to Caroline Knapp for copyediting the manuscript, and to Anne Just for providing the index. Special thanks to Daniel Puskar for reading an early draft of the proposal and finding its true direction.

This research was made possible by generous grants from the University of Michigan Center for Afro-American and African Studies in 2003, the U.S. Fulbright Fellowship Program and the NSEP David Boren Fellowship in 2004–5, the United States Institute of Peace Jennings Randolph Dissertation Fellowship Program in 2005–6, and most recently by the University of Notre Dame Institute for Scholarship in the Liberal Arts and the Ford Family Program in Human Development. The University of Notre Dame Institute for Scholarship in the Liberal Arts also provided funding towards production of the index.

Finally and certainly not least, I must thank my family. My parents, Joe and Doris Bolten, have been unwavering in their support of this project, as has my sister Laura Sinquefield. I must acknowledge the patience of my stepdaughters, Molly and Rosie, who always understood when I had to slip away to write for a few hours. The most important acknowledgement goes to my husband, Neil MacDonald, with whom everything seems possible. It is to him, and to my dear neighbor Mabinty, that I dedicate this book.

Acronyms

AFRC	Armed Forces Revolutionary Council
APC	All People's Congress
DDR	Disarmament, Demobilization, and Reintegration (program)
ECOMOG	Economic Community of West African States Monitoring Group
ECOWAS	Economic Community of West African States
NCDDR	National Commission for Disarmament, Demobilization, and Reintegration
NPRC	National Provisional Ruling Council
RSLAF	Republic of Sierra Leone Armed Forces
RUF	Revolutionary United Front
RUFP	Revolutionary United Front Party
SLA	Sierra Leone Army
SLPP	Sierra Leone People's Party
UDP	United Democratic Party
UNAMSIL	United Nations Assistance Mission to Sierra Leone

Timeline of the Key Events of War and Aftermath, 1991–2003

1991

March
Foday Sankoh and the Revolutionary United Front (RUF) invade Sierra Leone from Liberia. For the next several years, the war remains confined to the southern and eastern regions.

1992

April
President Joseph Momoh (APC) is ousted in a coup of junior army officers; Captain Valentine Strasser is later announced as the head of the National Provisional Ruling Council (NPRC).

1996

January
Maada Bio seizes command of the NPRC in a bloodless coup.

March
Tejan Kabbah wins a democratic election. His Sierra Leone People's Party (SLPP) takes power and Deputy Minister of Defense Sam Hinga Norman moves the civil militias into an official role fighting the RUF alongside the army.

November   The first peace agreement, the Abidjan Accords, is negotiated between the government and the RUF.

1997

May   Combined RUF and army elements march into Free-town and overthrow Tejan Kabbah's government. Kabbah and his cabinet flee to Guinea. The Armed Forces Revolutionary Council (AFRC), with Major Johnny Paul Koroma at its head, seizes control of the country. Combined rebel and mutinous army forces deploy throughout the country. Kabbah, from exile, announces the disbanding of the army.

1998

February   Troops from the Economic Community of West African States (ECOWAS) seize the capital city Free-town from the AFRC after fierce fighting. The AFRC flee up the highway into the bush northeast of Makeni.

April   Kabbah appoints Nigerian General Maxwell Khobe head of the armed forces; Nigerian troops deploy throughout the country.

December   Combined forces of the RUF and former AFRC members invade Makeni from the countryside and forcibly occupy the town, chasing Nigerian troops to Mile 91.

1999

January   The combined forces of the RUF and former AFRC members who bypassed Makeni march to Freetown, overwhelming ECOWAS forces. Thousands are killed as ECOWAS and the new Sierra Leonean army re-group to push the rebels out.

January–May   Various factions of the RUF and former AFRC fight for control of Makeni, a conflict known locally as the *infights*. General Issa Sesay of the RUF emerges the winner.

July Foday Sankoh and Tejan Kabbah officially sign the Lomé Peace Accords, ending the war, giving blanket amnesty to RUF fighters, and establishing the existence of the United Nations Assistance Mission to Sierra Leone (UNAMSIL).

2000

January UNAMSIL begins construction on combatant disarmament centers, one of which is built in Makeni.

May RUF troops attack the Makeni disarmament center, killing fifty peacekeepers.

June Tejan Kabbah announces that because Makeni is home to only "rebels and rebel collaborators," he will use the army's gunship to bomb the town.

June–October Gunship attacks on Makeni spark a mass exodus from the town.

November The government and the RUF sign a ceasefire agreement in Abuja.

2001

May The National Commission for Disarmament, Demobilization, and Reintegration (NCDDR) establishes an office and new disarmament center in Makeni.

2002

May Issa Sesay loses his campaign for a seat in parliament in national elections, which also return Tejan Kabbah to the presidency. Sesay dismantles all official RUF offices in Makeni and claims an end to the RUF in Makeni.

2003

March The new Special Court for Sierra Leone indicts Charles Taylor, Foday Sankoh, Issay Sesay, and nine others on charges of war crimes.

2012

May   The Hague's Special Court for Sierra Leone convicts Charles Taylor of eleven counts of aiding and abetting the RUF, including planning the Makeni invasion. Taylor is sentenced to fifty years in prison for war crimes that include supplying and encouraging rebels in Sierra Leone in a campaign of terror, involving murder, rape, sexual slavery, and the conscription of children under the age of fifteen.

Note on Sources

The material for this book is comprised of interviews that I conducted one-on-one with individual residents of the town of Makeni. After a significant amount of time getting to know someone (often months), I would ask permission to sit down together to conduct a life history interview, a conversation in which I guided them through questions, beginning with their early childhood and moving through significant events to arrive at the present.

Each person who tells their story here assented to having our conversation tape-recorded. As we spoke I also took notes on their answers, and followed up with clarifying questions once they had finished speaking about a particular event. The quoted text presented within the chapters is an edited version of the material we covered in these interviews, which often took three hours or more and contained the hesitations, repetitions, tangents, and banter of normal speech. In the editing process, I enforced a certain amount of chronological discipline on the interview transcripts, which often jumped around between events and timeframes. However, in order to remain true to the chaos of memory—often reflecting the chaos of war—I left some of these idiosyncrasies intact, giving the reader a feel for the rawness of these memories, even years after the fact.

In order to protect the privacy of the living and the dead, except in the case of famous figures mentioned in Sierra Leonean history and current events, all names have been changed to pseudonyms and many characteristic individual details have been altered to prevent easy identification. I conducted the primary interviews with each of my sources (identified here by their pseudonyms) on the following dates and in the following locations around Makeni:

Captain Mohamed Mansaray (soldier): June 3, 2005 in the jungle warfare classroom of Teko Barracks, Teko Road

David (rebel): June 4, 2005 in the offices of a community organization, Baio Street

Alimamy (student): September 1, 2004 in the Reconcile Café

Kadiatu (trader): June 13, 2005 in her stall in the lorry park

Adama (evangelist): May 4, 2005 in her home in the Lookintown neighborhood

Musa (father): September 17, 2004 in my home in the Lookintown neighborhood

Michael Kamara (politician): May 10, 2005 in the town council chambers on Station Road

When I returned to Makeni in May 2010, I sat down for conversation once again with the individuals who were still living in town: Alimamy, Kadiatu, Musa, and Michael Kamara, the last of whom I conversed with over the phone. Adama had passed away; David had returned to his home in the south; and Captain Mansaray was working as a contractor in Iraq.

Enough time has passed since I conducted the initial interviews that new interviews would likely reveal new information, altered interpretations, and changes in how events were remembered on the part of everyone I spoke to. Rather than capture "history," this book seeks instead to reveal how, just a few years after the war, people remembered the past, positioned themselves in the present, and thought about the future. Be that as it may, any inaccuracies in the text are my own.

Sierra Leonean Emotions, Sierra Leonean War

N: My mom and I were residing in a village very close to the border with Liberia. And when the rebels crossed into Sierra Leone I was captured. I was captured by the Revolutionary United Front of Sierra Leone, the RUF.

CB: *How old were you when you were captured?*
N: I was . . . I was . . . I was sixteen years old when I was captured.

CB: *Did they try to recruit you or did they just take you forcibly?*
N: Um, anyway I was captured. But this ideology they gave me, I actually accepted it and turned to them. Because in that situation, you had no alternative but to just accept and adjust to that situation. So I was able to accept, but there was also nowhere for me to go, so I joined them. So from 1991 up to the year 2000 I was with them.

This rebel, whom I call Noah, has a typical recruitment story among former combatants with the Revolutionary United Front (RUF), which waged a decade-long war of terror in the Sierra Leonean countryside. Young people were seized from villages, fed a revolutionary ideology, and given a "choice" either to stay with the rebels or to watch their families be slaughtered. Those who escaped were often apprehended by the army or by civil militias and killed as rebels. Those who remained survived, as Noah explained, by "turning to them," becoming part of a family forged within the RUF, developing bonds with other fighters and captives that endured long after the end of war.

I spoke to Noah, who wore sunglasses to cover scars from a shrapnel injury that destroyed his right eye, in a room surrounded by his RUF *brothers*—a Krio term for unrelated individuals whose friendships, in this case, were forged during the war—who had gathered to discuss their lives. Noah revealed that he had opportunities during the war to break with the rebels, but chose not to. When his damaged eye became infected, RUF leader Foday Sankoh took him to a hospital in Cote d'Ivoire for surgery. He returned to the RUF fold upon being discharged.

"Why did you go back?" I queried.

"Well, I was with Foday Sankoh the whole time. He brought me with him when he went for peace talks so I could have this surgery. He was there for a year for the peace treaties [in 1996] and to rest. So after I left the hospital I joined him."

"You stayed with him for a year?"

"He was my *pa,* he brought me to Cote d'Ivoire to save my sight. I stayed with him."

A young rebel affectionately refers to the movement's leader as his *pa,* even after he was brutally kidnapped into the movement's ranks and suffered debilitating injuries during the ruthless war it waged. Noah had a chance to escape but chose to stay, and when we spoke, three years after the war ended, had decided against returning to his natal village and was instead living openly with other former rebels in the town they occupied for three years. Was he immoral? Brainwashed? Evil? This interview, among many others, illuminated fundamental questions about how people make choices during war, and how they think about and narrate these choices in the aftermath. Noah was frank that he had been "captured" against his will and had become a rebel as a survival tactic, and yet he stayed, loyally, with his commander though he had opportunities for escape. How do we parse out the basis upon which he made these decisions, justified them, and later came to narrate them? Noah's story of his survival choices, how he rationalized those choices, and then transformed the relationships they engendered into positive, life-sustaining connections lies at the heart of a new understanding of the Sierra Leonean war.

In this book, I investigate the importance of understanding Sierra Leonean practices of *love*—a Krio term expressing the bonds of mutual identification, sacrifice, and need between individuals and groups of people—to comprehending how the war unfolded and why people made decisions, such a staying with a brutal rebel leader, that appear contrary to tenets of both survival and morality. *Love* is a Sierra Leonean concept of material loyalty—relationships forged and sustained in complex, often compassionate acts of resource exchange—and though its primacy is reinforced through serious social sanctions, it is constantly in danger of being usurped by greed. Greed is called *eating*—the hoarding rather than the sharing of resources. *Eating* inspires fear and anger in those affected, as their very survival may be threatened by it. In pursuing the lives they desire, individuals negotiate between these two extremes at the same time as they balance the competing needs of multiple relationships. As individuals prioritize some relationships over others, nurturing some people more than others, betrayals result, which trigger a rash of responses from confrontation to vengeance.

Recent Sierra Leonean history is characterized by extremes of *love* and *eating*. In the years before the war, the elite *ate* among themselves and cultivated *love* among important people—traditional leaders, the intelligentsia—by variously coopting and threatening them. Most people were not important enough for inclusion on any terms, leaving them feeling betrayed and alienated. Foday Sankoh preyed on alienated youth as he built the RUF. Whether they joined out of *love* or fear, many rebels became anxious to destroy "the rotten system." Soldiers, angry at government neglect and betrayals, initiated coups in 1992 and 1997, taking power and resources for themselves. The occupation of Makeni, the town in which I worked, endured for three years because of an ideological standoff in which the government argued that residents *loved* the RUF more than the nation. *Love* is a foundational tenet of social personhood in Sierra Leone, thus it informed individual actions and influenced major events during the war.

No matter what path they navigated in surviving the war, every person—rebel, soldier, trader, or student—made choices based on the rubric of *love*. Nothing, not even violence, exists without reference to the "parent culture" of fundamental cultural practices.[1] As anthropologist Veena Das explains, "There is a mutual absorption of the violent and the ordinary . . . events are always attached to the ordinary as if there were tentacles that reach out from the everyday and anchor the event to it in some specific ways."[2] The damaging effects of eating are as much a part of everyday life as is *love*, and violence can be merely a matter of numbers and chance: when too many people have too little, the smallest spark will ignite a blaze. Though the war emerged from a constellation of factors—including the ambitions of RUF leader Foday Sankoh and warlord Charles Taylor in neighboring Liberia—it was enabled by mass alienation from a system dominated by elite consumption. Once set in motion, its character was defined largely by *love* and *eating*, and these are the same practices through which rebuilding occurred. As individuals balance competing relationships and seek success, there is ever-present potential for betrayal and exclusion—or *eating*—making violence as great a possibility as peace.

THE INTIMATE RELATIONSHIP BETWEEN VIOLENCE AND THE ORDINARY IN AFRICA

There are many accounts of African wars exploring how people understand and negotiate life when assaulted constantly by the ravages of fighting and despair. Many accounts emphasize how people strive to create a meaningful world in the midst of chaos as a way to resist the tendency of violence, in situations when war seems to have no end, to become the "normal" world. Responses to violence are informed by one's worldview and cultural practices; in essence people comprehend war, negotiate violence, and seek a better life through cultural understandings of what a good world looks like. Whether emphasizing food production, ritual practice, aesthetic landscapes, or belonging, wars are endured and managed on the intimate scale of individual survival, through the same practices by which people live in ordinary times.

Carolyn Nordstrom discovered that civilians in Mozambique were determined to keep life as "normal" as possible during the war, by planting crops even if they would be ravaged, peddling fish though it meant crossing minefields to find customers, and using traditional healing rituals to "take the war out of people" who had been exposed to fighting.[3] Civilians mired in the fighting between the ruling Frelimo party and the Renamo rebels refused to allow their fear of continued violence to overcome their determination to reject war in their own lives, by doggedly insisting that if a house is burned it must be rebuilt, if a field is plundered it must be sown, if a child is seized by rebels, it must be embraced upon its return. Nordstrom described acts, both courageous and dignified, of carving out a space where the rightness of a peaceful world is asserted in the midst of chaos by undertaking simple, everyday actions of productive living.

Sverker Finnström found that in northern Uganda, where the Lord's Resistance Army has waged a devastating war since 1986, individuals sought "good surroundings" in which to make a viable future for themselves, just as they struggled constantly in "bad surroundings" in which peace and balance were not possible, even during lulls in the fighting.[4] People sought good surroundings by increasing their attention to the spiritual realm and reasserting their ties to history and the wider world. They paid obsessive attention to ancestral shrines within family compounds, always building, always visiting them. By calmly reasserting the continuum of the past and the present, living and dead, they reinforced for themselves the rightness of their lives, in a sense offering up to God the assertion that they belonged in the world. In maintaining their place in an aligned cosmos of past and present, people were better able to govern chaos.

In the small West African country of Guinea-Bissau, young militia members fighting in the civil war in the 1990s engaged in a process Henrik Vigh described as "social navigation."[5] Every choice a young fighter made was informed by the will to become an adult with prospects and possibilities in an environment that was itself constantly in motion, as the power of government and junta forces waxed and waned during the war and its aftermath. For Vigh, the social networks through which youth understood their chances for a "sweet life" were uncertain terrains whose own fortunes rose and fell with the smallest turn of war. Youth chose their networks and tied their prospects to those of their *parente,* their ideological kin, and through *dubriagem,* the Guinean practice of craftily "making do," worked towards a good future. Thus were the fortunes of the youth tied—whether during war or peace—to the intricacies of the networks and emotions governing their world.

To write about Sierra Leoneans struggling to maintain a viable world by emphasizing the ordinary would contribute little to our understanding of war. People everywhere gain mastery over the terror of war by undertaking the most banal, normal activities by which they order their lives, whether this is manifested as food production, cosmology, or social bonding. What I emphasize here is that the cultural practices of love governed the country's descent into war, were deeply implicated in the terror tactics employed by factions, informed survival tactics, and were the foundation on which individuals recreated a meaningful world. More than helping people cope with, understand, or master war, love was the *logic* of war and is the logic of the ordinary. According to their own narratives, what was extraordinary about wartime practices was the emphasis people placed on their will to transform relationships initiated out of fear—fear of being killed, of not getting enough food, of being alone in the world—into love.

These personal relationships were consistently prioritized over all others, even over calls by the president to gain victory for the nation by crushing the rebels. Thus was love "naked": intimate, stripped of pretense, and based on interpersonal bonds. No one accepted fear as the governing trajectory of their lives, nor did they accept bending to the will of the powerful—those most often guilty of eating—to determine their primary relationships. Through their work on their relationships, they worked on other people, attempting to transform those who ate into people who nurture. The question that remains is whether the will to do so remains in ordinary times.

I hope with this book to shed new light on the war in Sierra Leone, but also to open the possibility of rethinking the notion that emotions, morality, and decision-making in war are separated from ordinary life. It is impossible to understand the particular nationalism of the Israeli settler without understanding cultural Judaism. It is equally difficult to grasp the rise of the Taliban without appreciating the competing allegiances to which Afghanis have been subjected for hundreds of years. It behooves us not to assume that we understand love and loyalty, anger or grief because we assume emotions are "universal." Emotions are cultural practices emerging from and embedded in long histories of struggle and survival. Emotional practices possess cultural logic and shape the course of traumatic events, just as they bind those events to the "ordinary" life of aftermath. Understanding these practices creates the possibility of understanding the intricacies of what peace means in places experiencing war, and therefore how to enable and nurture it.

LOVE AS SOCIAL IMPERATIVE

The relationship between the young, half-blind Noah and Foday Sankoh comes into focus when, in Noah's narrative, he moves from "accepting the situation" to staying with Sankoh because he was his "Pa." Noah, who could have easily blamed Sankoh for his traumatic kidnapping, his years on the run in the bush, and his devastating eye injury, spoke positively of his commander. Here was a relationship forged in fear and inequality, and yet for Noah, by enabling potentially sight-saving surgery (whether Sankoh was being magnanimous or calculating), this relationship had transformed into one of love. The surgery was what Noah needed most, even if it required relatively little of Sankoh himself. And yet Sankoh gained a loyal cadre, proving his status as "Pa." Both Sankoh and Noah worked on each other, Sankoh to prove his moral status as an individual who cultivated love, and Noah to inspire the love that sustained his life.

It is by assessing their relationships that Sierra Leoneans understand and judge how well or badly life is going: are people nourished and supported, or are they thin and "lost" to each other? Love is an overwhelming sense of loyalty, inspired by one's emotional ownership of another, an ownership which is predicated on, in Andrew Oldenquist's words, "the object of loyalty possessing features that make it worth having."[6] What makes people "worth having" in Sierra Leone is, ideally, their need for nurturing, and their desire to reciprocate via relationships of mutual responsibility and generosity that contribute to flourishing and happiness by spreading risk and the unknown across people through space and time. Nonideally, individuals are "worth having" because of their resource monopoly; in such cases others risk their own survival if they do not ingratiate themselves with that person.

In Sierra Leone, a good person *loves* many individuals, has relationships of gratitude, obligation, nurturing, care, and mutual sacrifice. More than mere romance, love is a cultural practice, existing only as people *do* love rather than just *feel* love.[7] Sierra Leoneans understand and evoke love through the work they put into nurturing each other, to bringing people closer to them through their willingness to make their obligations reciprocal: "I love my brother so much," explained one former combatant with respect to his best friend, "even if he has only a few coins and I have not eaten today, he will give me his money. And when I have a little food, I share with him." Love is investment, trust, and interdependence. It is how people understand their fellows as worth having in their lives. One cannot love another without actively contributing to that person's survival, often making sacrifices on behalf of that person, knowing they are willing to do the same.

Loyalties are "nested," in Oldenquist's words, meaning that individuals have multiple loyalties at once, and these loyalties often compete with each other or are weighed against each other. Inevitably, someone loses. Not all relationships are made equal, and individuals are often forced to choose between them. Love of family is different than love of country; for example, the president was outraged when Makeni residents remained in town with the rebels, prioritizing their families' survival over the thriving of the nation, and bombed the town as punishment. Soldiers depended on salaries and rice from the government, and initiated a ferocious coup in 1997 after the government transferred these benefits to the civil militias. Betrayal is a deadly serious matter, resulting in the injured party punishing the transgressor or taking by force that which is no longer offered willingly.

In this social world, people are furious over the smallest betrayals and brood over broken relationships. Both actions speak to the vigorous defense of the need for balance, of maintaining harmony by giving and taking what is fair and necessary rather than what is desired.[8] People narrate the importance of working on their relationships even if resources are scarce. Love and care cannot be separated conceptually or in practice; love *is* care, it is one's explicit enhancement of another individual's life. People believe in love. They want care to be acknowledged, appreciated, and reciprocated in kind. Betrayals must be addressed and rectified, lest the system be tipped in favor of eating, of competitive, individual greed.

THE DESIRE FOR PERMANENCE AND THE WILL TO EAT

The ambivalence of a system based on mutual nurturing is evident in a symbol known to all Sierra Leoneans: the cotton tree.[9] When I learned Krio, the lingua franca of Sierra Leone, I bought a book of proverbs, and with my neighbor worked carefully through words and meanings. Among the moral lessons conveyed in proverbs, the cotton tree was the primary symbol of human aspiration, of the will to be *big*. It is a massive, statuesque tree, soaring in a perfect arc of branches high above the impermanent lives of people below. To reach the heights of human possibility, one aspires to be like the cotton tree: tall, old, nurtured into a state of permanence defying the vagaries of history and fortune, and offering under its canopy shelter and security. This permanence transcends death in the legacy one leaves as an ancestor. People aspire to be revered elders, surrounded by their descendants, and to be remembered and praised in death because they nurtured many people. According to one blogger, "Since a big cotton tree of great age, presiding over any town or village, must have been witness to . . . the succeeding lives of the present and many past generations, the trees tend to be held in veneration, almost as though they might be the after-life abode of ancestors whose souls may inhabit the mysterious deep recesses . . ."[10]

The cotton tree is a prime symbol of the need for nurturing, as it cannot grow without light, water, or rich soil. Even the most robust beings depend for their survival on outside inputs, and yet, to grow so large, dwarfing other beings, the tree must consume more from its surroundings than it returns. To seek permanence is to seek to tip that balance just a little bit, to quietly maneuver a better life for one's self by seizing those small opportunities to eat, while not jeopardizing the nurturing that enables life. As individuals strive for permanence, small slips toward eating can signal potential disaster. Two of my caretakers were close friends; their relationship was cemented the day one secured a coveted NGO job for the other. Then arose the issue of a mattress that one acquired and sold without sharing the profits. I knew their friendship was in grave danger the day the mattress seller approached me, wringing his hands in despair because the other had cooked a meal and was eating alone. The situation was aggravated by the fact that he was hungry, and the other knew this. They had always shared food, and he had never imagined the relationship ending. He had spent the money from the mattress on a new pair of shoes: were these petty desires threatening a friendship, or was it more important that he be presentable at school? One must always weigh the consequences of investing in the self rather than others.

To test the boundaries between nurturing and eating is acceptable, but to swing wildly towards eating alone is not. Individuals who live alone, have few friends and do not share are feared as witches; unearthly creatures who thrive not by nurturing other people, but by consuming them in midnight acts of ritual cannibalism. A person who lives in this manner is considered inhuman, and must be expelled or killed.[11] Even if one is not feared as a witch, people who consistently eat more than they love are called *wicked*. Wicked individuals are shunned, gossiped about, and taunted. These sanctions are grounded in the belief that because an individual cannot survive without relationships, complete marginalization will coax them back into the fold.

The problem with these sanctions on wickedness arises when wicked people have external sources of nurturing. When people do not need others to survive—when they have access to aid money or diamonds, for example—the social world itself is at risk because sanctions cannot harm them.[12] This imbalance is created when individuals with multiple relationships shed the less nourishing ones because they are unnecessary. This loosens the bonds of the system itself, creating and enhancing social inequalities. The RUF gathered willing recruits early in the war by scooping up alienated rural youth who were left out of the system. Sankoh promised them socialism, in essence a return to redistribution and mutual nurturing. In the global linkages occurring with the peace process, alienation is once again a credible threat, as many possibilities exist for people to gain permanence outside of their Sierra Leonean social worlds, thus allowing them to shed their relationships. One anthropologist worked in a village struggling to recover, as local elites lobbied for better positions vis-à-vis the NGOs working there. Asking them what their biggest problem was, she was told, "We no longer love ourselves."[13] If people refuse to look to each other for their relationships, instead seeking permanence from the outside, they once again invite the violence bred by betrayal.

"WHEN THE COTTON TREE FALLS, IT IS STILL HIGHER THAN THE GRASS"

The cotton tree represents the permanence sought by everyone. However it is also symbolic of the fallibility of love as cultural practice. Part of the tree's importance is its relative rarity, symbolic of the unusual ability of one to thrive when most others do not. Sierra Leoneans recognize that not everyone achieves permanence, and that this permanence requires the skillful manipulation of relationships to one's best possible advantage. Just as people strive toward this goal, so do they fear the tendency in others, for perhaps they are being taken advantage of, if only slightly. To pursue extraordinary permanence through one's relationships is to strive to be a *big* person.

To be *big,* though sometimes a comment on one's physical girth, is to possess and manage a great number of relationships through which vast resources flow. Wealth is measured in both people and material, and historically one needed both to be *big.* Big people—chiefs, successful traders, politicians, or wealthy farmers—function ideally as a safety net for the less wealthy. It is their responsibility to ensure that others are taken care of, and they receive the steadfast loyalty of those people in return. Those in a big man's purview can rely on assistance with ventures such as marriage and education, and help during troubles such as crop failure or deaths in the family. In return they offer labor, and political and social support. This system of bigness resonates with theories of power based on popular legitimacy. For theorist Hannah Arendt, true power comes only through legitimacy, which is predicated on the will of the majority. A big person retains his status through the will of his people. If he does not nurture satisfactorily they retain the option of deserting him, and his power deserts him with them.[14]

A big man who betrays his people, for example a politician guilty of embezzlement, is at risk of the most serious sanction of all, being "pulled down." This is the act of socially and financially toppling someone who hoards success. The people most likely to "pull down" someone are those who feel they are in a relationship of mutual nurturing with that person, have themselves contributed in good faith, and are therefore entitled to share in every success. The pulling down can take many forms, from the spoiling of resources that someone secretes away instead of sharing to public shaming of an individual who is clearly wicked or "greedy" and has done their people "wrong."[15]

The quest for bigness, though a risky venture if one spreads his or her resources too thinly, is the quest for physical and symbolic permanence on a grand scale. Symbolic permanence can persist even if one fails. One of the most repeated Krio proverbs states, "*Cotin tri fɔdom tɛ, i ay pas gras,*" which means, when the cotton tree falls, it is still taller than the grass. Once a person has imprinted himself in the social world by means of a quest for permanence, he retains symbolic permanence even if he ultimately fails and is deserted. He has contributed to others' well-being, giving a symbolic bit of himself in nurturing them.[16] Many of my interlocutors emphasized this proverb when outlining the causes of the war, not because it was an explanation unto itself, but because it illustrated how bigness could be abused. According to one student, "These big men in Freetown believe they cannot be touched. They will eat facially [in front of others] because their big friends will protect them. They only have to care about themselves." Bigness and permanence are so culturally prized that, if there are no limits on what one can acquire, there are also no checks on one's ambition.

Historians of Sierra Leone have set forth myriad causative factors for the war, though the actual fighting started when Foday Sankoh crossed the Liberian border with a motley band of Sierra Leoneans and Liberians in March 1991 and attacked villages in southern Sierra Leone. Often emphasized are the greed of a few individuals, including Liberian president Charles Taylor, for the country's diamond wealth; Taylor's vengeance against Sierra Leone president Joseph Momoh after the latter sent peacekeepers to Liberia; the misplaced ambitions of violent proletarian youth for a "revolution" where they could partake in power; the well-placed ambitions of rural youth trapped in a system of institutionalized slavery that prevented them achieving adulthood; and the quest of those same rural youth to belong to a functioning system that valued them.[17] I do not believe there is one main causative factor. However, in their narratives individuals were preoccupied with the predilection of the already big—whether in Freetown or Liberia—to eat more than their share before the war.[18] Bitterness over these betrayals, alienation from the potentially rich relationships that were possible in the capital, and Foday Sankoh's willingness to manipulate these feelings in the countryside were instrumental in setting the war inexorably in motion. It is to the long history of this moment that I now turn.

FROM NURTURING TO EATING: A SHORT HISTORY OF POLITICS IN SIERRA LEONE

Sierra Leone, a nation of multiple ethnic groups, gained independence from Britain in 1961. Before departing, colonial administrators installed electoral democracy as the de facto political system, overlaying it on a local historical system of hereditary chiefdoms. There was never a sense of how well or badly democracy would mesh with traditional forms of gaining power, namely the process of becoming big through nurturing and resource distribution, though both systems emphasized support for a leader predicated on the distribution of good. Colonial administrators oversaw the election of the first Prime Minister, Sir Milton Margai, a medical doctor and member of the Mende tribe. Margai died in 1964 after three years in office, leaving little precedent for his brother Albert, who succeeded him, to follow.

Albert's primary loyalty was to his Mende tribe, a loyalty which was first manifest in his purge of all non-Mende from his cabinet. Unlike his brother, whose cabinet was comprised of the most able politicians, for Albert, politics was about looking after one's own ethnic group. He used appointments as personal favors, and balked at initiating programs and infrastructure outside of his home region. Dissatisfaction grew amongst lawmakers from the Temne and Limba tribes, who were increasingly marginalized under Albert's government. They were galvanized under the banner of the rival party, the All People's Congress (APC), in advance of the national elections in 1967, which became a referendum on Albert's mandate. The leader of the APC was former trade union leader Siaka Stevens.

After questions about the legitimacy of the elections, a coup, and a countercoup, Siaka Stevens was eventually named prime minister. It was under Stevens that politics became personal relationships writ large, with every Sierra Leonean either involved or excluded from his personal/political circle. His rule has been termed the *shadow state*.[19] The "shadow state" refers the private networks running parallel to the official state machine, where real power is revealed in the transaction of favors, which usually include state resources, for loyalty. Stevens extended his power over people who depended on resources, while at the same time allowing official state structures to decay. The shadow state resulted from Siaka Stevens's desire to circumvent love for all Sierra Leoneans in the pursuit of bigness. Instead, he ensured his political security—his big status—by concentrating care among influential people, and punishing everyone who did not aspire to be loyal, or who did not matter.

Not everyone offered Stevens their love, which spurred the adoption of more authoritarian tactics. Stevens flushed all high-ranking Mende officers from the army and replaced them with loyal Limbas. He created his own security forces from unemployed youth in Freetown, thus coopting a potential source of discord. Using IMF debt renegotiation, he finagled the transfer of a majority interest in the country's diamond mines from DeBeers, which had begun the mining industry in 1932, to his government. He then attempted to transform the country into a one-party republic, with himself as president-for-life. Several members of his own party defected in protest and formed the United Democratic Party (UDP). When it became clear to Stevens that they were undermining his support, he destroyed the party and scattered the leaders into exile.[20] Following another coup attempt, he executed several top officers in his army, and used the momentum of his intimidation tactics to establish a republic in 1971.

Over the next six years Stevens effectively ran a one-party state by cowing opposition through threats of retributive violence. When an attempt was made on the life of his prime minister in 1974, Stevens reacted by hanging eight prominent citizens.[21] University students protested violently in 1977, and Stevens reacted by forcing a referendum for a one-party state, arguing that only with unity would the country be able to function without political violence.[22] Students protested again in 1984, so Stevens shut down the universities for two months and banned those newspapers that posed vociferous challenges to his regime. By systematically eliminating individuals who threatened his power and refused cooptation into his regime, Stevens closed the door on all opposition. Lavish rewards were offered to dissidents who joined his circle; doing so often brought them out of politically induced poverty. Those who benefited from their associations with Stevens called him "Pa," the father of the nation.

Stevens was careful to distribute resources wisely, lest he undermine himself by forgetting to love his most strategically important friends. Whether or not teachers or police officers received their salaries did not matter, as their love was not critical to the stability of his state. Security was critical, however, so Stevens nurtured love among the army with lavish salaries and gifts of rice. He allowed his most loyal followers to build their own cliques within their ministries; a cabinet appointment was both lucrative and a chance to be big in one's own right. With the shadow state, Stevens revealed the dark side of love: it can be grounded in fear, rather than nurturing. His power was vested as much in his ability to take as it was to give, thus stripping people of their will to love him except as a way to maintain what little they had. Though his strategy was ruthless, it worked.

Stevens was the most successful big man in Sierra Leonean history: he amassed a huge personal fortune, gained a powerful and loyal following, transferred power to a lackey (Joseph Momoh) who protected his interests when he retired, and died wealthy without the country ever experiencing war.[23] This speaks volumes to his skill at abusing a political system and manipulating cultural practices to his own ends. Stevens gutted the official state apparatus, including its checks and balances—all real activity took place behind the scene, between a wealthy, beneficent *pa* and his loyal and grateful inner circle. Those on the outside did not matter, and their access to resources was so limited as to destroy any possibility that someone might create credible opposition. However, this did not prevent ambition entirely. After Stevens retired, a different beneficent *pa*, Foday Sankoh, emerged to take advantage of the widespread alienation felt by those who had been sidelined by the shadow state.

FROM ROTTEN SYSTEM TO EXPLOSIVE REVOLUTION

Joseph Momoh took over from Siaka Stevens upon the latter's retirement in 1985, and did nothing to alter the most grievous abuses committed by Stevens's political elite. When Stevens left office, his inner circle controlled the majority of the country's resources, and local people in the diamond- and timber-rich rural areas were bitter about the plunder of their lands. These rural areas existed in abject poverty and residents were justifiably angry. According to one army officer who was stationed in a rustic outpost in 1990, just at the cusp of war, people were agitating for change. The assassination of loathed Liberian dictator Samuel Doe prompted many to react angrily to their own president. People asked this officer, "Why can't we have a war here too?"[24] They were bitter that Momoh was content with the inertia of the Stevens regime and refused even basic reforms. They were vulnerable to anyone who appeared to offer love.

Great leaders and great nascent dictators alike seem to sense the winds of change, for better or for worse. Foday Sankoh, unfortunately for Sierra Leone, presented himself as a leader of the people who would throw out *di rotin sistem* (the rotten system) and replace it with socialism, a system that guaranteed that everyone received their fair rewards. The plan had admirers. According to a self-described fervent Communist I call Keke, who knew Sankoh at the time, "We used to talk politics, the country at large, what the APC was doing, and a lot of these things he was so pissed off about. So we decided to come together and see what we can do to reform this place."

Their conversation took place in 1985, when Sankoh was a photographer. Sankoh had been a corporal in the Sierra Leone Army but was dishonorably discharged after participating in a mutiny in 1971. Keke himself was a discouraged organic intellectual: denied higher education because of his lack of connections, he spent his time reading Marx, digging illicitly for diamonds, and writing scathing commentary on *di sistem* for newspapers. He and Sankoh conversed as part of a group of self-described revolutionaries who had contact with the Soviet Union and spent their time "educating people about socialism and how it would do good for the poor."

What frustrated Keke as much as his social exclusion from the Freetown elite was the inability of his Marxist study group to gain sympathy and recognition from the embassies of the Soviet Union, Cuba, and Libya. Colonel Qaddafi brought a group of radical students and professors from Freetown to Libya for training as revolutionaries in the early 1980s, however—in an ironic twist—he seemed to have less interest in recruiting uneducated people to the cause.[25] Excluded even from recognition as revolutionaries, according to Keke, "We decided to take it the hard way to see how best we can get what we want and do what we want to do."

The "hard way" became the Revolutionary United Front. If it seemed easy to train in Libya, gather Communist support, and pressure Momoh from there, the "hard way" involved kidnapping, looting, maiming, and murdering in the hinterlands. Why would intelligent revolutionaries take out their anger at urban excess by raping and pillaging through the dejected and impoverished countryside? Keke's explication of the logic behind the RUF was saturated with his frustrations at his inability to gain access to anything, even revolutionary groups. Those in power had no reason to want what Keke offered, therefore he had no foundation on which to seek permanence. It was as though he and his fellow outsiders had been cast out of the world that mattered.

Keke possessed the intelligence and ambition to be successful, but would never be so because he was born poor, without resource-rich relationships, far from the centers of power. Not only was every door closed to him, there was also no one person to blame, and no anger directed towards him by those people who collectively benefited from a system—the shadow state—that made his life hell, no one person at whom he could react.[26] *Di sistem* was an outrage on love, and Keke was livid about the large-scale betrayal, the abuse of the world, that his countrymen had endured. Keke lost his faith in big men as a worthy part of the social world because they were responsible for its exploitation.

The fact that the RUF attacked the same neglected, impoverished countryside from which its members hailed can be explained only by the fact that Foday Sankoh and Charles Taylor were skilled at taking advantage of frustrated youth. Sankoh and Taylor had met in Libya in the 1980s, and remained friends as Taylor plotted to seize control of Liberia by overthrowing Samuel Doe. Taylor's war in Liberia sent thousands of refugees into Sierra Leone, further stretching the country's delicate financial situation. Momoh contributed peacekeepers to an ECOWAS (Economic Community of West African States) force in Liberia, prompting Taylor to announce that Sierra Leone had thus made itself a legitimate target of violence.[27] Sankoh warned Momoh over the BBC news that Momoh had ninety days to leave office or face a revolution; the RUF invaded Sierra Leone from Liberia nineteen days later. Speaking from Taylor's base in Liberia, Sankoh then announced over the radio that his people's struggle had begun. Though no clearer details emerged of the motives of Taylor and Sankoh, there can be no doubt that they felt the atmosphere was ripe for taking advantage of the instability that Momoh had ensured through dogged adherence to the shadow state.

The only way Sankoh could gain a foothold for the RUF was by attacking the neglected and remote countryside. These attacks were more likely to be successful, as government troops were concentrated in Freetown. Also present was the potential to recruit—whether willingly or by force—vast numbers of youth who might, because of their own disadvantageous positions, be convinced over time to become loyal to the RUF. Sankoh took advantage of people's physical vulnerability to build the RUF's numbers with little resistance from the military, after which he built a cult of personality around himself as a caring and beneficent father figure. Many RUF fighters called him *pa*, the affectionate title given a big man. Even during war, the social world was reproducing fundamental features.

The ideology pushed by Sankoh illustrates his willingness to play on people's belief that the social world itself was broken. Sankoh claimed as his goal the destruction of *di sistem* in all its vagueness, rather than targeting individuals and stating specific aims. Years later, the fighters I spoke to repeated the end of "the rotten system" as their goal. Keke emphasized ridding the country of the APC, but the APC was only one label that could be affixed to every manifestation of the exploitation of love. And the manifestations were omnipresent: the impoverished villages, the plundered and neglected environment, and the stagnation of rural life. The ease with which the RUF gained traction was not only due to the south's remoteness from Freetown physically and ideologically. The RUF gained momentum by preying on the basic tenets of love: commanders used people's own best defense against uncertainty and poverty—their love for each other—as a recruitment and retention strategy. If Sankoh could destroy natal families, youth would have little choice but to adhere to their new RUF family.

LOVE AS WAR STRATEGY

Available evidence suggests that Sankoh had no ideology; instead he was merely using the RUF as an instrument to achieve big man status for himself.[28] His awareness of the ease with which violence is cultivated in impotent rage cannot be denied. However, Sankoh also used love to create a functional fighting force: the RUF grew by preying on the need of children especially to be in nurturing relationships. RUF commanders ripped families apart to force children's adhesion to the RUF, and this, in all its terrible brilliance and effectiveness, only reinforced the importance of relationships. The RUF endured political upheaval with two strategies: introducing the socialist ethos that served as an alternative to *di rotin sistem,* and, when that ethos faltered due to a popular coup, destroying primary relationships to break the resistance of would-be recruits.

Many youth were vulnerable ideologically to the RUF. I sat down one day with a former RUF fighter named Abraham, a true believer in the RUF ideology and the need to liberate the nation from greed.

He was kidnapped as a small child: "After they had captured us they gave us the ideology. I had been a good student, and the government promised me a scholarship. I filled out the form, but they didn't give it to me, they just left me waiting in my village. So the RUF were lecturing us about the political system here in this rotting country, this rotting system. They told us that they had brought liberation for the young generation. At least they would drive out the rotten system and put things in place. Then they lectured us that after everything, we would have free education and free medical to develop the country. I knew from that day that I would be with them. And I was with them until the day of disarmament." The ideology was the glue that, at the beginning, held the RUF together: an inclusive socialist counter to an exclusive dictatorship, an end to a compromised sociopolitical world. For many of the combatants I spoke to who were early recruits, the RUF's ideology was compelling. Abraham was smart, ambitious, and frustrated by his inability to succeed on his merits. The RUF provided an alternative way of thinking about his place in the world, and a way to finally act on it.

Abraham thrived as an RUF bush camp administrator, which illustrates how adept Sankoh proved initially at managing his cadres according to the ideology. Rather than make everyone a fighter, he played to individuals' own skills and dreams. Young people who excelled at math or accounting became administrators; nurses and doctors were stationed in the clinics; teachers in the rudimentary bush schools. Whether recruits were volunteers or captives, they could see the logic of the ideology at work in the camps, where services were free and everyone benefited from distributions of food, clothes, and medicines. They offered their skills and they were cared for. Taken into the bush at the point of a gun, many stayed with the RUF for the duration.

The fact that Sankoh pressed an ideology in order to gain legitimacy with his cadres and the international community, elaborated a socialist ethos in the camps, and kept a movement together over the course of a decade is precisely what separates the war in Sierra Leone from a tragedy that unfolded on the other side of the African continent around the same time. The RUF fought using an intimate understanding of sociality and loyalty: Sankoh fought with and through people, and anyone was a possible recruit. The genocide that took place in Rwanda in 1994 illustrates the opposite phenomenon: an extermination campaign designed by a modern elite to keep themselves in power, executed in the hope of consolidating ethnic solidarity, and using the machinery of the state to accomplish these goals.[29] President Habyarimana enabled the genocide by creating and elaborating divisions between loyal Hutu on one hand, and the minority Tutsi party and Hutu opposed to his regime on the other. His party used the national radio station to dehumanize the "outsiders," calling them a national blight of "cockroaches." Genocide itself then became possible with the creation of what philosopher Giorgio Agamben calls "bare life": a state where life no longer has any value because it has lost its legal and political salience.[30] Once Tutsi were stripped of their status as citizens, their lives possessed no value in Rwanda, therefore it was acceptable to kill them without consequences. Even during the worst excesses of war in Sierra Leone, there was never a sense that anyone—militant or civilian—was no longer Sierra Leonean and thus eligible for extermination like an animal. The terror tactics sown by factions were psychological tools designed to cow populations into submission, allowing perpetrators to pay themselves back for what they rationalized as the corruption of the state that had left them impoverished and marginalized. The ideology of socialism was the face of this rationalization; it counters genocide in every way.

In 1992 the power of the RUF ideology faltered as a result of a successful coup in Freetown. A group of young, underpaid, underresourced and unhappy army officers drove from the eastern front of the war to Freetown and marched on the presidential palace. Supported by university students, they overthrew the government and sent Joseph Momoh into exile in Guinea, where he eventually died. The National Provisional Ruling Council (NPRC) was just what the country seemed to need after years of dictatorship: young, idealistic army officers initiating immediate political change. The coup's face, twenty-six-year-old Captain Valentine Strasser, announced over the radio that the new government would bring a rapid end to the war, usher in an era of accountability and development, and return the country to democracy.

According to anthropologist Paul Richards, the coup was a direct result of the RUF's success at recruiting youth who wanted to belong to something meaningful. Soldiers—paid by and loyal to the APC—knew they were fighting a losing battle for the hearts of Sierra Leoneans. The ideology gave the RUF much greater recruiting success than an army defending a dictator; indeed if troops entered a village to fight the RUF, they could not be certain whose side villagers were on. With this trend continuing, the army would most certainly lose the war, and they took drastic action.[31] Essentially, the army officers who were fighting both physically and ideologically knew they could only triumph by removing the RUF's raison d'être: *di rotin sistem,* the APC regime.[32]

The popularity of the NPRC—especially among youth—was a blow to the RUF. Many rebels admired the NPRC until it resolved to defeat the rebels. When I asked one coup-admiring rebel why he stayed in the bush when the RUF's goals were being met, he said he was hurt that the NPRC chose to fight the RUF rather than reach out to them as fellow brothers with the same goal of changing the country: "They did not allow us to be with them, they did not call upon us. We were still fighting. They said they are going to flush out the Revolutionary United Front members from this country." RUF members felt betrayed. The *rotin sistem* may have been overthrown; however, their fellow revolutionaries chose to turn on the RUF rather than embracing them as brothers.

Attacked physically and ideologically from all sides, the RUF retaliated. Gone was recruitment. Kidnapping, which they called *adoption,* took its place. Only continued marginalization served as a reason for the RUF to fight. The NPRC was on the brink of destroying the RUF in 1995, however, because the coup's leaders were more focused on maintaining their power base against the exiled APC than they were on military victory, they offered the RUF a peace agreement: amnesty in return for unconditional surrender. The RUF rejected this and chose to fight on, in spite of their precarious position. They felt personally injured by the NPRC, which they saw flaunting its own ideals of inclusivity by hunting the RUF. The RUF had two points of momentum in their favor: one was the increasing decadence of the regime, and the other was the success of the new *adoption* strategy. I will touch on decadence first.

The tendency of those who taste power to enjoy the good life a little too much needs very little explanation, and was a recurring theme in Sierra Leone's history. The leadership of a 1965 coup insisted on their interest in functioning democracy as they lived in palaces, drove luxury cars, and were eventually deposed. With the NPRC, reform gave way to decadence as officers moved into mansions, drove the latest cars, and enjoyed themselves beyond the means of most citizens. Growing disenchantment with the NPRC preceded a palace coup in 1995 that drove Valentine Strasser from power. The NPRC began losing ground to an RUF that had discovered renewed vigor in their fight, as the NPRC turned out to be no different than the APC. The RUF ideology—

whatever its role at that point in justifying the war—could be pushed once again.

Between 1992 and 1995, however, this was not the case. The ideology was useless against a popular government, and recruitment faltered as a resourced and ideologically revived army began crushing them. Unable to attract willing recruits to the cause, the cadres turned to *adoption*: children and youth "chose" to join the RUF family as their own family members were murdered, and then were "adopted" by individual commanders. The brutal logic was impossible to deny, and was explained by a former combatant I call Saidu, whom I met in his village in Kailahun, a remote district on the Liberian and Guinean borders. He never overcame the horror of his RUF conscription:

"I was so small when they invaded! They rounded up the boys. The rebel war entered and they captured us and told us that we would join them! They used force; they said that if we didn't join them they would kill us. So I joined them and I went with them during the wartime. When they went to war I had to fight. I was only thirteen years old then, but I fought because otherwise they would have killed me. I thought the ideology was good but we didn't have the power to agree or disagree with it. You can't deny them, because if you deny them you will die. It was a war. So you just have to accept it. Because if you don't accept it, they will do you bad, they will kill you.

"And my sister and brother are dead. It was the war that killed them. They were both shot, right when the war entered this place. The first day, the rebels killed my sister, and they chased us and held us and told us that if we didn't join they would kill us. So for us, we joined them just to save our lives. I had tried to run! They just chased us and captured us and dragged us back to the village. That was when they shot my brother. They left us alone for a bit and we ran again, and again they brought us back. They shot another boy. Then we realized there was no way out."

Saidu's love for his family was consistently punished, leading him to accept the RUF as his primary loyalty instead. The RUF was able to seize control of his emotions, however because they encouraged him to attach to his commanders, they clearly never wanted to destroy the system itself. Saidu spoke about the importance of his RUF brothers during the war, and how people in his village accepted him once the war was over because he wanted to take care of his father and surviving sister; thus he was a good person, not wicked. He had accepted the war in order to survive, but had done so through his will to love.

As one schoolteacher explained when describing why children became combatants, "whatever the situation, children can accommodate it in their hearts." Having been brutalized into severing ties with their families, children as young as seven sought someone to look after them, and often found comfort and support in older rebels who nurtured them with resources and training, however paltry. Rebels often described leaning on their senior brothers. According to one, "My own commander was Bai Bureh [named after a legendary warrior].[33] We were from the same village in the south, and he is like my big brother! He was adopted first. During the war he was kind to me. He usually gave me good advice: I should take time to fight the war, and I should handle civilians gently, not kill innocent people, not burn houses because I wanted to . . . and so on and so forth." This advice seems rudimentary, but for young, vulnerable children, rebel guidance was the only care they received, and they responded to it.

We cannot simplify the situation of children in war zones. They are not solely victims of war: they have the ability to think, act, and decide on their own. Anthropologist Susan Shepler has worked with child soldiers in Sierra Leone since disarmament, and writes explicitly about the context of Sierra Leonean childhood during the war: "Of course the lives of children during the war were hard, but we must not see them simply as victims . . . before the war, the everyday life of Sierra Leonean children was often quite difficult, many laboring to support their families as active participants in social life."[34] In Sierra Leone, work is part of childhood, and children play active roles in social and family life. Children played an equally active role during the war as they worked on their own relationships of love.[35]

The bonds children had with their commanders mimicked those they had with their parents in many ways, which is why they often endured throughout the war. Once their parents were dead, children formed relationships with their military commanders out of sheer vulnerability and economic desperation.[36] Children had to belong to the RUF as they had belonged to their own families: they needed to be needed. Their relationships with commanders followed the logic of love, where working children received food and protection. And, because these relationships mimicked children's familial relationships well enough, when faced with the alternative option of being killed as a rebel by the army, civil militias, or even one's own former villagers, there was no question about staying with the RUF under the protection of an armed and relatively benevolent commander.[37]

THE RUF PREYS ON LOVE

Just as love dictated how people survived the war, so did the RUF's ability to prey on love work to their recruitment advantage. It was not the wicked individuals, those who prioritized their own survival and ran away, who were kidnapped by the RUF. Rather it was the youth who remained in their villages to protect vulnerable family members who were captured. This information emerged through a conversation with a former RUF commander, a schoolteacher I call Calvin, who was seized early in the war: "I was trained as a teacher and I lived and worked in Kailahun, and it was there that the war met me. The war caught me because my parents were old. They did not want to go anywhere even though I suggested to them that we should leave, but they cried. They told me I was the only person who could help them. They begged me, 'Where are you going? How are you going to leave us? Are you going to leave us to be killed?' So from there, with tears in my eyes, I decided to stay so that I could take care of them."

It is rare to find an only child in Sierra Leone, so I asked the obvious question. "Didn't you have any brothers or sisters in Kailahun to help you?"

"I had brothers and sisters; initially we were all together, but most of them fled. So I took the burden of our parents. There was no way for us to go to Guinea, no way for us to go anywhere, so I decided to stay. I was with them, but eventually I had to become a member of the RUF. And I was in the safe hands of God Almighty, even though at the end of the day I eventually lost them because . . . well . . . when the government troops advanced in 1993, I was, I mean, *all of us* took off for the bush in order to save our lives."

All of Calvin's siblings chose to run. He was captured because he loved and stayed with his aging parents. It was early in the war, and the RUF was using this remote outpost as their main base. Because he was stationary, Calvin could take care of his parents in spite of ongoing skirmishes with the army. His halting reference to the government in 1993 recalls the year after the coup, when the new junta was determined to crush the RUF. The NPRC asked for assistance from Nigeria, which sent jets to bomb Kailahun. This memory is so painful because of Calvin's decision—with the cluster bombs falling—to abandon his parents and run to the bush. This single moment of choice, when Calvin prioritized his own survival over that of his parents, haunted his narrative. There were many others like Calvin, people who were swept up in the war precisely because of their love for others, whose only unspeakable acts involved decisions to run when others could not.

Calvin was known around Makeni as a powerful RUF figure during the occupation, however he was a respected and accepted member of the community in the aftermath. His ex-combatant status did not define him; more important was the proof that love and work were his priorities, whether during the war or in ordinary times. In Makeni, Calvin is known as the RUF officer who convinced the aid trucks to come, as a man who proved his worth by showing his love for his coresidents in the town. Calvin never felt the need to justify his combatant status to me; rather he emphasized the fact that his teaching job would allow him to educate his son and rebuild the family home in Kailahun. His statuses as RUF recruit and commander did not define his life, but were expressions of the foundation of love as a governing tenet in his life.

NARRATING LOVE: TRUTH, FACT, AND THE CONTOURS OF A MEANINGFUL WORLD

This book is comprised of narrative accounts of survival during the war. I did not witness any of the events people describe; therefore I am unable to attest as to whether or not the accounts provided are *factual*. Without a shadow of doubt, however, I can assert that they are *true*, as they reflect how people remember and reconstruct their worlds. Memory is an action; the past comes to life in the telling, and is different with each invocation. People never remember exactly what happened, but will describe what is important for them to tell and for the listener to hear: a narrative that reinforces present life through the interpretation of past choices.

Memory is thus more about the present than the past. A person's memories are their own reality in the moment they relate them; in essence, what individuals told me was how what had happened in the past was important to them in the moment they described it, and how it situated them in their social world so that it was possible for them to move forward.[38] Everyone engaged in some form of "social forgetting," where the act of *not* vocalizing something—if it is socially important that it not be stated—is as important to remembering the war as an act of articulation.[39] This deliberate "unspeaking" cannot unmake the past, but it can prevent a past that would torment the present from gaining the power to doing so. People rarely remember trauma, for example, or find a way or a will to articulate it. As Marc Augé suggests,

"Remembering or forgetting is doing gardener's work, selecting, pruning. Memories are like plants: there are those that need to be quickly eliminated in order to help the others burgeon, transform, flower."[40]

Equally important are memory's paradoxes. People rarely remember chronologically, especially when delving into a chaotic or traumatic past. Events and participants double back on themselves: one experience of violence may be so near another emotionally that they are narrated together, though they may have taken place years apart. Similar events are clustered, all the stories relating to a single person might emerge simultaneously, long stretches of little activity may be glossed over, while important events of a few days or hours take time to unfold in the telling. This is normal in all narrative processes, rather than being particular to war.

Every story gave the narrator an opportunity to orient himself or herself harmoniously with respect to the contours of love, and this is revealed in the emphases people placed on those who accompanied them through their survival. More than honesty, bravery, daring, or strength, people spoke of their experiences through their relationships, rationalizing where they prioritized some individuals over others, emphasizing where they sacrificed for those they love, brooding over betrayals. Therefore, whether or not an account is factual, the *truth* emerges in its emphasis on a commitment to a social world where people take account of each other as fellow humans, rather than as adversaries.

The controversy surrounding Nobel Peace Prize winner Rigoberta Menchú's autobiography stands as testimony to the importance of truth. Menchú, a Mayan activist in Guatemala, narrated the story of her family's defiant struggle against Latino hegemony—resulting in the harassment, torture, and killing of many family members—in the international bestseller *I, Rigoberta Menchú*. The account was later revealed as containing numerous inaccuracies, manipulations, and, according to one critic, outright lies, which prompted a flurry of criticism among academics and lay readers: they had been *deceived*. However, Menchú enhanced the account with details that amalgamated the experiences of her fellows in order to outline the truth of the situation: the brutality was real, even if the precise details were not factual. These atrocities happened, even if they did not all happen to her.[41] Menchú succeeded in alerting the world to the Mayans' plight; therefore the account is worthy, if not factual. These stories are also worthy, for we all strive to place ourselves rightly in a world that enables us to thrive with each other. Thus these chapters narrate the rightness of love, and the struggle individuals engaged in to nurture love when forced to make a choice—and to justify these choices where they failed. I have no doubt that individuals omitted some details and augmented others, however this does not make their narratives less valid. How they want to be known is more important to understanding what is socially emphasized than the details of what actually happened.

The social narrative that emerges from these collected stories is a political project of talking back to the SLPP government, which effectively banished the town of Makeni from the nation. Whether an individual narrates preaching at the RUF hospital, trading in looted goods, "joining" the rebels, or being savagely beaten by them, each one highlights an individual's challenge to President Kabbah's own narrative of Makeni as "a place of collaborators." Individuals were not blind to the ramifications of engaging with the RUF, but each did so in order to save themselves and their families, and used the fact that the president forced them to do so in order to articulate a critique of a government that cared more about the political imperative of consensus than it did about the welfare of its people.

In the chapters that follow, I illuminate the struggles to maintain and defend the world during war and aftermath through the voices of seven people: a soldier, a rebel, a student, a trader, an evangelist, a father, and a politician. Over the course of my nearly two years in Sierra Leone between 2003 and 2006, I befriended and worked with a spectrum of people in Makeni. I chose these seven individuals partly because of their eloquence, and partly because of the diversity of their experiences. They have only three things in common: their narratives highlight the cultural practices and exigencies of love, each issues their own challenge to elites who eat at the expense of their people, and when I met them they all lived in the town of Makeni, in northern Sierra Leone. Trauma and confusion silence them in some places, and in these moments I use the voices of others with similar, equally resonant narratives. Each person has his or her own chapter. This allows their perspective, their fragmented memories and partial knowledge of events, and the reasons for their decisions, to emerge clearly. Each chapter also highlights different perspectives on the struggle to balance the various demands of love in personal and social survival. In many ways, the two were indistinguishable during the war, and after.

I have no doubt that some accounts—the student, the politician—were exaggerated. Indeed, the ability to tell a good story is a valued skill in Sierra Leone. I included these narratives to illustrate how people achieve balance between honesty and the will to be known as loving individuals. The student witnessed and participated in some truly terrible events, and the politician was well aware of the suspicion with which most Sierra Leoneans view ambition, especially where it involves the will to be big. Both teetered on the edge of respectability during the war, and in their accounts they emphasized the positive and rationalized the negative. If they did not participate in everything they narrated, they still wanted me to believe them, highlighting their embrace of the contours of the social world, and their will to be situated in that world. This is *truth*.

In the next chapter I introduce Makeni, a town stigmatized by the rest of the nation because the ex-combatants who had engineered the occupation were not driven away after the war. The town is a standing testimony to the fraught nature of nested loyalties, as individuals struggled amongst themselves and with the government to define the morality of choices made during the occupation through the rubric of love.

Chapter 2 follows Captain Mansaray, a loyal army officer ambushed by affiliated troops who is charged with treason after successfully defending himself. He is released from jail by a murderous coup, and must decide whether to align himself with the "thugs" who saved his life. Through his story we see the role of love and betrayal in determining the shape of coups, mutinies, and peace accords.

In Chapter 3 we meet David, a schoolboy who is captured by the RUF in one of their first incursions over the Liberian border. He spends the next ten years with the rebels, pursuing a "normal" life of farming and relationships in the chaos that keeps forcing him, against his will, into a barbaric, sickly, and lonely life on the run in the bush.

Chapter 4 is the narrative of Alimamy, a student who emphasizes how he clung to his identity as a loving son and hardworking pupil to save himself from emotional breakdown during the worst excesses of the rebel occupation of Makeni. In his story he highlights the resonance of love: strangers emerge to assist him because they respect his father.

In Chapter 5 we meet Kadiatu, a mother and market *big woman* who befriends the rebel leadership in Makeni in order to trade looted goods and feed her dying children. She argues forcefully that free markets are moral, that the only good social world is one where no one eats from other people's relationships, as a corrupt government does.

Chapter 6 follows Adama, a lonely widow who transforms her faith into an instrument of survival by preaching to and feeding dying rebels. After returning to Makeni from asylum in Britain, Adama struggles to reestablish the loving relationships that sustained her during the occupation, as her wealth makes her a target of jealousy among her neighbors.

Musa, an expectant father, is the subject of Chapter 7. Vulnerable to harassment and RUF recruitment because of his age, Musa actively negotiates a persona for himself of loving son and doting father trying only to nurture his own, and not fighting for big man status with rebels. He earns consideration from RUF commanders as a "gentleman," as they respect his humility and dedication to his family.

Chapter 8 is the story of Michael, a politician who emphasizes throughout his narrative his primary love for the town of Makeni itself. Acting as a double agent for the British government, he infiltrates the RUF and fights on the town's behalf, even as Makeni is stigmatized for sheltering rebels. Michael justifies his pursuit of bigness as a politician because of his fear of a lack of love in his own family.

The people who narrate their stories in this book did not have the luxury of understanding what was happening as the war raged; their information was always partial and often based on rumor. Individuals made survival decisions based on their emotional cultural practices. They forged relationships in defense of their lives, weathered the storm of war, and made sense of and justified those choices in the aftermath. They often confuse time frames and events, which is part and parcel of war-related trauma. I will do justice to the discombobulation of war by keeping some of this confusion intact. However, I have imposed a framework on the stories to keep them moving in time. I bring in the voices of other people who can speak to these issues when my interlocutors themselves lack the ability to speak with clarity on their situations. However, my aim is to let the survivors narrate the contours of love and betrayal themselves.

Not one of these stories is itself a complete picture of the war. None of the people in these pages know each other. This is not a family portrait, nor is it a history of the war; it is a tapestry. I did not select these narratives because they fit together conveniently, but because they gave me the power to illustrate the singular importance of understanding love in Sierra Leone. These narratives are personal. Each illustrates some significant events and omits others. I use memories as keystones from which to build some history into the picture, so that it is possible to understand how cultural practices were foundational to the war on scales large and small. Each story bears its own version of truth. None are verifiable as completely factual, but that does not matter. People do not live their lives based on what happened, but how they remember, interpret, and analyze what happened.

The people who color this book are the living incarnations of the struggle to maintain a good world through love, even as the tenets of that world made war possible. They were able to survive as passionate, emotive beings, coping with brutal events through anger, care, and faith in their world. Their stories illustrate the simple fact that human beings working through love and defending the worth of their world in their relationships are living proof that war will never defeat human possibility, even as that same world is one where war is possible. That fact is a grain of perfection we can grip tightly in our quest to understand what it means to be human: we are complex, passionate, social beings, and our survival is predicated on our retaining this basic feature. Passion, in whatever desperate ways it manifests itself—love, hate, punishment, care—is not a flaw of the all-too-human. It is a complex act of social and physical survival on which the world is predicated, and must be understood and respected as such.

War did not defeat Sierra Leone; it will not defeat humans anywhere on this earth. The ability of survivors to create and nurture relationships with others in the aftermath was predicated on the fact that they live on a foundational practice of love, however imperfect. Whatever imbalances throw that world into chaos can be addressed, as individuals work on their basic cultural practices as agents in an everchanging world. People are willing to fight for those they love and to be part of a world founded on love. In this we can see the brilliance of being only human.

1

Understanding Makeni
and Nested Loyalties

Marginality and Collaboration
in the Northern Capital

My initial trip to Sierra Leone in 2003 was spent largely in Freetown, mulling over research possibilities. I focused on the idea of studying Makeni because it was stigmatized, though it was a regional capital city. From that moment, everyone I met in Freetown, from the U.S. ambassador to university professors, dispensed advice on working in Makeni. The majority warned me to stay away altogether. They related what I would find when I arrived: a dangerous place, full of thieving youth, shameless rebel collaborators, arrogant RUF commanders . . . a backward town, morally corrupt and ideologically marginal, harboring the dregs of society, the criminals whose tolerance of violence turned a rebel insurgency into a bitter, interminable standoff. On the whole, Freetonians reviled Makeni because of the occupation, which was viewed as iconic proof of the township's perpetually antagonistic relationship with the rest of the nation. Receiving these admonitions politely, I resolved to experience the town with an open mind, cognizant that strong feelings dominate thinking about Makeni. I had touched on an issue about which no one was neutral, though the issue was formed in a confluence of historical events, and not just the war.

In short, from the beginning of the colonial administration of Sierra Leone, Makeni was its most economically, developmentally, and politically marginal and vulnerable urban center; in essence the "least loved," most precarious place to live in a nation characterized by the precariousness of existence. As one of my interlocutors explained it, "Makeni was never loved like Bo or Kenema. You can see this in how poor the town is." Lack of love and poverty become conflated: the town is poor because the rest of the nation does not love, and hence nurture it, and the nation does not love Makeni because poverty hampers its participation in the national development project. Lack of nurturing is both cause and consequence of marginalization. Without the ability to reciprocate, there can be no display of gratitude. Without gratitude, there can be no love.[1] What residents of Makeni wanted, and what they lacked consistently under successive governments, was a leap of faith that begins with investment: they wanted government to take the first step in nurturing as a parent would with a child, and hope that the investment will pay dividends in gratitude. As neither side had taken the first step, the town and country were at an impasse.

This was difficult to see in the immediate wake of the war, when aid created a boomtown atmosphere and carefree largesse was rampant. Makeni in 2003 was undergoing the largest demobilization and reintegration effort in the northern province, the second largest in the country. Young men were pushed through skills training hundreds at a time, six months at a stretch, and the town's economy benefited from their casual spending of transition allowances. The bulk of ex-combatants were in relationships with local women, and their money flowed through their girlfriends and wives to their families. With money present, everyone in Makeni gained from the generosity of someone else. The hateful selfishness purported by residents of Freetown seemed absent.

Once the international community retreated, however, the prioritization of nested relationships became more obvious. Individuals became care*ful* rather than care*free*—in essence, with fewer resources available, maintaining the most important relationships mattered, and the obvious gifts of bounty that occur with plenty disappeared. Many petty relationships broke down, but it was those that mattered—the marriages that produced children, as an example—over which people fretted and sacrificed. As people could not nurture through large investments such as school fees, tokens of love—important because the sacrifice involved more than their monetary value—became the order of the day. But how far can a little bit of money or a shared meal go in sustaining families, or pursuing dreams? Can small acts of love maintain a social world? As residents discovered long before the war, mutual love cannot occur without investment, and this is also true on the scale of communities and states.

Makeni did little to participate in the national development project because it was poor. It was poor because it had always been an accidental town, unincorporated into the ethos of the nation, and because it was betrayed by its first political hero, the dictator Siaka Stevens. Makeni was, in essence, the unwanted stepchild. This was not a natural state of affairs. Rather it stemmed from the notion that Makeni had nothing to contribute. Bereft of natural resources, the town grew on the vagaries of trading and transport, tying its fortunes to the market rather than a base of production. It was more prone to drought and crop failure than other parts of the country, and because of the early conversion of many local people to Islam, was attractive neither to missionaries nor British administrators for education and development. After Sierra Leone achieved independence, successive governments blamed Makeni for its own "backwardness," speaking derisively of residents' tendency to think in terms of their intimate relationships rather than contributions to the nation. "Makeni people care about money and not education," is a common trope. It speaks to someone who thinks about feeding their family, but not nurturing a future doctor.

As a consequence of consistent neglect and tribulation, the nurturing that Makeni's residents did for each other was small-scale and immediate. Their ability to practice love was limited heavily by their poverty and economic uncertainty; one can literally see a person's poverty in how they prioritize their many relationships and the nurturing they can accomplish. One may be asked to share in a meal but not a harvest. A parent gives a child clothes but not school fees. Resources must be carefully divided amongst chosen loved ones; the greater the number of relationships, the less each person receives. Sometimes the effort of nurturing is more than one person can handle, given their own small resources. An elderly farmer who decided not to exert his last efforts planting rice one season did so because he was tied to too many people. If he tried to feed them all, everyone would receive very little. At the end of the day he would have "planted hunger," and it was better for each person to try to feed himself than for him to disappoint his loved ones. If one has anything, one must share or risk sparking feelings of betrayal. He chose instead to avoid their anger by having nothing himself and hoping they would understand.

The rest of Sierra Leone views Makeni as marginal because the residents often prioritize their family and friends rather than the nation. The common wisdom is that as a regional capital, Makeni should make an identifiable contribution to national welfare. What is missing from this judgment is an understanding of the invisible everyday poverty that masks sacrifices people make for their family and friends. The consistent threat of destitution and hunger generates different criteria by which people judge each other. Nonresidents' lack of familiarity and empathy with the tremendous cost of small-scale nurturing leaves the town open to being judged on the fact that, during the war, people cared more about their own families and friends than they did about what the rest of the nation wanted. In their narratives, residents emphasized the rightness of concentrating on family, directly challenging the rest of the nation for failing to embrace this.

To be acceptable to the rest of the nation during the war would have required a wholesale rejection of the RUF, in essence, an uprising. Such a townwide effort was impossible: residents were so demoralized and jumpy due to the constant threat of attacks and internal fighting that, according to one person, "any sound of gunfire caused us to hide under the bed!" Instead, everyone closed ranks around their most treasured people, choosing to save themselves and their families by acquiescing to occupation. The repercussions were harsh.

To understand how this process unfolded requires delving into exactly what Makeni is as a place, who lives there, and how the ostensible willingness of residents to accept ex-combatants was a predictable outgrowth of existing marginalization. When asked to prioritize saving their loved ones or ending the war for the country, most everyone chose, in Andrew Oldenquist's words, their "naked" loyalties: family and friends.[2] Just as Sierra Leone was an artificial construction of colonialism and politics, so love for the nation was a secondary, more cerebral consideration than the primary impulses of family. Nationalism would have been stronger, perhaps, if people felt they belonged to the nation.

LOCATING THE SCENE

If trade were utterly reliable as an economic pursuit, Makeni would be wealthy beyond residents' wildest dreams. The center of town is dense with markets and storefronts selling every ware imaginable. If the movement of people could make a place wealthy, Makeni would not have a trouble in the world. From the center of Makeni, one can proceed on a direct route to every other corner of the country, making it the nation's internal transport hub. Everything about the town itself reflects the constant movement of people and goods that define its identity as a trading center, but also define its fragility, how susceptible it is to swings in market demand and thus to poverty. The town's iconic center is Independence Square, from whence one can travel northeast to Kabala, east to the diamond area of Kono, south to Bo, and west to Freetown. Just off this square is the lorry park, a plot of land surrounded on all sides by stalls of wholesale and transit-oriented goods, teeming at all hours with hawkers, taxis, motorcycles, and travelers. Framing the town to the north and south are two large hills that dominate the landscape. Residents think of them as a married couple, cradling and nurturing the town, physically defining a permanence of place that cannot be achieved by buildings alone. The larger of the two, a solid mass of granite emerging from the ground, is Wusum, the male hill. His mate, Mena, the female hill, rolls gently along the highway, dotted with trees, vegetation, and boulders.

The town's population is contained loosely by these hills, but otherwise spills out in an unplanned jumble of construction, ranging from mud-brick and thatch huts to multistory concrete edifices. Most of the new construction lines Azzolini Highway (named after the first Catholic missionary to arrive in the town in the 1940s), which runs between Freetown and the mining area of Kono, and cuts between the two hills. Large commercial structures hover over the road, hoping to attract custom from travelers looking for food, accommodation, or gasoline. Much of the actual activity on the roads takes place along their verges, where children play, women sit with baskets of produce, and laborers wheel overloaded carts of wood, rice, and other sundries into town. Much of the wheeled traffic on side roads consists of commercial motorcycles, which rose in popularity after the war because they negotiate poor roads with greater ease than do their four-wheeled counterparts. Along with houses and shops in various states of construction or decay, the streets and small waterways are lined with tiny "kitchen gardens," the opportunistic growing of rice and vegetables wherever a seed can take root. Chickens, goats, and sheep peck and browse between buildings and among voluminous piles of garbage, often fighting semiferal dogs for the chance to do so. Nights are pierced by the snarls of dogs battling each other for the day's waste.

The town does not look wealthy, or healthy. Aside from the flies and putrid puddles advertising a lack of waste disposal, many crumbling buildings, pockmarked with scars of war and time, stand waiting in vain for intervention. Most of the new construction is commercial properties, the majority of them owned by absentee landlords trying to profit from the safe distance of Freetown. Children play in the flooding created by the garbage-choked drains when the annual rains arrive. The rest of the year it is oppressively hot, and prone to the abrasive, invasive dust that annually sweeps off the Sahara with the Harmattan wind. People seek relief in scant shade; many of the trees have been felled for firewood and construction, leaving the landscape largely barren of green cover. The fruit-bearing trees are usually spared the axe, and when in season, the glut of fruit presages outbreaks of intestinal diseases, as flies feed off rotting peels and pits. With water supplies dwindling, households converge on the few wells deep enough to continue supplying daily needs. There is nothing comfortable or easy about living in Makeni. Every season has its own problems, every part of town susceptible to the same problems as any other.

When I first arrived in Makeni in 2003, the population was estimated at two hundred thousand. This was remarkably high for a city that lacked natural or economic attributes: the density reflected the ravages of war more than a natural dynamic. The population was partially a reflection of an influx of displaced people who, having lost rural homes or livelihoods during the war, hoped for waged employment. Many were ex-combatants who disarmed in Makeni and decided to remain in town. Others were attracted by the commercial possibilities inherent in the influx of aid organizations, still others for the prospect of employment from all of the above. In many ways, the population grew because of the possibilities inherent in having so many people in one place.

The town was founded by a group of elders from the Temne people, whose ancestors migrated south from Guinea several hundred years ago. Up until the war Makeni remained largely Temne, with a sizeable minority of Limba people, whose villages dot the landscape north of the town. Other ethnic groups represented—Fula, Kuranko—came largely as seasonal traders, or to take advantage of the educational opportunities that first arose with the Catholic missions. Though the war began in 1991, it reached Makeni first in the form of refugees from the south and east, who contributed a sizeable population of Kono, Mandingo, and Mende people. Though many of the displaced returned home and the Temne once again assert their dominance, the town retains the cosmopolitan feel of a metropolis. Unless one is certain of someone's ethnic background, all conversations begin in Krio, the national lingua franca.

Temnes are known as keen traders. Early colonial accounts of the town marvel at the resourcefulness with which trading took place, from tailors setting up shop on their verandas to small girls toting wares on their heads, circulating through town. One can find anything from to-matoes to automobile parts in the central market, where there are also bustling trades in used clothing and the local batik and tie-dyed textiles. Those without access to market stalls set up shop wherever space is available; often people start their trading with small boxes from which they sell candy, matches, and soap. The glut of traders causes stiff com-petition, so profit margins are slim and traders work to turn custom-ers into *padi*—friends. Affective ties, more than shrewdness or chance, keeps one's income reliable, if not large.

The town is politically scarred; residents are largely loyal to a party that for many years humiliated and ignored them. It is nearly impos-sible to walk down a street without seeing a flash of red, the color of the APC. In the years after independence, the party became attractive to Temnes who had been excluded from the Mende-based political sensi-bilities of the SLPP. Residents voted en masse for Siaka Stevens in 1968 and hoped he would reward their support with development projects, even as it was clear that he was using his presidency to eat. In 1977, sev-eral cabinet ministers defected. Objecting to Stevens's ironfisted control of the political landscape, they formed their own breakaway party, the United Democratic Party, and held meetings in Makeni.

Stevens punished Makeni violently, as he saw the mere hosting of an opposition party as personal betrayal, an act of disloyalty deserving retribution. He publicly withheld key development projects including a new power station, and admonished residents that he was punishing them for being ungrateful and disloyal. Stevens solicited residents to beg his forgiveness.[3] In spite of both Stevens and his successor Joseph Momoh neglecting the town, residents steadfastly support the party not because of its policies—Sierra Leone's political history is one of "hometown" politics of in-group development—but simply out of fear that their fate would be infinitely worse under an SLPP government. This is the essence of negative love, of clinging to the least of all pos-sible evils.

LOCATING MYSELF

I conducted the bulk of my fieldwork between May 2004 and August 2005. The town was replete with foreigners, as the aid boom was in full swing. Many people mistook me for NGO staff until they noticed that I did not have a vehicle. They then assumed joyfully that the Peace Corps was returning, and I was the sign of more volunteers to come. There ensued several months of patient explanation that I was a student rather than an aid worker, and that my purpose was to research the history of the town and its people, especially with respect to Makeni's awkward postwar position.

Knowing my occupation and interests was not enough for residents to understand why I was living in Makeni. They had to make sense of why I would choose, of all places in Sierra Leone, one of the poorest in which to live and work. The implicit consensus was that I sympathized with their plight vis-à-vis the rest of the nation; that I loved Makeni more than any other place. I was therefore *their own* anthropologist and historian, living in Makeni in order to write the truth of their story for the world. People spoke of me as their defender; I was even introduced to their member of parliament as "our anthropologist."

The implications of this for my work were profound. Rather than struggling to find interlocutors, I was a magnet for individuals eager to tell their stories. I spent most days walking around town to attend events or pass time with acquaintances, and was often greeted by a new person who was curious about my work and wanted to offer his or her own story. I spoke to many of these people, but was unable to sit down with all of them. I spent time observing classes in the schools, meetings at the town council, religious events, graduations and ceremonies, and political rallies—and just hanging out with people. My concerns about the social stigma that might result from my speaking to former rebels, soldiers, and other combatants were unfounded, as these people were viewed as part of the fabric of the town, judged as individuals just like everyone else.

The ease with which I recorded life histories, especially with respect to war experiences, implies that residents of the town were acutely aware of the stigma they faced in the country. They wanted to be heard and validated—a story is not real until it has an audience—but they also wanted to defend themselves against accusations of collaboration with the rebels and the accompanying shame of being traitors to the nation. They viewed me as their mouthpiece. I did my utmost to do justice to them and to the project of understanding love as a social framework by telling their stories, all the while being aware of the fact that narrative is a political tool by which people justify their actions. If Makeni was "backward" and unloved, residents were happy to explain that the government was at fault. After all, they were not in a position to provide electricity, running water, paved roads, and public buildings on their own. A government that shirks its responsibilities towards its citizens must be publicly proclaimed wicked if it is to see the error of its ways and return to practicing love.

"BACKWARD" MAKENI: POVERTY AND THE LIMITS OF LOVE

It was clear that residents were not proud of Makeni. Comments regularly flew about how "backward" Makeni was compared to the other regional capitals of Bo and Kenema, both of which had grid electricity and paved roads. Residents claimed that no government ever loved Makeni as much as it loved the other two towns, feeding Makeni only the last and least scraps of development. Extensive archival work revealed that from the beginning of the colonial administration of the protectorate in 1896 to independence in 1961, the town was never as nurtured—with resources and investment, or with development and infrastructure—as the other two towns to which it was frequently compared.[4]

Makeni is slightly north of the geographical center of Sierra Leone. It is not in the belt of rainforest that dominates the southern and eastern parts of the country, nor is it technically in the arid, cooler north, where lower densities of mosquitoes and tse-tse flies make raising cattle possible. It is in an open wooded savannah, where for most people, mixed crops of vegetables and tubers are the most reliable food source. The area is covered with the seasonally flooded swamps known as *boliland,* in which, with tremendous effort, rice and other floodplain crops can be grown during the annual rains that fall between May and September. It lacks, however, a feature that was critical to initial administrative decisions about the suitability of the area for agriculture: rivers.

The British colonial administrators who arrived at the end of the nineteenth century were keen to use the country's hinterland for crop production and resource extraction. They found the south and east suitable for growing tree crops and harvesting timber. The rivers that flowed extensively through these areas and the northwest also made them attractive for the introduction of mechanized swamp rice farming. Makeni had neither rainforest nor rivers, so very little agricultural infrastructure was introduced, aside from some abortive attempts to produce cotton.[5] There was, however, a demand from Europe for palm kernel oil, which prompted the administration to build a railroad to transport kernels, stopping at a point equidistant from the largest palm groves. Palm kernels were plentiful in the north, and the place chosen for the termination of the railroad was Makeni. The town grew as traders and transporters flocked to the booming economy.

The problem with boomtowns is eventual bust. The railroad was planned in 1896, when the demand for palm kernels in Europe was astronomical. By the time the rail line was complete in 1916, demand had subsided, and palm kernels could be extracted at considerably cheaper cost in Southeast Asia. The trade in Makeni senesced, and so did administrative interest. As the area was not contributing anything to the colony's exports, there was no need to invest in physical or human infrastructure, no matter the size of the population. Development such as roads, schools, and hospitals were largely absent for the next thirty years.[6] Makeni was treated as an accidental town, an area of no strategic importance because it contributed nothing to the productivity of the protectorate.

Only the fact that its population continued to swell forced the administration to take notice. It was given the status of northern regional capital in 1948, when it was the second-largest urban center outside of Freetown. Hospitals and administrative structures were built slowly, and always after similar structures were well in place in Bo and Kenema. The latter towns were booming centers of large-scale production and trade of rice, timber, and diamonds. Makeni, by contrast, produced nothing. In 1949 an edict from London essentially forced the administration to deliver the same legal structures to Makeni as were already in place in Bo and Kenema. Even though Makeni had been granted regional capital status because of its population, the administration in Freetown overlooked it as site for a policing system, and instead installed one in a secondary town closer to the diamond region.[7] This is only one of many examples of Makeni not being loved by the administration because it was not contributing, a dynamic which resonated with the system of loyalty politics of nurturing and withdrawal practiced by Sierra Leone's governments since independence.

The administration on its own could not fully colonize Sierra Leone. Britain relied heavily on missionaries to establish schools, promote religious conversion, and pave the way for administration, extraction, and development in the hinterlands. Makeni was again disadvantaged by its physical location: relatively close to the Guinea border and within the traveling realm of the seminomadic Muslim Fula traders. Much of the Temne population was Muslim by the time of administrative incorporation into the protectorate. Feeling that conversion was more likely among the "animist" populations than among those already converted to a monotheistic religion, Christian missionaries congregated in the Mende south. Missionaries built critical infrastructure such as schools and hospitals, and the presence of expatriates in the south and east encouraged the government to supply the areas with roads. Makeni did not receive its first permanent missionary presence until 1950, when a group of Xavierian priests led by Father Augustus Azzolini arrived. His order built St. Francis School in 1951, added a junior secondary school in 1955, and a senior secondary school in 1958. At the time St. Francis opened, only two hundred children in the region attended school, most of them at the iron ore mine complex in Lunsar. By this time, the Bo School for Boys had been training the sons of the southern elite for almost fifty years.

Though initially responsible for Makeni's population explosion, the railroad became more of a hindrance to development than a boon. By the time it reached Makeni in 1916, palm oil prices had dropped to the point where the railroad struggled to break even. The administration hoped to make money by converting the trains to carry passengers. As a last-ditch attempt to make a failing transport industry profitable, the administration refused to connect Makeni to the protectorate's ever-growing road system, hoping this would force people and freight onto the train.[8] Minutes from meetings of the Roads Board from the 1930s show that the suggestion to link Makeni up to nearby protectorate roads was consistently tabled, as such a road would absorb traffic that would otherwise use the railroad.[9] The suggestion to attach Makeni to the rest of the road system by toll road was bandied about for several years. Not until the early 1970s, when a plan to dismantle the railroad was already in the works, was Makeni linked up by road directly to Lunsar, a mining town less than fifty miles away.

Makeni residents found themselves politically disadvantaged at independence in 1961, when Sir Milton Margai, a Mende doctor, became the first Prime Minister under the banner of the SLPP. Margai wanted a unified nation, but his untimely death meant his brother Albert—known to be more "tribal"—assumed office. Unlike Milton, Albert restricted his cabinet to trusted Mende advisors. Siaka Stevens formed the APC as a counter to the Mende tribalism of the SLPP, and it became a coalition party of the Krio, Temne, and Limba. Stevens obscured his own ethnic heritage, which allowed him to court the loyalty of multiple tribes. He curried favor in areas of the country where his popularity was not assured by his Temne-Limba leanings, and so, paradoxically, under his rule Makeni also received the last and least bits of development. Stevens punished the town after the political defection of his ministers in 1977: the UDP was demolished by Stevens's thugs and its leaders imprisoned and eventually executed. Stevens required a public apology from residents before admonishing them that the development of the town relied on their "self-help" measures, which the government would consider supplementing.[10] In essence, he abused practices of love to chastise and shame the town.

Residents were elated when Stevens retired in 1985 and named Joseph Momoh, a Limba from the nearby village of Binkolo, as his successor. They assumed that, as he maintained family ties in Binkolo, Momoh would participate in political favoritism—hometown politics—from which Makeni might benefit. Momoh appointed several Makeni natives to key positions in his ministries, however it was soon clear that these appointments were rewards for Momoh's inner circle, rather than acts of love for the town. On his first visit, the new minister of state presidential affairs reiterated that he was not a servant of Makeni, but of the nation, as was the president himself. Residents must stand behind their president, but they could not expect the town to benefit.[11] According to one resident who served on the town council, this was a veiled warning that Makeni needed to prove its love first before it would receive development. Indeed, Momoh did not grant the town any infrastructure projects in his five-year tenure as president. My interlocutors who remember his presidency took this extremely hard, as, according to one, "We did not know why our own son would not help us. We always stood behind him."

In this all-too-brief history of Makeni between 1900 and 1991, there is a pattern of consistent, deliberate neglect because of vagaries of history and geography: riverless, Islamic, resource-poor Makeni held no attractions that would make investment, and thus building bonds of love, worthwhile for any administration. The town was never nurtured partially because residents scrambled to support themselves, produced little, and through forces of circumstance, contributed very little to the colony, and later to the nation. Nurturing is a two-way street, and administrators and politicians expected residents to contribute first. Inhabitants yearned to belong to the nation, but they were weary of apologizing for prioritizing their families and of begging for investment. The only relationship they inspired was the negative kind: punishment for falling out of line.

Education was an uncomfortable fit for Makeni residents because it requires long-term sacrifices of both money and manpower that could otherwise be used in business to support families. Successive governments pushed education with a diffuse notion of training leaders for the nation, with rewards delayed until students secured precious jobs, from which money and security would eventually return to the family. However, jobs were scarce and few families could invest in schooling a child. Education made little sense in the resource-restricted space of interpersonal care defined by poverty; by sending a single child to school a mother hampered her ability to nurture the rest. As a trader who trained her daughters in the market stated, "If I teach my daughters business we will earn money together for our family until they get married. If I put them in school, they will cost us money from now until they get jobs, and we will eat little. And there are no jobs."

Makeni residents had little to give each other and less to give the nation in the wake of the war. This did not make them bad people, or "backward." With fewer resources, every act of nurturing required greater sacrifice. Those sacrifices were made on behalf of one's naked loyalties, and not the state of Sierra Leone. Residents believe that, in contrast to their own lack of resources, Sierra Leone had much to give them—as evidenced by the fact that Bo and Kenema had all their schools rebuilt by the end of 2004. What they could not understand was why the government did not invest in the town; hence the feeling that they were being forced to be loyal out of fear that their small concessions would be lost, because they had nothing to offer that would inspire love. They were adamant that the catch-22 could only be solved by the government making the same sacrifice the trader could not justify for her child: invest first, and give slightly less to other regions. Whatever that investment, Makeni would never have as much to return to the nation. Hence, there was little logical reason for the government to give, and it was right that Makeni should be behind. This paradox is one of the primary frailties of love, and it creates feelings of bitterness, whether in war or in ordinary times.

OCCUPIED MAKENI

Though rebel forces did not occupy Makeni until 1998, residents felt the effects of war years earlier. Once the NPRC coup took power, it purged regional administrations of APC politicians. The coup, run by young officers with an agenda of political reform, was initially popular. Unlike most previous governments, the NPRC officers lacked clear regional or tribal leanings. The coup assigned officers to administer each region, and, aside from some arguing over the fact that Makeni was not allowed its own civil militia, the town was fairly calm throughout the initial years of the regime.[12] The refortified army dedicated itself to defeating the RUF, and in the first years of the junta, tribal and regional differences were cast aside as the nation pulled together to fight the rebels. All of this changed, however, with the peaceful transfer of power from the NPRC to new SLPP president Tejan Kabbah in 1996.

Kabbah opened his presidency with a national tour, during which he addressed the emotional issue of the war. For most towns his words were encouraging. For the people of Makeni, however, he saved vitriol. Citing the fact that Foday Sankoh and one of his commanders were from the north, Kabbah told the assembled crowd that the people of the north—and therefore Makeni, as the capital of the region—were responsible for the war and owed the rest of the nation an apology.[13] Intellectuals from Makeni reacted violently to what they referred to as "the Hail Theory of War," citing multitudinous facts, from the physical origin of the war in the south to the largely APC sympathies of the north as counterarguments, but the protests fell on deaf ears. Writers from around the nation cheered Kabbah's willingness to galvanize the country's sympathies against the RUF. Though the south and east may have gained new resolve, the consensus in Makeni was that it was being scapegoated.

Kabbah's speeches were not enough to keep everyone happy with the government. Within a year the Armed Forces Revolutionary Council (AFRC) seized power. This coup was a combined effort of the RUF and mutinous members of the Sierra Leone Army, which had fallen out of favor with the government. Kabbah had encouraged local civil militias to take up the bulk of the fighting on behalf of the government, and followed up this call to arms by slashing army salaries and rice rations. Cast out of government favor, many bitter soldiers were vulnerable to the RUF call to take matters into their own hands, and they succeeded in chasing Kabbah from Freetown in 1997. His government-in-exile in Guinea gained the cooperation of the ECOWAS to retake power early in 1998. Once he returned from exile, Kabbah concentrated his military efforts on fortifying Freetown and protecting the towns of Bo and Kenema, leaving only a skeleton crew of Nigerian troops in Makeni. The RUF attacked Makeni on December 23, 1998, and after a skirmish in the barracks, the remaining Nigerian troops fled. With no other force to protect the town, it was taken easily by the rebels.

The occupation of Makeni lasted three years. In 1999 and 2000, residents cowered in terror as various groups of rebels vied for control of the town. Some groups were comprised of mutinous soldiers led by opportunistic RUF commanders. Others were groups of "real rebels" taking orders from Foday Sankoh himself. Nowhere in this time did Kabbah order an invasion to liberate the town, even as one of his ministers assured residents of Makeni just four months into the occupation that the town would soon be rescued.[14] Those promises came to nothing. Citing the starvation that was occurring, NGOs engaged the RUF in conversations about providing humanitarian aid in the town as, simultaneously, the government suggested peace talks. The RUF gained political legitimacy with these overtures, which treated them as a force to be negotiated with, and they thus had no reason to end the occupation without real concessions. The occupation continued, and residents were in a bind. Those who remained were immobile for various reasons including infirmity, lack of family elsewhere, and the prohibitively high "tax" levied on fleeing civilians at RUF checkpoints.[15] Not knowing if or when the town would be liberated, people did their best to survive the daily indignities of living under occupation. The more people an individual took responsibility for, the more they were required to interact and cooperate with rebels, who controlled most of the resources in the town. In short, the greater the number of relationships individuals had, the more they were vulnerable to criticism of happily "collaborating" with rebels.

Foday Sankoh signed the Lomé Peace Accords in 1999, and used the accords as a political tool to further alienate the country from Makeni. In November he visited Makeni to ensure people that the UN troops stationed in the town were there to maintain security as peace took hold. He stated that he was not prepared to fight again and that the combatants would disarm. For a month after his appearance in Makeni, he jockeyed for leverage with the government by asking the United Nations to leave Makeni, arguing that residents were more comfortable with RUF security than that provided by foreigners. He cited the fact that residents were celebrating the day he arrived on his national tour to promote the peace accords as proof that they were all rebels, which was soon refuted in a statement issued by residents.[16] They felt Sankoh was deliberately trying to maintain the RUF headquarters in the town, so that if the town were disowned completely by the rest of the country, he could carve his own fiefdom out of the wreckage. A week later, a government press release announced that the northern region was the only part of the country being excluded from an international aid plan, because its security situation was not up to standard. Because of Sankoh's statement, Makeni received no humanitarian relief.[17]

Despite the lack of aid, the United Nations moved military observers into the town to set up disarmament camps. The camps were designed to provide fighters from all factions a place to hand over their weapon in exchange for protection, shelter, food, and a disarmament and transition package. Several RUF commanders in Makeni were not invited to Lomé for the peace accords and feared that Sankoh was selling them out for his own benefit. They rejected disarmament, and in March 2000, RUF cadres surrounded the camps demanding the return of their "kidnapped," disarmed brethren. In one night of siege, they killed fifty Kenyan peacekeepers and took over one hundred more hostage. They destroyed the camp and rekidnapped seventy-two child soldiers. Kabbah was enraged, and highlighted this in a radio broadcast as proof of the residents' collaboration with the RUF—and proof that Foday Sankoh had spoken the truth. To rid the nation of this blight, he would bomb the town to bare ground.

The government had a single helicopter gunship, which was flown by a South African mercenary. On its first trip to Makeni, the gunship distributed propaganda. It flew low, showering the town with leaflets titled "Lion News." "Lion News" was touted in the newspapers as instructions for rebels on why they should disarm and exhorting the benefits of peace. The leaflets themselves paint a different picture. The threatening nature of these exhortations sparked a mass exodus from the town, a "pathetic human chain to nowhere" of over thirty thousand people, including the old, infirm, and starving, who left a town under threat of imminent death without any idea of where they would go.[18] The propaganda drop was followed the next day by a series of bombings, which lasted for several weeks.

The bombing was the final damaging event in the relationship between Makeni residents and President Kabbah. By sending the gunship, Kabbah stated unequivocally that he believed Makeni had betrayed Sierra Leone and deserved punishment. This action enabled the RUF to portray itself as the rational, positive alternative. Though residents had wavered on the point of whether or not the government loved the town enough to liberate it, the wholesale destruction offered by the government left no doubt in people's minds that the relationship was unsalvageable. The RUF seemed reasonable and compassionate in comparison; they remained steadfastly in the town, offering instructions to

Members of the RUF:
Government Forces are
advancing and are strong.
If you fight you will DIE

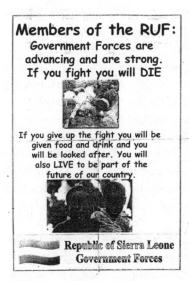

If you give up the fight you will be
given food and drink and you
will be looked after. You will
also LIVE to be part of the
future of our country.

**Republic of Sierra Leone
Government Forces**

**RUF leaders
get**

**Everyone else
gets**

**Republic of Sierra Leone
Government Forces**

FIGURE 1. Two sides of a leaflet dropped from the gunship, tattered and soiled from repeated handling. Photo by author.

How to Surrender

Keep your weapon, but take the magazine
off and throw it away

Wear or carry something white and walk
or drive towards a Police or Government
Forces location. Make sure your weapon
can be seen clearly.

Follow their instructions. You will be
looked after and given food and drink.

**Republic of Sierra Leone
Government Forces**

**RUF:
this time we've
dropped leaflets**

Next time it will be:
a half inch Gatling machine gun *or*
57mm rockets *or*
23mm guns *or*
30mm grenades *or*
ALL OF THEM!

**Republic of Sierra Leone
Government Forces**

FIGURE 2. Ostensibly "exhorting the benefits of peace," these leaflets caused Makeni residents to flee the town. Photo by author.

people about when and where to hide when they heard the gunship, and resolutely remaining in charge, like a captain going down with a sinking ship.

The bombing was the one instance where Kabbah forced residents to choose his government over their own families, in essence stating that the nation should be residents' primary love. This is an extraordinary idea: that the president was somehow sovereign and could demand such love in a democracy. By gathering their families and leaving the town, residents proved that Kabbah could not force this; they would not be stripped of their status as citizens and forced into a new state in which they possessed only Agamben's "bare life" and could be killed without conscience. They fought back by deserting Makeni, even as this resulted in the abandonment of dying children, the elderly, and the sick by the side of the road. The abandoned were mute testament not to the indifference of their families, but to the outright cruelty of the president: these were the people for whom the strong stayed in Makeni, and now it was the president who had forced their deaths. The RUF, remaining in Makeni and running the town as usual, was not subject to such accusations of betrayal. People did not suddenly love or support the RUF; however, Kabbah made the rebels appear the more rational of the two adversaries. If it is true that Makeni people felt some affinity with the rebels, it only became true when Kabbah destroyed all possibility of love for his own regime.

THE COLLABORATOR LABEL: DEFINING THE NATION'S ENEMY

Whether or not individuals cooperated with the rebels during the occupation, Makeni struggled to shrug off the stigma of collaboration in the aftermath, once ex-combatants had been reintegrated. Reintegration was designed to retrain ex-combatants in the locations where they disarmed, and return them to their natal villages with their new skills. Makeni's problem stemmed from the fact that most of these ex-combatants did not return home because they preferred urban life.[19] Unfortunately for the town's reputation, this was interpreted by Kabbah as proof that residents were happy to have them; that they did not care what it did to their reputation to appear so welcoming to the men who had ruled their town for three years.

There are many reasons ex-combatants chose to stay, stemming mainly from the fact that many combatants had been in Makeni for a long time, and had started families they wanted to be near.

Ex-combatants were also aware that they would only find employment in their skills—especially in domains such as driving and mechanics—in urban areas. They could not return penniless to families who hoped they would shoulder the burden of caring for aging parents and younger siblings, and so they chose to stay in town looking for work rather than returning home ashamed and empty-handed. These former combatants themselves defended the townspeople against accusations of collaboration, and their perspectives came from many different angles.

One ex-combatant spoke of the need to actively work on peace by not forcing anyone to uproot himself. The very act of expelling someone reveals a spark of anger in the heart, and this is anathema to peace: "When disarmament went on, [RUF commander] Issa Sesay told us that the war is over, so really everyone should try and go back home. So we were under that pressure. The paramount chief of this chiefdom, Chief Kasanga, outwardly told his people, his community, that we should not be driven. 'The war is over, the ex-combatants have disarmed,' he said. 'They have demobilized and reintegrated. If somebody wants to stay here, let him stay, because we are now under law. If anyone wants to stay and abides by the rules and regulations of the community, we will leave them alone. If somebody wants to go, if he does not want to comport himself to the rules of this community, then go. He should go away.'"

He continued, "So the chief said that good people can stay, but we were under other pressures. At that time they were driving us from their houses, they said we should leave their houses. But Issa . . . this is his hometown. So he was passing around the idea of peace, that we should not be driven forcibly, and at that time people loved him so much because he was nice to them during the occupation. So whatever he said, Issa, they took. So people were favoring him. Some people were not in favor of that, because they said that so many Temnes are scattered all over this country. So if the same is true, let these people come back and the Mendes should go. The special reference was for the Mendes; that we should go home. It was like cleaning the town.

"So the paramount chief advised. He said no, that will not happen. If that happens, it will bring tribal conflict. This is a big problem and we don't want to bring it here. So as far as he is concerned, and this is his chiefdom, he will not allow that to happen. So we can stay here now, peacefully. Of course in any community there must be bad people. Some ex-combatants, they are wicked. And due to their behavior during the war, most of them did not stay here. They were afraid of their shadows. So most of them went home."

There are two important points to note from this narrative. The first is that the speaker did not feel at ease, contravening the notion that residents welcomed ex-combatants. The second is his conclusion that an exodus of ex-combatants would appear to be an ethnic cleansing, as the bulk of the ex-combatants were Mende. The chief perceived this as potentially fueling ethnic conflict in the town while the Mende SLPP was in power, a result he wanted to avoid. In his estimation, the town would suffer greater condemnation for an ethnic cleansing than for letting ex-combatants choose their own path. Many did choose to leave, as they had families and dreams that they wanted to pursue elsewhere. The ex-combatant assumed that most "bad" people would end up leaving town of their own volition, as they had either gone crazy from the acts they committed during the war, or they had no friends at all in town, or both. Driving ex-combatants out would achieve nothing.

A different ex-combatant defended people in Makeni who stayed during the occupation. He framed the occupation as solely a rebel act, claiming that the government falsified information about the attack on Makeni to blame the town for an event that was so clearly a rebel invasion that it was impossible to believe otherwise. Ex-combatants stayed in town due to the vagaries of fortune, not due to any concerted effort on the part of civilians to coax them to remain. The lack of development in the town was punishment for nothing, the act of a vengeful government:

"When we came out of the bush we made this place our headquarters. So people started talking, saying all Makeni people are rebels. They are all rebels because look: all the ringleaders were born there. So they are all rebels. So anything we do here they don't want us to succeed. But it can't be this way. The government can't keep blaming us and giving us a bad name because so many people didn't have anything to do with it. And because they blame them, the rebels, they are making sure that development and work don't come here, they are trying to make things difficult for us. We are trying to overcome that bad name; we are doing everything we can to prove to the rest of the country that it wasn't the fault of Makeni. Former rebels are moving back home, people are going back south . . . but during the war, the chance wasn't there to go home. And we had a plan to go back but things after the war kept foiling it and we just sat down here."

Civilians in Makeni were circumspect on why people stayed during the occupation, once it was clear that the rebels were in control. It was not easy leave the town, especially for those who lacked the infrastructure, people, and means to support themselves elsewhere. According to a teacher, "People used to come and go from the town when it was occupied, but under very difficult circumstances. You know, there are certain people who . . . not that they did not want to leave Makeni, but I think they were looking at this from two schools of thought: where to go, and how to find a living. I think that was the concern of people. Those who moved, a good number of them did not even have a focus. It was like they just 'go for go's sake.' They follow others. When they see a particular group moving, they are left with no alternative but at least to follow them. That is how it used to happen. And for those who stayed, it is not as if they never wanted to move. They wanted to move but maybe they were old or crippled. How to move then?"

It was those who lacked the ability to leave who were most vulnerable to being called rebels: in essence the old, the poor, and those who cared for them. The teacher affirmed this point:

"Some were having relatives . . . one thing about Africa, people respect tradition. And they respect age. And it is a kind of insurance policy here: parents take care of you until you reach adulthood, and much is expected from you again in return. And if at all you have nothing to give to them, especially in relation to cash, or whatever, but if you have a way of staying around them, maybe you have to do that. I think they often appreciate that so much: your presence alone around them . . . it means you have concern for them. And as a result, some people had to stay because of that, because they loved their parents.

"Like myself, my dad was in M—— and I was in Makeni. But there was a roadblock between M—— and Makeni, and one could not venture to M——. And even when I had left Makeni, I always thought: I had an obligation that I must come back to see my daddy. And I was told his condition was deplorable. So I went and saw my daddy, though I had to walk the whole way in very dangerous conditions. And he was not in very good health. I motivated him, I tried to make him see reason so that we go together, but he preferred to stay. He said, 'No, it is better if you go, I prefer to die here.' Old people . . . they don't like to move! He said he had lived his life and it was fair for him to die, but I should leave and save my own life. So he stayed in M—— right through, he survived the whole thing! And the moment I got a teaching job in Makeni I came back to see him."

Recalling Calvin's story in the Introduction, where he describes staying in Kailahun to care for his parents, the fact that so many people chose to remain in the town under occupation rather than scatter speaks to how love requires sacrifice that defies danger. The fact that residents allowed ex-combatants to remain, on the grounds that the decent people would stay and the bad would eventually purge themselves, is the natural rhythm of harmony restoring the social world: those who embrace relationships can stay. Makeni residents were acting resolutely from love in both instances, a more compassionate stance than that offered by those who frame the situation as one of collaboration and national betrayal. For Makeni people, anything could be endured if their loved ones survived. It did not matter who was ruling the town, as long as individuals could provide for their loved ones. It did not matter who stayed after the war was over, as long as those who did were good people. It was more likely that a fragile peace would be preserved if ex-combatants were not driven out in anger. According to the teacher who could not coax his father to leave, "I think Makeni people must be more liberal than other people. We do not just support someone in government because they are our tribe. You get Makeni people voting for the SLPP if they think it will bring good things. No one in the south votes for the APC. So maybe we are a bit liberal to accept the ex-combatants."

In essence, it was the willingness of people in Makeni to remain true to the basic tenets of love—a faith that if someone proves they are "worth having" based on their willingness to nurture, they can be brought into the social fold—that placed them on the outside of a government where loyalty was based absolutely on tribal affiliation. As one of my Mende friends stated thoughtfully, "Loyalty to the SLPP party, it's like a religion among the Mende. You do it because that is where you belong, it does not matter what they do for you now, because the only way you will get anything in the future is if you stay with them. Kabbah was the *big man* in this party and he believed that everyone owed him this love because he was also the *big man* in the nation." In essence, loyalty to the SLPP begins as a negative relationship, as fear of being left out. People are steadfast in their hope that they can transform this relationship into one of love. Kabbah thought that loyalty to his government was a higher priority than love for one's family, with the result that this marginal, problematic town was one of the last places in Sierra Leone to receive relief aid at the end of the war. Makeni residents had not earned his nurturing, and so they earned his bitter disapprobation.

2

"I Must Be Grateful to Them for Freeing Me"

The Soldier

The intricacies of love and betrayal cannot be better illustrated than through the relationship between government and soldier. More than a mere employment contract, the commitment to soldiering requires the will to sacrifice one's life in service of the government, with the expectation that the government will in turn provide a lifetime of care. In Sierra Leone, this bond resonates with intimate, interpersonal practices of love. Therefore, betrayals that occur between parties initiate reactions that unfold similarly to the traumatic breakup of a relationship. The experiences of Captain Mohamed Mansaray, who was tried for treason after a skirmish with a civil militia, faced execution, was rescued by a murderous coup, and was then reinstated as an army officer, illustrate the importance of the rubric of love in comprehending how soldiers understood and acted on their loyalties. Though foreign governments recommended against it, the Sierra Leonean government acknowledged the importance of cultivating love among disgruntled soldiers—welcoming even the mutinous back into the ranks—to bringing about a final end to the war and initiating sustainable peace.

Captain Mansaray was jailed for killing "friendly fighters," supposedly aligned civil militia members, and was saved by a coup of soldiers aligned with the RUF. This prompted a soul-searching decision about whether to shift his allegiance to the "barbarians," or to remain loyal to a government that had betrayed him. He protected himself by working for the coup until its leadership proved itself unworthy of his love. He then escaped to Guinea and "waited for my fate to meet me." The general of a reformed army knew he needed his former soldiers to win the war, and so called them back to the barracks, no matter what acts they might have committed for the junta. In Sierra Leone, it is understandable that soldiers' love for a government that does not appreciate them would waver—a government that wants a loyal army must embrace these soldiers, rather than expelling them for betrayal. I argue that to bring soldiers back to barracks was an act of nurturing and appreciation that prioritized cultural practices of love over the legal discourse of impunity.

AN OFFICER'S CONFIDENCE

When I met him in 2005, Captain Mansaray was in charge of training young soldiers at Teko Barracks, on the outskirts of Makeni. A tall, witty, and confident man, he was charged with training inexperienced and cocksure young recruits in the arts of jungle warfare. He approached our interview the same way, striding in from a training session, throwing his beret on the table, sitting down across from me and taking control of the conversation with, "I hear you have been looking for me." His approach to our conversation made it clear that he had told the story many times; I was receiving, more or less, the "official" narrative of soldier loyalty.

Mohamed was only interested in talking about the war. His childhood did not matter, nor did his family, who remained absent from his narrative. Here was a single man, enmeshed in his army family, focused only on the turbulent relationship with his *pa,* the president. We began with his rationale for enlisting. This decision was wrought in heady and yet terrifying days, during a coup that inspired the young to serve. The army was a popular career in the 1990s, as the NPRC had ensured that those chosen for officer training were the best and brightest, and were treated well:

"I was enlisted into the army as an officer cadet in 1994. There was only one reason to enlist in the army at the time: the war was raging! I saw it as one of my duties as a citizen, my national duty, to serve my country. I enlisted to defend our motherland. I was lucky that I was able to do the full ten months of training. Later in the war as things began to go badly, the cadets received less and less training. More people were dying, and there was a need to send officers to the warfront as quickly as possible. Some barely knew how to fire a weapon! But I felt confident when I graduated. I was commissioned as a second lieutenant in 1995, and I was posted to Bo, in the south of the country."

Mohamed's narrative was precise in the way that most Sierra Leoneans, especially army officers, were with respect to where they were at any time and who was with them. However, the statistical log often overshadowed how he felt at any point in time, a common trait among officers, one of whom said, "For our soldiers, we must be precise. It is not our job to say how we feel." His story involved a painstaking reconstruction of both the list of his commanding officers at any point in time and the precise location of his brigade and platoon. I had to prod him on the details of his emotional state when he made decisions—where he clashed with the RUF and what the outcomes were, how it was that he always seemed to be able to bring his platoon through battle more or less unscathed. He emphasized that he had little difficulty persuading soldiers to follow him into battle.

His confidence brimmed even as he remembered his first experience of active battle as frightening: "My heart was racing when I first heard the gunshots; I felt a little paralyzed by it. The RUF was coming, and here I was, just out of school and now in a battle! But then I saw the faces of my men and knew that I had to lead them into this battle, or we would all just die as victims of it. They were going to wait for me until I seized control of the situation. So I guess from there I lost my innocence of war. And after a time, I developed some zeal and enthusiasm and I was able to overcome my fears." His enthusiasm was based in part on the fact that the RUF was, up to that point, still a small rebellion contained to the south. Mohamed's battalion was stationed in the southern central district of Bo. Taking Bo would have been a major victory for the RUF, and the NPRC stationed several battalions in the area to repel the advancing rebels.

The RUF leadership knew that its ability to hold the imagination and loyalty of its young cadres lay largely in its ability to conquer and capture the icons of the APC's power. Aside from concentrating on Bo, this led them to organize major attacks on diamond fields, elite schools, and industrial sites. The RUF attacked the campus of Njala University, less than eighty miles from Freetown, and vandalized empty buildings that had been evacuated early in the war.[1] In 1996, Captain Mansaray was sent with a skeleton company to defend what was left of it. We did not discuss why his posting at Njala was significant, and it is for this reason that I must leave his story briefly in order to flesh out key details. Between when Mohamed joined the army and his posting to Njala, the initial coup had been overcome by a palace coup and democratic elections, and the focus of the fighting shifted from the army to civil militias. These events are critical to comprehending Mohamed's experiences.

THE DISGRACE OF THE NPRC AND THE IMPORTANCE OF NJALA

In the 1990s Njala was the only college affiliated with the University of Sierra Leone located outside of Freetown. This was one of the major attractions for students from rural areas: a child's dream of attending Njala seemed real; its presence a reminder that success was possible outside of the APC's power base. The attraction for the RUF of capturing the campus—literally as well as figuratively—was undeniable. Njala would be an ideological publicity coup for Foday Sankoh in his bid to control the countryside. However, as the war dragged on, the political landscape altered to the point where the RUF was not the biggest threat to Njala, nor were they Captain Mansaray's primary concern. Mohamed shuddered visibly when he began to speak about his first battles at Njala, for they were not with the RUF, but with the civil militias. The most dangerous aspect of the civil militias for the army was their separate loyalty to the government, a loyalty that did not include fellow fighting factions. In the political climate of the time, the rise of these militias complicated the preeminence of the army as a fighting force; the army's soldiers were, literally, fighting to maintain their position against interlopers.

At the time Captain Mansaray was sent to Njala, the army's future was uncertain. The NPRC had become decadent and had fallen out of favor with Sierra Leoneans. The junta had left the army field units in the same position—underresourced, underpaid, outmanned, and outgunned—as they themselves had been four years earlier. With the army's reputation and capabilities once again compromised by the lavish lifestyle of its leaders, the RUF began to rebuild. Feeding on Sierra Leoneans' fading faith in their leaders, RUF cadres began retaking positions they had lost. Valentine Strasser promised that the NPRC would organize elections as soon as the war was won, even as that end became more remote. Something had to give.

Strasser was deposed in a palace coup in January 1996 by a coalition of officers led by his vice president, Julius Maada Bio, and Tom Nyuma, the chief of defense. The coup joined a long chain of similar political events in Sierra Leone, as one person's quest for bigness and permanence was invariably overcome by the similar ambitions of another, drawing on the same limited resources. In such a situation, as long as no one commands complete loyalty—the way Siaka Stevens did—he is in a precarious position. Big men are prone to backroom deals, coalitions, and other would-be big men keen to seize an opportunity. The biggest threat to big men is their closest allies, who can woo the same followers.

Sergeant Bah, a soldier who was ordered to seize the barracks from NPRC commanders, participated in the palace coup. Sergeant Bah is a large man with an open, freckled face, serious about his responsibilities and loyal the chief of defense, Tom Nyuma. He was suddenly thrust into a position of overthrowing the government because he was hanging around his battalion headquarters outside of Freetown that morning:

"Tom Nyuma marched into battalion headquarters and ordered the second-in-command to bring two trucks of soldiers, about 120 of us, to the front gate because he said we were going on a military exercise. None of us questioned why he was ordering us to do this, because he was the man in charge! You as a soldier have no right to ask anything, especially of Tom Nyuma because if you questioned him he might just decide to kill you. We had heard these things about him. So we saw the big transport trucks and figured this was an official exercise, and it was just our battalion that did not get the news. Tom Nyuma had us armed with AK-47 rifles and rocket-propelled grenades, and then he ordered us to get on board. We expected that because it was an exercise we would head east and go to the hills, or maybe south into the jungle. So it was a big surprise when the trucks went west, in the Freetown direction.

"I should have been suspicious about an exercise because there was not supposed to be anything scheduled. It was a graduation day for new soldiers, and the ceremony had just been completed at Benguema Training Center. President Strasser and Vice President Bio were at Benguema while we were heading towards Freetown. When we arrived in Freetown, the trucks dropped us at this bridge very close to Cockerill Barracks, which is the army's headquarters. Tom Nyuma ordered us not to move, so we waited there until Strasser and Bio returned from Benguema. From our position, we could see the helicopter that was bringing Strasser and Bio back from Benguema landing inside the barracks. It was after it landed and everyone went inside that we were given the order to move."

Sergeant Bah looked a bit sheepish at this point, as though it should have been obvious what he was being ordered to do. But he persisted that until the coup actually happened, it had not seemed possible. "I didn't know that they had intended to overthrow Strasser on that day! We were just following orders! So they drove us near the barracks and ordered us off the trucks. They said we must move in a single file, which according to my training, was like saying, 'Get ready for a battle!' So we moved, and Tom Nyuma said that this was the place where we would be performing our exercise. He said, 'Now we will move!' We moved in single file all the way to Cockerill."

Here it is difficult to differentiate between the actions of a soldier and the actions of a man loyal to his *big man*. Though Tom Nyuma inspired loyalty through fear—he was rumored to search for soldiers who had gone AWOL from the front, personally beat and imprison them before eventually sending them back—Sergeant Bah described the platoon that was specifically chosen for this duty as one of noncommissioned officers. Through many years of training, they would have acted automatically on orders.

"As we are moving, any officer we saw, Tom Nyuma would order his arrest and we would hold him and hand him over to our lieutenant, who would take care of him. No one was hurt while we were doing this; I think none of them could believe what was happening. This went on until we reached the headquarters, where we were suddenly face to face with the security force of Chairman Strasser. They were falling in their battle lines, with their heavy support weapons. But they were not many more than we were. So immediately Tom Nyuma rushed at them and yelled at them, 'Why are you just standing there? Come to attention!' They all came to attention. He said, 'Ground arms!' So they placed their weapons on the ground. He said, 'Half step, backwards march!' So they marched backwards, and he then gave a salute for us to advance. He said, 'Take all these weapons,' and we took all the weapons off them. We disarmed them diplomatically!"

The coup was remarkable for the fact that the force of soldiers' fearful loyalty to Nyuma assured its bloodless nature. In what other situation would an armed group of soldiers, clearly aware that something was amiss, surrender their weapons to an advancing force of their colleagues? Such was the power of Nyuma's reputation for severity that he could, with a company of loyal and unsuspecting soldiers, seize control of the government. It echoed Siaka Stevens's own hold on the nation.

"The moment the bodyguards were disarmed, Tom Nyuma rushed into the conference room. We rushed in too. And the captain gave us orders to deploy around the room, which we did, and we took control of all the men. None of them were armed, and it seemed that they all knew what was going on. None of them fought us. At that moment, Tom Nyuma and two other officers took the headdress off Strasser.[2] Suddenly he was no longer our president, he had been defeated and was just a man again. They pushed him into a helicopter, and they took him from Cockerill directly in the Guinea direction. Nyuma told us that this was a coup that was organized successfully. And from then, Maada Bio was appointed as the new chairman."

Bio followed through on the promise of democratic elections, which were held three months later. Alhaji Ahmed Tejan Kabbah, a former UN diplomat and advisor to the NPRC, won the presidency in a sweeping victory. The SLPP party, out of power since 1967, was ushered in with great fanfare. Kabbah had campaigned on promises of ending the war, but was faced with doing so with an army that had nurtured the nation's love for several years. He needed to transfer this love onto himself, and thus was faced with the predicament of both discrediting the army and retaining a loyal fighting force with which to end the war. Soldiers themselves had already been implicated in actions that shed doubt on their love for their countrymen, which Kabbah exploited in his bid to transfer the people's love to himself.

SOLDIERS BY DAY, REBELS BY NIGHT

The RUF suffered tremendous losses in the early days of the NPRC regime as a revitalized and resourced army pushed them to the margins of the country. On the brink of destruction, the rebels fought a dirty public relations campaign aimed to turn rural people against the army. They confused the issue of who was plundering and burning villages by wearing looted army uniforms into raids and combat. Many of the former RUF cadres that I spoke to admitted that much of their supply chain came from ambushing army convoys and relieving them of food, weapons, and other supplies. One former combatant related a story of taking the kit bags of several soldiers because he had not had soap or wearable clothes for months. His rebel platoon was clothed haphazardly in looted uniforms and ragged civilian clothes. Another confirmed that RUF commanders often wore full army uniforms to display their status. Civilians confronted with these uniforms were confused: was it rebels or soldiers who were causing mayhem?

Because the uniforms were not worn in regulation fashion, soldiers themselves stated that they could immediately spot a rebel in soldier uniform, because he looked "ragtag." Those rebels who had procured clothes by looting or, sometimes, by taking them off soldiers they killed, rarely had the full uniform, and those who did lacked the knowledge to wear it properly. Civilians, however, could not necessarily differentiate between a rebel in solider uniform and a soldier who had been in the bush for months. Indeed, as the RUF was increasingly successful in raiding convoys, soldiers at the front began to look more ragtag, and did loot villages to supplement their depleted and burgled supplies. It was becoming impossible, whether by dress or behavior, to differentiate between soldier and rebel. Civilians began accusing soldiers of being *sobels:* "soldiers by day, rebels by night." They feared *sobels* as much as they feared the RUF.[3]

The emotional and psychological effects of these developments were devastating for army morale, and soldiers began to act as they were treated: as hated enemies of the people. The army's cause was not aided by its lack of resources. Because soldiers were deployed far from their homes, a lack of maps and local knowledge became an almost crippling handicap to troops who lurched, hungry, despondent, and logistically blind through unknown territory. Cut off from their supply chains, many fended for themselves in RUF-devastated villages. From this arose a new mantra among civilians: "rebel attack, soldier clear." Writer Ishmael Beah, in remembering his time as a child soldier in the army, described a life much as it would be within a rebel cadre. The two fought each other as enemies, but as individuals had only their friends to rely on, they also looted with impunity. To defend their villages against attacks—whether by rebels or soldiers—youth began organizing themselves into civil defense militias. The most famous of these was the Kamajors, which took its name and initial members from a traditional male society.

The Kamajors did not rise as a self-interested fighting faction until President Kabbah recognized them officially as a military force comparable to the national army. To the end of his presidential tenure, he defended their intentions as loyal defenders of liberty. Because this is Captain Mansaray's narrative, I will analyze his story about the Kamajors, and how the government's support of this self-interested faction was the reason the army—and its ability to fight the RUF—was destroyed. From soldiers' perspectives, the rise of the *sobel* was a disease caused by a disinterested government. Instead of nurturing their ragtag forces, the government expelled them and embraced rural youth as the basis for a new army.

One of Captain Mansaray's commanding officers, Major Manneh, stated that *sobels* provided an opening for the new government to exercise their political muscle and "make the people love them, and wipe away their memories of how much they had loved the NPRC." Major Manneh is an articulate man, a college graduate who joined the army in the 1980s because he needed money to hospitalize his ailing father. He related a story from the eastern district of Kenema, famous for its diamonds, where the new government took advantage of a weakened army to assert themselves against the NPRC:

"The RUF had attacked Kenema and they were dressed like military police. And people were saying, 'It was the military that attacked.' This was the point where the politicians could have explained to people that it was not actually the army who attacked, however they wanted people to think it was us. The military did not have a media officer, as all our money was spent on fighting the RUF, so we just kept silent. So we did not succeed in convincing people that we were not the ones carrying out the attacks. The politicians who were bent on holding on to power decided to use that incident to castigate the army. They were calling us *sobels,* slandering us. We lost credibility, the people lost their faith in the army and they turned their backs on us. From that point people in Kenema would talk to the RUF instead of the soldiers. They just didn't know any better."

Major Manneh was clear that, placed in terms of love as the matrix by which people create, negotiate, and understand all relationships—even relationships writ large like that between a politician and citizens—the reason for Kabbah's desire to discredit the army was logical. Soldiers' loyalty was to whomever recruited them.

"The government considered the army to be that of their predecessors, of both their enemy political party and of a coup.[4] They believed everyone who was recruited was loyal to someone else. How could they work with this same army? So in preparation for the elections, when they knew they would take power, they publicly questioned the army. This way they could get the international community to hound the NPRC to hand over power. They succeeded in doing this, but then they were stuck with an army they had told everyone was incompetent."

In essence, a new government had to contend with the loyalty its citizens, whether civilians or soldiers, had to previous governments. People had to love the SLPP as they had initially loved the NPRC. As the previous government was a military council, when they were framed as betrayers of the nation because of their excess, by extension, the whole army was as well. The *sobel* phenomenon—though there were mutinous soldiers who did join the RUF—was a foundation for transforming loyalties. However, the government needed a force to fight the RUF. The surge in militias defending their villages provided the perfect platform to shift responsibility for fighting, and the benefits of salaries and food—government "appreciation" and gratitude—from the army.

The Kamajor militia lacked military training, but the mystique of their hunting magic and their vast numbers made them a viable alternative to the military in people's imaginations. Born from secret societies deep in the bush, Kamajors were steeped in rituals designed to produce fearless warriors. According to lore, a Kamajor who maintained the sacred taboos would be invincible in battle, impervious to bullets, and clairvoyant about the positions of his enemies.[5] People feared these spiritually powerful warriors, and with Kabbah's blessing they became the primary fighting force.[6] The deputy minister of defense, Hinga Norman, provided the Kamajors with arms, rice rations, and public praise. Young men flocked to their ranks, as they finally had a clear way to act on their desire to protect their own villages. Captain Mansaray narrated his encounter with the Kamajors as a case of youth anxious to prove their love for their big men by attacking a soft target: the army itself.

THE PREEMINENCE OF IDEOLOGICAL BATTLES

As we focused on his own experiences, Captain Mansaray became uncomfortable talking about the deteriorating relationship between the army and the militias. He perceived a clear-cut case of divide and conquer, with Kabbah forcing people to support a faction handpicked as the best alternative to an army that he had discredited. This sowed discord in villages, where the families of soldiers were ostracized and sometimes attacked by those who supported the militias. The government had chosen to nurture the Kamajors, therefore it became impossible for people who claimed to love Sierra Leone to also support the army. Loyalties were being challenged.

The soldiers perceived a breach of loyalty when Hinga Norman introduced the Kamajors as a fighting faction. Norman gave the army explicit instructions to cooperate with the Kamajors, and to not hinder their activities in their home territories. He lavished the Kamajors with gifts of weapons and food—supplies that were diverted from the army—and publicly slandered the army. As Major Manneh remembered, "In my presence the then-deputy minister of defense verbally attacked our commander. Norman told him, 'I will do this and this to you, and this and that,' in front of other people! They told us in front of the Kamajors that they did not trust us!" According to Major Manneh, if Norman intended to empower the Kamajors to the point where they became the preeminent faction fighting the rebels, he was bolstering that effort by shaming and discrediting every soldier, loyal or not. Mohamed became aware of these growing rifts just as he was taking up his post at Njala University.

"Things started to go bad when it became clear that the Kamajors were waging an antiarmy campaign. They started attacking some of our guys. They set up checkpoints on the roads where they hijacked soldiers on official business, by pulling someone out of his vehicle and killing him. We couldn't trust them anymore, and the bad blood began to grow. They kept saying they were our friends, and yet they did these things to us! Covertly, their agenda was to become the primary fighting force in the country, and get all the benefits and trust of the government. They were fighting us for supremacy. And for us in the field this took the form of them killing our men. We lost two men traveling home on leave. It was very unsafe for us to go alone. The moment you left your platoon to go visit your home they would ambush you. It was made even worse by all of their hunting magic." He shuddered. "When one captain was killed, nobody, *nobody*, ever found his body."

The Kamajors were widely thought to nurture their magic through cannibalistic rituals, where ritual consumption of body parts conferred invincibility. More than the everyday fear of witchcraft possessed by Sierra Leoneans, the belief that Kamajors were hunting and killing soldiers—literally eating their rival faction—denoted this as a new kind of warfare, one of gaining strength and even immortality through the consumption of enemies. Mohamed was terrified of this development.

"He was killed and we cannot find his corpse. A lady from his village informed us that he has been killed and they have eaten him secretly in their initiation ceremony. She was terrified, but wanted us to know. So I informed my headquarters, and the battalion commander sent in his best officer to investigate. He asked the chief if he could produce the body of the soldier. But everyone in the village denied that they knew anything about him. It remains a mystery, up until now. We must believe this woman, because she would not tell us unless we agreed to protect her from the Kamajors. If we announced that she had informed us about his death, then they would probably hang her and her family. So we kept secret everything we knew."

Kamajor medicine men conducted elaborate initiation rituals in which new recruits were imbued with protective magic. Many went into battle in unusual costumes, with elaborate headdresses and bullets sewn inside their clothes to protect them. The Kamajor leadership boasted that bullets could never kill a trained, disciplined, and initiated Kamajor.[7] A Kamajor death due to bullet wounds resulted from him breaking sacred taboos, such as drinking alcohol or sleeping with women. The stories of human sacrifice and cannibalism—meant to enhance a warrior's strength—were omnipresent in my interviews referring to Kamajor rituals. Both witches and Kamajors eat people, but only Kamajors might also protect. Their sinister liminality terrified people, which was why Mohamed trusted the woman who came forward.[8]

Mohamed and his platoon were infected by the fear the Kamajors generated, to the point where he advised his soldiers never to travel alone. He believed he had no reason to fear Kamajors when army and militia units were stationed together to protect a position, until one night in 1996. Though sinister, isolated acts of betrayal among rival factions were understandable. However, a large-scale attack was beyond the boundaries of mere rivalry for the government's love and appreciation. This was an outrageous betrayal.

"On 28th of October, 1996, I was on the Njala campus when the Kamajors attacked soldiers at Taiyema junction, about seven miles from our location. One soldier was brutally murdered, three were wounded, and the rest fled to Bo town. I wasn't to know that part until later, but just after that attack the Kamajors continued with the advance, and they attacked Njala. They came in with whoops and cries and they were firing all over, and we realized we were surrounded. I ordered everyone to stay low, load their weapons, and fire on anyone who fires on them. We defended ourselves successfully; no one among my men was injured or killed, though that was not true for our enemies. I did not realize until they fled and we started recovering the bodies of their dead that these were in fact Kamajors that had attacked us. Oh God, I was in trouble!"

Mohamed narrates a precise series of events of the battle—his soldiers were attacked, and fired only to defend themselves—as though he was sitting in a courtroom, remembering "the facts" to a jury. If he only realized after the fact that his company had annihilated Kamajors, this would make his stance legally defensible, and not an act of betraying his president—and thus his country—by killing a supposedly friendly faction.

"At that time, we were still supposed to accept that the Kamajors were not our enemies! But we had to defend ourselves. If someone fires on you, you return fire. And they had assault rifles; it was not like they attacked us with bush knives. And, well," he tucked his head shyly before continuing, "we were attacked by over a thousand of them, and we were only about sixty. But once we were in our trenches, we were able to inflict massive casualties among them. They believed that they could not be hurt or killed by bullets, so a lot of them died. Truthfully, we embarrassed them. They were unable to take our location, and they had to flee. That afternoon, they came back and attacked again, and we defended that attack too. They were unable to take our camp, and they were also unable to take back their dead. I think they wanted to erase the proof that they could be killed. But we still had those bodies, and we buried them."

With his shy pride in his company's success, the tone of the narrative switched from jury testimony to explaining to me, an outsider with no Kamajor allegiances, just how successful a battle it was. Mohamed swiftly returned to the sobering facts of aftermath.

"I informed my commanders that people dressed in Kamajor attire attacked our location. I described them as enemies, because I knew that a friend would not fire at me. The situation report I sent to headquarters emphasized that enemies dressed as Kamajors had attacked us. So it's like . . . ah . . . what should I say? Perhaps they were rebels! Concurrently they too were making a report that soldiers at Njala attacked them."

Mohamed is an intelligent man, and he was aware of the ramifications of accusing the Kamajors of attacking him. Hinga Norman had made it eminently clear to the army that he trusted the Kamajors; that the burden of proof for an attack lay solely with a coup-mongering, *sobel* organization. It emerged that Mohamed was wise to use vague language in his report, as it showcased his honesty and humility, rather than his willingness to point fingers, and resulted in an equally honest investigation of the attack:

"Our own bosses in Bo took action. The Kamajors and the army met with the police and tried to come to common ground. An investigative team arrived at the site to see whether the soldiers attacked the Kamajors or Kamajors attacked the soldiers. The team reported entirely in our favor. In Taiyema and in Njala, they reported that the Kamajors had attacked."

As unsatisfying as their findings were for Hinga Norman, the exoneration of the army indicates that civil servants were still loyal to the prior government, the army-run NPRC. Mohamed's triumph meant very little to Norman, who was not going to be humiliated by his own organization being convicted of attacking an army position. He had risked his reputation by touting them as a viable military alternative, and so immediately went on the offensive. Captain Mansaray was at the sharp end of this attack.

"Norman was in Bo at this time, and he was raging. He accused us of killing his Kamajors and warned that we would surely go to prison. So he called the brigade headquarters to speak to the chief of staff. He told the chief that he wanted to speak to me directly. So we met and he accused me of killing his men. I said, 'We have not killed some men, sir.' I said, 'We were attacked by enemies who were dressed in Kamajor attire and they were killed in action.' I said, 'You cannot tell whose bullet killed somebody.' So that was my defense, and he accused me of trying to be too clever! But I told him, 'If you are not satisfied, then you need to talk to the wounded soldiers in Bo.' So he went to them."

By telling Norman, "you cannot tell whose bullet killed somebody," Mohamed was playing to the mystique of Kamajor invincibility, while simultaneously diverting culpability for homicide and a breach of loyalty. He was wary of offending Norman further by doubting Kamajor magic. However, with this turn of phrase he reminded Norman that before battle, Kamajors performed rituals on their own bullets in order to make each one fatal to its target. Mohamed was inferring that in the confusion of a firefight, perhaps it was the Kamajors' own errant, all-powerful bullets that killed them.

In taking this line of defense and by subtly throwing their invincibility into question, he forced the Kamajors to retract their story, a clear point of pride with Mohamed. "The Kamajors later said that these people at Njala were not Kamajors, they were RUF guys wearing Kamajor attire. It was only logical, because their people do not die and they are also never wounded. So therefore it must have been rebels. A common ground was found, and so we decided that among troops loyal to the government, if anyone led an attack on the other, he would be killed instantly. And the Kamajors sealed this pact with magic."

The importance of the factions finding common ground cannot be overstated. It highlights that the meeting was not about determining who was correct, but ensuring that both sides remained loyal to the government. Allowing the Kamajors to retract their story enabled them to retain the façade of legitimacy and the mystique of invincibility. Norman also achieved a temporary détente with the army. Since the clear supremacy of Captain Mansaray's troops over the Kamajors proved that the army was a superior fighting force, the war against the RUF would be best won with soldiers not irretrievably alienated. For a brief moment, Norman's determination to defeat the RUF overcame his will to promote the Kamajors. This was soon, however, overcome by the desire of many Kamajor leaders to wrest military supremacy from the army permanently, and corner the market on the government's "appreciation." Mohamed was in Bo when the Kamajors made their move.

"On the 30th of October, I was in Bo, waiting for orders. The Kamajors were grouping from all the villages, walking to Bo for a large offensive at the army headquarters. They said they had an order from Hinga Norman to attack all soldiers. We were all concentrated at headquarters at the time, because there had been a few incidents where a soldier was lynched or killed in the township, which resulted in the commanders ordering us all to move back into the barracks and stay together. So the Kamajors launched an offensive on the headquarters, and the paramount chief who led the attack was killed."

Due to their origins in the guilds of hunting and warfare, the Kamajor fighters themselves were essentially apprentices to the masters of these crafts, in some cases to paramount chiefs. Such a master—the most skilled at his trade—initiated all the others. Akin to a chief surgeon or judge, he was the standard by which others judged their skills.[9] If a Kamajor master was killed, this spelled doom for his minions, mere apprentices to the magical warrior craft.

"Paramount Chief Lekano was a Kamajor. He was killed, *and* he had been one of the people that brokered the peace so that anyone who attacks will surely die. He led the Kamajors to our location, and he was killed. Yeah. He was killed. But that meant tough luck for the army. Because Hinga Norman came back to Bo with the chief of defense staff and the inspector general of police to launch an investigation. So the officers and the Kamajors scrambled to broker a new peace and select a council of elders from among both organizations, to make our own deal and bring some quiet."

This peace never took hold, because, as Mohamed soon discovered, Norman was not going to give him, or any other officer who had fought the Kamajors, the chance to be heard. More than just destroying Kamajor hunting lore, that testimony would have destroyed all confidence people had in the new fighters, and thus the government itself. People would have called for the return of the NPRC. Mohamed did not know that Norman was going to use legal means to quiet all challenges to the

Kamajors' supremacy. I asked him if he would have run if he had know Norman was coming after him. His response: "Maybe."

NEVER BETRAY THE GOVERNMENT: MANSARAY ON TRIAL FOR TREASON

"I was called to the police station for an interrogation. And I made the same statement that I made earlier. After two months, in early December, I was called to Freetown. We were conducting operations when I heard that I should go to Freetown to answer for a few things about what happened at Njala on the 28th of October. So I went to Freetown, I was taken to the military police, and they were very quiet about it. Nobody said anything to me, except that I should go to the Criminal Investigation Division [CID] for the army.

"So I went to the CID and they said that I would be detained for other charges. It seemed like they didn't know what to do about the situation. So they brought in this civilian witness. This witness said, 'I will explain what happened to you.' And he told them about the attack. And they decided to arrest him and charge him with aiding an attack on the Kamajors. We were all detained at headquarters for four months and eleven days, and later arraigned in court. They brought us all up on murder, wounding people, and other related charges. And we pleaded not guilty, and were sent to jail to wait."

Mohamed's face betrayed confusion, hurt, and disbelief, as though he himself still could not come to grips with the events of his trial, even at the moment of narrating them. He had assumed once the initial investigation had concluded that he was exonerated and could return to his duties. Only when the witness was also charged did it dawn on him that Hinga Norman would finish any questions about the army with a public treason trial. As far as Norman was concerned, a trial would send a clear signal to the military to step aside and let the Kamajors fight the war, or suffer the consequences. Mohamed was a metonym for the army being cast out of the government's circle of nurturing.

The trial took place in a confluence of troubling events. In November 1996, President Kabbah and Foday Sankoh signed the Abidjan Peace Accords to officially end the war. The terms of the accord stipulated that the RUF would lay down arms and transform into a political party. A new army would be open to any RUF member who wanted to be a soldier. Though these events signaled to the international community that Sierra Leone was taking steps towards peace, in the context of local practices, they indicated instead a struggle over who would be officially embraced and nurtured by the government.

In a slight to what was rapidly becoming one of the largest fighting factions, not only were Kamajor representatives absent from the negotiation and signing of the Accords, but no provisions were made for their demobilization and reintegration. The assumption was made that militia members would simply disperse back to their villages and take up farming and hunting once again, as war was simply a natural extension of their everyday practices. The Kamajors had nothing to gain from the peace accords, and everything—power, arms, money, legitimacy, and pride—to lose. The only way they could justify their importance was by continually attacking the army—and the army's credibility. This meant that in spite of a public treason trial, Kamajor-military skirmishes increased in frequency and intensity. Norman could not round up and gag every witness; thus popular perception of the lines between Kamajor, rebel, and soldier blurred with each passing day.

Hinga Norman had also overstepped his bounds and put President Kabbah in an awkward situation. As president, Kabbah was the commander in chief of both the military and the Kamajors. In spite of the lack of love, it was his military, and his officers, being hauled to trial. Mohamed was one of a dozen officers awaiting trial, and the army was becoming restless. Soldiers gathered in protest, and it was clear to President Kabbah that the Kamajor-army squabble was militarily unsupportable and politically untenable. One or two companies of disgruntled soldiers was one thing, several battalions worth quite another. After months of brief proceedings in which defendants pled "not guilty," media coverage of the trials had reached a fever pitch and Kabbah was forced to intervene. Ignoring the trials would have spelled doom for his presidency, as it would have confused the issue of whether or not the president was himself loyal to his fighters. Mohamed became much more animated in this part of his narrative:

"The next time we appeared our lawyers came to defend us, and it seemed that the president was really interested in the matter because there were reams of papers, letters, appealing for us, and the soldiers themselves were complaining to the SLA [Sierra Leone Army] leaders that Captain Mansaray and his men should be released. They were arguing that we were unlawfully detained. Because when Kamajors were killing soldiers, nobody said anything. When soldiers defend themselves, people will take us to prison. Our second appearance in court, there was no case file. The president had it. He was studying the file, trying to figure out how he can intervene politically. He was under a lot of pressure from the community. Before our next appearance our lawyers asked for the case file. It was still not there, and there was still no evidence against us. So we waited, and the court was adjourned again."

President Kabbah was stalling the proceedings to gain some political ground. When he took office in 1996, Kabbah hired a South African mercenary outfit, Executive Outcomes, to work with the Kamajors to fight the RUF, and he had enough success with this arrangement to lure a weakened Foday Sankoh to the negotiation table in Abidjan. However, once the Accords were signed, Executive Outcomes left. Within six months, the RUF was once again fighting at full strength. Sankoh blatantly ignored the tenets of the Accords and ordered his cadres to continue engaging the army and Kamajors.

Mohamed asserted that Sankoh had no interest in becoming the leader of a political party. The Accords could not give him anything that he did not already have, namely a fighting force, command and loyalty, and a steady income from mining diamonds. Sankoh was a big man, and had no interest in accepting amnesty from the government of a nation he wanted for himself. What Kabbah could not have known at the time, however, was the willingness of elements of the discredited, disdained army to join Sankoh in this quest. On May 25, 1997, the Armed Forces Revolutionary Council (AFRC) was born, and with it Captain Mansaray's liberation at the hands of society's most criminal elements.

THE AFRC: HOW SOLDIERS INTERPRET FAILURES OF LOVE

All Mohamed can remember about the day he was broken out of prison was the mayhem. "I remember the sounds of gunshots, of people shouting. . . . I remember hearing the front gates of the prison blown open with a grenade, hearing the guards leave their posts with cries of fear and go running for their lives. I remember seeing some guys in ragtag breaking open the door of my cell." These were low-level soldiers, not officers, who freed him. The unfolding coup was a precise illustration of how the perceptions among soldiers of *who* had failed in their duty to love and care for the fighters shaped their reactions to this failure. The soldiers blamed their own chain of command for the abuses they suffered at the hands of the Kamajors, and to them Hinga Norman and President Kabbah were not politicians so much as the top two members of this chain. The coup was a reaction to a betrayal by big men, who were failing to care for their loyal cadres.

Mohamed, as an officer who had valiantly protected his soldiers from Kamajors, did not expound on these failures in his narrative. However, Major Samura, who also commanded soldiers in battle, admitted that the coup was logical and predictable: "I know why the coup happened. The soldiers were very angry with us. They did not have the power to be angry with the Kamajors, or the government, just us. Because in their eyes, we could have done something about their deplorable situation. When soldiers were making complaints against the Kamajors, we sent these complaints through our chain of command. And we believed at first that Hinga Norman was taking action. But nothing happened when things started going very badly. The president finally ordered an investigation into this issue, and Hinga Norman selected the people involved. Unfortunately the investigation was biased and it ended up in chaos. And just a week or two after that committee was set up this AFRC coup happened."

This investigation was President Kabbah's attempt to address the treason trial and the fate of Captain Mansaray and others, and it occurred without the jailed officers being interviewed. It came to nothing, and that was the trigger that set off the coup. As far as the soldiers knew, it was their big men who were responsible for caring for them on the battlefield, and the only officers who had stood up for them were in jail, betrayed by the government. Major Samura was stationed in Freetown at the time of the coup, and he knew of these internal failures to love, protect, and nurture. "It was just corporals and below who staged the coup, the low-level enlisted men, and they targeted officers specifically for torture and murder. They said that they had done everything correctly in complaining to us that the Kamajors had been killing them, and we have been charged with their welfare but we were complacent. They saw that we had done nothing, when in fact we did everything within our power to do, which wasn't much. We only had the power to send their complaints up the chain."

Major Samura defended the officer's inability to act, even as he sympathized with the soldiers' plight: "In the military, I don't go to the head of joint force and tell him what is happening when my chain of command are all present: my brigade commander, my commanding officer, these are the people in my chain. I cannot just move from the platoon and go to the lieutenant and then it is done. You will never hear of these things in the military. But unfortunately the soldiers, well, they cannot understand because they were impatient and emotional. And that caused the AFRC coup."

Whether or not he understood his iconic status as a champion of soldiers' rights, Captain Mansaray thought that he was released because he was an infantry officer at the front. The soldiers hunted down staff officers, who were responsible for pay, provisioning, and welfare.[10] "Some of the AFRC said that these officers were not helpful when democracy was there, that was their grievance. Some said the NPRC officers were treating them badly. They were trying to reclaim rations and pay. And to be honest with you, those things were happening. Some soldiers were working for four or five months without receiving their salary or food. What used to happen under Stevens was that at the end of every month a private soldier would get a bag of rice added to his salary. Under Kabbah, some officers were withholding salaries and rice from their soldiers. These were some of their frustrations that boiled over in the coup. Me personally, I was lucky. Nobody molested me or attacked me because I had never been a pay officer or a quartermaster. So I had no problem with them."

Captain Mansaray described graft and embezzlement not as illegal or immoral, but as a breach of the relationship that should exist between officers and soldiers. Indeed, the *sobel* phenomenon itself was a result of failures of care: soldiers took what they needed because they were not receiving it through the chain of command. In this intimate way of thinking, it is one's immediate relationships that are responsible for one's survival—and those relationships that must be confronted when care fails. Both Captain Mansaray and Major Samura articulated the fact that uneducated soldiers, fighting on a remote front, had no knowledge of the larger battles being fought over military primacy. Nor did they know that the lack of rice was partially due to Kabbah's own policies. Siaka Stevens instituted the rice ration to inculcate loyalty among the cadres—nurturing that predictably secured their gratitude—and Kabbah diverted these resources to the Kamajors.[11] What soldiers themselves saw was their commanding officers not taking care of them—whether or not they were able to—and it was those officers who bore the brunt of their anger.

The ragtag, barefoot, and dirty foot soldiers who marched triumphantly into Freetown went on a looting frenzy. These were the *sobels*, taking back what they were owed by a military, and thus a country, that had turned its back on them and withdrawn care and appreciation. Looting was vengeance, and it was encouraged by would-be big men of the coup, eager to secure their status by caring for the cadres, by allowing them to *eat*. Corporal Tamba Gborie, who led the attack, had been

Valentine Strasser's bodyguard during the NPRC. He had lived a lavish lifestyle in Freetown, and wanted, in the words of one soldier, "to be fat again."

The coup would have been overthrown had it not had mass support within the army, articulating just how angry soldiers were. As Major Samura stated, "a coup relies on soldiers. You must have soldiers supporting it otherwise the structure will topple." Corporal Gborie proved that the coup was, in part, a backlash against officers who would not stand up to the mistreatment of their soldiers by the Kamajors and the government by choosing Major Johnny Paul Koroma to lead the AFRC. Koroma sat in the cell opposite Captain Mansaray in Pademba Road Prison. He was also on trial for treason, though his charge was attempting to overthrow Kabbah's government. Major Koroma was the perfect officer for the job: demonstrably willing to seize control of the country, and angry enough to be amenable to any course of antigovernment action. In the coming months, Koroma provided the façade of legitimacy that an officer brought to a coup, and ordered his soldiers to do whatever they wanted.

APPRECIATING THE MURDEROUS MOB

Captain Mansaray was in prison on May 25, 1997. He did not hear Corporal Gborie make a breathless radio announcement that the government had been deposed in a coup, a curfew was being imposed on Freetown, and Major Johnny Paul Koroma was in charge. Once freed from his cell, however, he knew that everything had changed. He stood on Pademba Road, dazed and uncomprehending, as the city erupted in chaos around him. Koroma's first act as head of the AFRC was to invite the RUF to join a coalition government. They were natural partners, as both were the sworn enemies of Kabbah's government. The RUF marched triumphantly into Freetown, and Foday Sankoh, though in jail in Nigeria on weapons charges, was named vice chairman of the junta and vice president of the country.

Captain Mansaray did not know any of this. All that he knew was that he had to get off the street and away from the fray. As he gathered information, he pondered his position with respect to the criminals who had probably saved his life. Was he grateful to them? He assumed they had freed him and spared his life in the officer witch-hunt that followed because he was a hero to the soldiers, defending them valiantly against the Kamajors. Mohamed decided to wear his uniform when he emerged from hiding. The soldiers recognized him, and not only spared his life, but also invited him to join the looting. Mohamed told me that he refused to do so, believing that this was "temporary madness" and he wanted to preserve what was left of his good name as an officer. "I was not ashamed of being an army officer. It was up to them to decide what to do with me."

Mohamed had to negotiate a position that ensured his survival, balancing his gratitude to the AFRC against the possibility of further treason charges; he also had to justify his position to me, an outsider with full knowledge of the horrors of the junta. He did not sugarcoat the fact that he chose to work for the junta, offering his loyalty out of fear of being attacked because he was an officer. Once the looting had settled, he reported for duty to the headquarters. The officers who acknowledged the coup and reported at Cockerill Barracks in Freetown were given assignments—many of them promotions—and those who resisted became targets. Hunting officers became an AFRC sport. Officers were targets in part because they were blamed for the army's misfortunes, but also because certain officers possessed enough clout with soldiers loyal to Kabbah that they could stop the AFRC with a countercoup. Aside from strategic promotions in order to fill the dwindling chain of command, Johnny Paul Koroma did not attempt to coopt people. He gained a loyal following out of officers who feared him, because anyone who refused a position in the AFRC was executed.

Mohamed narrated that although he owed the soldiers who had saved his life his gratitude and loyalty, this did not mean he aligned with their position. "To be honest with you, initially I was grateful. I was grateful to them for getting me out of prison. And that was how it ended. Nobody asked me how I felt about the coup, nobody wanted to know if I thought it was right, me who had benefited from it. But when they were in power, it was like . . . the guys were not mature enough to run the government. They were abusing power." In spite of his reservations about the junta, he worked under them for many months, loyal out of fear. Captain Mansaray was the chief of security for the Freetown ports, though he did not discuss his time in this illustrious promotion. He rushed through his description of the entire year of the junta in just a few sentences.

Embarrassment, trauma, and regret are all possible reasons why Mohamed refused to link his own story with the story of the AFRC, even as he linked his life with them. He had to stay with the junta in order to survive. Soldiers targeted officers who broke ranks; murder was not uncommon. As one of the men they had sprung from prison, Mansaray in particular would have been targeted had he refused to pay his debt to the regime for saving his life. However, he was frank about his opinion of the AFRC. "Well actually they were ruthless! Most of them were not educated, they knew nothing, and they saw the only way to rule was by harassing top people. And with this technique they were in power for nine months. But if they had not been ruthless the senior officers would have overthrown them, I am sure of that. Because they scattered the senior officers and forced them into hiding, there was no way for them to organize and overthrow the coup. That was how the coup stayed in power." Mohamed eventually voted with his feet. As the coup faltered under internal squabbling, he quietly traveled north to his ancestral village in Kambia, on the Guinean border. Captain Mansaray spoke of working for the AFRC out of gratitude and fear. Whatever the true nature of his feelings, by leaving he proved his unwillingness to transform fear into love, as for him the AFRC possessed no other qualities that made them worth having. None of the soldiers who knew Mansaray were troubled by his outward allegiance to the AFRC; one's life is a debt that cannot be paid any other way.

Other officers narrated joining because they felt betrayed by the government, and wanted to rebuild their sense of pride within an organization that relied on their talents. The AFRC gave them this opportunity. Major Kamara, a powerfully built, melancholic man, admitted that he initially worked for the junta willingly, out of sheer rage at battling Kamajors and suffering humiliating marginalization under Hinga Norman. "I was in Bo when the AFRC came up. At that point, Kamajor attacks were rampant. As far as I could see, the military had been marginalized. I saw this as a conflict of interest. The Kamajors wanted to usurp our authority, take our role, and that the government is taking sides with them! It did not help that the deputy defense minister was a Kamajor. And the anger boiled over and resulted in the 1997 revolution." He sighed, expressing regret that he joined out of anger. "Listen Catherine, I have never been a member of a coup and I will never be a member of a coup in my life. I am a career soldier. But I must confess that the situation was terrible . . . some of us were not pleased with what was happening!"

Major Kamara, like Captain Mansaray, had been at the epicenter of army-Kamajor battles. He asserted that he was the first army officer to have to defend himself from a Kamajor attack, though the lack of mass casualties meant the episode slipped under the radar, unlike the attack at Njala. He and his commanding officer brooded over their lack of support from the government, how their soldiers were being neglected and attacked, and were dying, with no consideration from the government.

"The perception among people of substance in the military was that we were being marginalized. So when the AFRC took over, my battalion commander was promoted to brigade commander. He recommended me for promotion, and I went from captain to battalion commander! It was a promotion I am striving now to achieve under normal circumstances!"

As the junta showed its true colors, Major Kamara rethought his choices. "Because of the composition and attitude of the AFRC, the justification for the coup dropped! They looted embassies, and they did not comport themselves, because they were not officers! In fact, I had a bodyguard who became one of the coup plotters. They made him a cabinet member, and he could not read! I was now taking orders from him? But for many enlisted men, they never took the time to think: is this somebody I should be giving my loyalty to? As the junta began to fall apart, the junior men targeted us, their officers, as well. For them it was better to save face than to be embarrassed by us leaving."

Major Kamara, like Captain Mansaray, abandoned his post. He collected his family, ran to his village on the northeastern edge of the country, and vowed to wait there until democracy was restored. He hoped that when his time for judgment arrived, people would sympathize with the fact that he was reacting to constant affronts to his dignity and ability to nurture his family. He stated that the AFRC allowed him to "stand as a man" for the first time in almost a year, and he hoped that they would understand his need for "appreciation" and to feed his family. His story is not unfamiliar in Sierra Leone, where dignity plays a key role in relationships. As fragile as relationships themselves, love is only assured as long as individuals are dignified givers and receivers of nurturing, who feel appreciated and needed in their relationships. As the teacher explained in the introduction, his father just wanted him to be around, even if he had no help to give. For many people dignity is the most important aspect of care. As Captain Mansaray and Major Kamara decided, continued loyalty to the AFRC was to embrace eating and violence as acceptable practices. There were many ways to save one's life, but perpetual loyalty to the junta was, for these officers, not one of them.

THE INTERPERSONAL POLITICS OF WAITING

As the coup raged on, Mohamed was in his village, waiting. "I was just waiting for my fate," he said, waiting for a decisive outcome. President Tejan Kabbah was working frantically from exile to bring down the junta and restore his government. An impassioned plea to the United Nations resulted in the AFRC agreeing to accords, which were signed in Conakry on October 23, 1997. One provision of the accords was the total demobilization of all fighting factions, including the century-old Sierra Leone Army. The AFRC protested—it was illegal for Kabbah to dissolve the army because it was a constitutionally protected force. The accord faltered as the junta crumpled under internal squabbling, with Johnny Paul Koroma arresting Tamba Gborie, a coup architect, on charges of "nefarious misdeeds" for cooperating with the accord.[12] Whether or not Kabbah officially disbanded the army, the AFRC, it seemed, would soon collapse under the weight of its own internal incoherence.

Determined to push military action as the only possible end to the junta, Kabbah rallied support from his ally General Sani Abacha, coup leader and self-appointed president of Nigeria. Under the guise of the Economic Community of West African States (ECOWAS), Abacha armed the community's monitoring group (dubbed ECOMOG) with Nigerian soldiers. By January, over ten thousand troops had amassed outside of Freetown, and with the help of the Kamajors, drove the AFRC from Freetown, securing the capital on February 12. The AFRC was not annihilated, merely chased up the highway past Makeni and into the bush. Nonetheless, ECOMOG declared victory. Kabbah returned triumphantly to Freetown. General Maxwell Khobe, leader of the Nigerian forces, was declared a national hero and given command of all Sierra Leonean forces.

The news soon reached Captain Mansaray's village. Terrified of potential repercussions against former junta officers, no matter how unwilling, he fled over the border into Guinea, living for a year as a refugee. This year warranted no other mention in his narrative, as though time spent helplessly waiting on one's fate is not worth pondering, let alone speaking. Being in Guinea only meant that he was not in Sierra Leone to be prosecuted. It was a temporary, safe state of limbo.

Having fled, Mohamed did not know that General Khobe had instituted the immediate reformation of a new army, the Republic of Sierra Leone Armed Forces (RSLAF). The new RSLAF was comprised of soldiers and officers who had surrendered to the Nigerians and wanted to fight for Sierra Leone. According to current officers, the RSLAF was formed for two different practical reasons. The Nigerians could not have achieved military victory without soldiers who knew the terrain, and these men had to be grateful, loyal soldiers. To reject all former soldiers would have deepened the hatred they had for the government and the nation, and would have inevitably prolonged the war. The embrace was an apology; it signaled a willingness to heal bruised relationships, nurturing them with rice and salaries.

Major Kamara was one of the first officers to join the RSLAF. He had been in his village, and was one of a coterie of soldiers-in-limbo who surrendered at the local army headquarters and were dispatched to Freetown for screening. "I was not found wanting by the Nigerians," is all he said about the screening process, which was aimed more at determining a soldier's willingness to fight for Kabbah than at airing their past deeds. He was immediately assigned to a battalion and sent to secure the airport. Major Kamara spoke of civilians hating and fearing soldiers, but Khobe pushed ahead with their deployment, if only for practical reasons: "I think ECOMOG realized that there is no way they could control the situation without the services of those who know the terrain and the people, who have the will to fight for their country. Soldiers with battle experience were handpicked."

The need and trust displayed by the army command had not reached civilians. Harassed and tormented under the junta, they were furious that soldiers had been forgiven and deployed once again. Major Kamara was now terrified of civilians. "We were in buses to go east, and there was a huge civilian outcry against us. They were saying, 'We don't need you! Go away!' They shouted and threw rocks at us. We used to stay in our vehicles for safety! We tried to tell them that we were not evil, not all of us were interested in the AFRC. But when we arrived in Kono, the rebels and junta soldiers attacked us twice, and we were able to repel them. Then the civilians realized: these are combat-tested soldiers."

Major Kamara considered himself lucky that his battalion was attacked in a heavily populated area, as his men had a stage on which to prove to themselves and to civilians that they were worthy of being soldiers once again. They sacrificed themselves to protect civilians, and the trust that could pave the way for relationships with their people was planted anew. The new RSLAF was not the old army. Needless to say, there were no Sierra Leonean officers with positions of influence in Freetown; all commanders were Nigerian. Trust was a slow process, and the officers had to build it through hard work over time. The news of the new army drifted to Guinea, and Captain Mansaray made his way back to Sierra Leone.

TRUST IN THE SIERRA LEONEAN LEGAL WORLD

What would prompt Captain Mansaray to return to a country that had betrayed him, imprisoned him on trumped-up charges of treason to satisfy the ego of the deputy minister of defense, and forced his adherence to a murderous junta that saved his life? Mohamed himself did not know what his status was with respect to the laws and political situation of his country when he returned. Was he a war criminal or a victim of the war? Was he a hero for standing up for his soldiers, or was he treasonous?

Western justice systems have clear policies on treason—under which Captain Mansaray was guilty for working under the junta, if not initially—however, justice systems initially evolve as a reflection of cultural and social values.[13] In addition, dire situations where survival is paramount do not lend themselves easily to legal parsing. Peter Uvin remarked on proposed war crimes tribunals in Burundi that in order to satisfy the parameters of the listed "crimes," nearly everyone in the country would need to be arrested and tried.[14] Defining criminality from chaos would have been unhelpful in Sierra Leone, and this is clear when examining Mohamed's story, where even admissions of guilt seem courageous and elicit sympathy. He narrated working for the junta as the most troubling aspect of his past; it ate away at him because his countrymen judged him. It was disturbing not from the perspective of the junta being legally "wrong," but because it mutilated love: the junta was "worth having" only because of its power to kill. This was reminiscent of the culture surrounding dictator Siaka Stevens: the dark side of love lurking in the recesses of the ordinary, always with the potential to emerge.

The approach to rebuilding, beginning with the army, occurred in a distinctly Sierra Leonean social world shaped by love. In rebuilding the army, politicians defined their soldiers as loyal sons who had been betrayed, scattered, abused, neglected, marginalized, and made angry and vengeful, rather than as criminals. This was not a rubric of good and evil. This was a conscious decision to return people to the fold, because bitter alienation always results from betrayal. Captain Mansaray returned to Sierra Leone, in spite of considering himself persona non grata with President Kabbah's regime.

"I decided to remain in Guinea indefinitely, and came back only with the signing of the Lomé Peace Accords, in December 1999. I *had* to come back to Sierra Leone. This is my country and I have skills to serve it. I am an officer, and if they are determined to have an army again then they need us. In 2000, when restructuring started, I presented myself at headquarters and they accepted me back. The British came to help, and I was assigned to a British training team. I was one of the first thousand officers and men to be trained. After training I was immediately posted on as an operations officer."

Mohamed was clearly proud of this achievement, showing no surprise at his return to the army officer corps. His confidence radiated from everything that had happened since that time, in spite of the apprehension that likely ruled his emotions the day he returned to the military. Fear had to become resolve immediately, as his first operation was critical to national security. The dust of the war had not settled completely: there was still trouble brewing outside Freetown in the form of a group calling themselves the West Side Boys.

COALITIONS OF ANGER AND DESPAIR

The West Side Boys were comprised of the remaining AFRC/RUF cadres fleeing Freetown in the wake of the failed January 1999 invasion. They seized a village in the Okro Hills, just east of Freetown, and survived as criminals. The Boys were the final angry holdouts from an organization so incoherent, by this point, that it endured only in the hate generated from being cast out of all nurturing relationships. Disheveled, defeated, angry, and alone, they banded together as a gang, the losers of a long and brutal war with no recourse to sustenance except through violence.

Although most pieces on Sierra Leone's war only mention the Boys in passing, my military interlocutors were obsessed with them because they represented how a social world of love is so vulnerable to war: hate stems from betrayal.[15] Major Samura was part of the group that repelled the Freetown invasion, and explained why it was critical not to forget the Boys: "The majority of them, maybe 80 percent, were former army. And maybe 10 percent were civilians and 10 percent RUF. I was deployed at the Okro Hills, just as the British wiped them out. I know their commander, Bazzy, who is now awaiting trial. He is a small boy socially, a corporal with no connections, and he was angry! Some of the civilians were our own children, the children of loyal soldiers. But when the government said they would disband the army, they thought, 'Our parents no longer have jobs, so we will join the rebels.' So that 10 percent, at least out of the 10 percent civilians, you have at least 6 or 7 percent that are soldiers' children and dependents. That was why the Okro Hill issue was serious."

Captain Mansaray agreed: whether or not the West Side Boys were perpetually criminal, officers perceived their very existence as a grievance against an uncaring government. They personified every error made by President Kabbah when he lashed out at the army. What choice did they have, with their livelihood gone? Would that make peace more likely? Mohamed was thoughtful: "They joined the West Side Boys because when the Nigerian force overthrew the AFRC, the army disbanded. Many of them were in exile in Guinea. Those who could not leave the country went to the bush to form their guerilla armies like the West Side Boys. And this only happened after the 1999 invasion of Free-town. When they left Freetown, they established the West Side. Most of them were soldiers, children of soldiers, and sympathizers. They were reacting to what was happening in Sierra Leone: soldiers were killed, lynched, burned down . . . even some who surrendered were killed. They were afraid and decided to form their group, that guerilla army. As an army they could defend themselves and make their grievances known. Their main cause was their instatement in the national army." The Boys wanted incorporation. As they had nothing positive making them worth having, they would demand it at the point of a gun.

Perpetually drunk and drug-addled, these young people who were chewed up and spit out by the war gained notice when a British army convoy accidentally drove into the hills. The Boys captured the patrol and held them in captivity for two weeks, until a special forces rescue mission, called Operation Barras, annihilated them in an early morning raid. Captain Mansaray was a member of the battalion sent into the Okro Hills to clean up after the mission, and he found very little left. Those who had not been killed had surrendered or fled. Those who surrendered were tried and imprisoned.

In spite of the success of Operation Barras in crushing yet another fragment of rebels, this incident left a critical question hanging: when would there finally be no remnant of rebel gang, no node of violently energetic discontent, to flare up and cause havoc once again? The government had offered all regular members of the fighting factions amnesty with the Lomé Peace Accords in 1999, but what about everyone who could not identify clearly with a faction? What about the children who grew up amid the betrayals and havoc of war, who felt that violence was the only way to be counted? The remedy, to eliminate the possibility of future violence, reinforced the importance of love and loyalty.

THE JUSTICE OF PRACTICAL PEACE

Sierra Leone faced many serious problems in the wake of the war, all related to the fact that the nation was replete with traumatized, embittered fighters who knew that it was possible—even desirable—to address social exclusion through violence. The war had endured for so long that it was now the children of those cast-out soldiers—personified by the West Side Boys—who used violence to demand recognition. To heal this nation and prevent future flare-ups of criminal violence required that that world, instead of punishing individuals whose actions occurred in a broken social world, be mended, and that only those responsible for damaging it or taking advantage of the damage be punished. The results were the Military Reintegration Program and the Special Court. Military reintegration resonated completely with the Sierra Leonean world of love and belonging, and was an almost unqualified success. The Special Court, mixing aspects of big men politics with Western punitive justice, was and is still controversial.

The nation could not function with the social stigmatizing of the ostensibly criminal, especially as much of the criminality, particularly among soldiers, was firmly rooted in failures of the social world extending up to the highest levels. Whether or not soldiers "deserved" the rice rations they had received under Siaka Stevens, diverting the rice to the Kamajors was an inflammatory act that hampered the war effort and contributed to a coup. To take food from soldiers and their families is more than simply redirecting resources, it is a social betrayal that sows bitterness and, potentially, vengeance. And so, having finished the initial reintegration, in which officers and soldiers were rehabilitated because the Nigerian army could not fight the rebels without their help, Kabbah initiated the Military Reintegration Program. Army enlistment was opened to members of any fighting faction: RUF, Kamajor, and AFRC. The government offered all these fighters care and dignity in return for loyalty and work. In spite of the initial discipline problems, all the officers I spoke with agreed that reintegration was the only way to move forward. It may have been just, especially from a Western perspective, to reject or jail the factions and reward only those who were perpetually loyal to the state, but at what price to future stability? The peace was fragile, and had no room to court hate.

Was the government purchasing loyalty? Yes. But it was the best possible outcome. Not only did it give former fighters a reason to give up their anger, it also helped rebuild the social world on the premise of love, by which people are fed, cared for, and given an opportunity for a dignified life. Peace, in order to be durable, must be practical. Practicality is more important than abstract ideas of justice, which can neither feed people nor nourish a sense of belonging in a nation. Courtroom justice instead feeds off the desire for vengeance, thus creating space for future violence.

However, in order to secure his position as the biggest big man, Kabbah also wanted to punish those who had challenged his authority. He secured funding for a Special Court for Sierra Leone, which was established in 2002 under a mandate from the United Nations to try those "most responsible" for the war. Reneging on the amnesty clause of the Lomé Accords, Foday Sankoh, Issa Sesay, and three other RUF commanders were indicted for war crimes, as were Johnny Paul Koroma and three other AFRC members. Charles Taylor was indicted for abetting Foday Sankoh, and, in a decision that illuminated the culpability of the Kamajors, Deputy Minister of Defense Hinga Norman and two other Kamajor leaders were also indicted. Though Kabbah's reputation was bruised by Norman's indictment, the latter died in a Guinean hospital, never to stand trial.

The Special Court has spent over $220 million convicting nine people, with Charles Taylor's trial in The Hague resulting in conviction on eleven counts of aiding the RUF, including planning the Makeni invasion. RUF commander Sam Bockarie was murdered before being captured, both Sankoh and Norman died in custody, and Johnny Paul Koroma's whereabouts—and if he is still alive—are unknown. Sierra Leoneans are divided on the issue of the Special Court. Some argue that the only way to check the excesses that are possible in the turbulent world of love is with public productions excoriating individuals who defy it, as they would witches. However, others feel the Court perpetuated the inequalities of the social world, rather than fixing them. As one man wryly noted, it was only prisoners, lawyers, and judges who were fed from the $220 million. He felt that if the United Nations had divided up that money among civilians, it would have been much better spent. That would have repaired years of unjust eating by the elite.

These debates over the usefulness of the Special Court became part of a long discussion over the goals and accomplishments of transitional justice measures in Africa and elsewhere in the world. In South Africa, where the Truth and Reconciliation Commission was charged with addressing the momentous abuses of the apartheid regime, arguments raged about whether or not perpetrators should have to admit guilt, whether perpetrators should be offered the chance of amnesty for admitting culpability, and whether victims and the families of victims should be encouraged to forgive.[16] Aside from the media attention paid to victims who publicly forgave their victimizers, thus validating Archbishop Desmond Tutu's exhortations that forgiveness was the duty of all victims *and* the only way to promote healing and coexistence, large questions lingered over the TRC's concrete accomplishments. Years later, everyday apartheid is entrenched in much of South Africa, its murder rates are the highest in the world, and economic barriers deter integration as well as legislation once did.[17] The TRC seems a minor event in everyday life, where the public performance of truth and forgiveness, though apparently addressing emotional turmoil, did not address the injustice of poverty.

With the Special Court also fading into the background of everyday life in Sierra Leone, it is clear that the government was able to promote durable peace, in particular by addressing coups as issues of love and belonging. When I met him, Captain Mansaray was a valued and respected officer, charged with shaping the skills and professionalism of the young recruits whose discipline he wrestled with, but whose personal histories he never questioned. And no one in his chain of command questioned him, either. When I asked another officer if there was any suspicion of someone who had worked for the AFRC, I received the curt reply, "*Di wa don don* [the war is finished]." Captain Mansaray's conduct during the war had no bearing on the present. The war was to blame, not the man, and his willingness to serve, loyally, was what mattered. This mode of justice is neither punitive, nor retributive, nor reparative—because it does not have to be any of them. It is the acknowledgement that Captain Mansaray was neither traitor nor demon, but was acting and reacting in ways resonant with everyday sociality; a direct challenge to Kabbah's cries of treason. What makes Mohamed extraordinary was the fact that he never acted in anger or vengeance, only in defense of his life. There was nothing to be forgiven.

3

"They Said Nobody Would Hide from This War"

The Rebel

David was an utterly average RUF ex-combatant. He was not the barefoot, scruffy, illiterate, and angry ragtag who sprang Captain Mansaray from prison. He was not a machete-wielding madman, red eyes bulging in a drug-induced haze, as in cinematic depictions. He was ordinary, with the appearance of an impoverished but poised everyman. He dressed and carried himself with an air of fastidiousness, as though self-possession were his only source of control. David had spent ten years as a rebel, and he narrated a story of trauma, in which RUF life was a constant assault on his desire for stable relationships.

Carefully dressed in an ironed yellow polo shirt and khakis, carrying a book bag, with an easy manner, David looked more like a student than a man who had spent over a third of his life with the RUF. However, when he smiled, it failed to touch his eyes. Though it was early in the day, David carried himself with the stoic fatigue of one who has been on his feet too long. When he slumped in his chair, closed his eyes and ran his hand over his head, the mood of his story had been set. Sitting in front of me was someone who wanted to convey that he had seen too much and borne too much. The purpose of his narrative was to distance himself from the brutality of the RUF. He framed his story as a battle to retain his sense of self in the face of the RUF's desire to make him miserable and ill. This was not a confession of misdeeds for which he would ask forgiveness; he was asking instead for consolation and validation. David spoke of his unwillingness to be on the run, losing people to the war, with his life ebbing away because he was alone. In this narrative, he was not a handmaiden to war and devastation. Rather, he was a survivor, victimized by the RUF, and attempting to realign his life with that of a productive social world. It was a common theme among ex-combatants, and he knew this. "Everyone here has a story. We don't much like listening to each other, but it will be nice to talk to you." He flashed a beautiful smile, this one touching his eyes, and began.

"I came from Pujehun district in the southern part of Sierra Leone. I am thirty-four years old now; it seems like a long time ago that I was a small boy. I attended primary school, and when I finished I had to move to a large town to go to secondary school. When I was a small boy, it was difficult for me, because my parents were very poor. They had no money to pay for school. My mother grew some vegetables to feed me and to pay my school fees, but we barely coped. When I got to secondary school, I was fortunate because my elder brothers were digging diamonds, and they paid for school. I got to form five [eleventh grade], and then sat my exams to see if I could go to university."

David's early life is characterized by the work of his family, held together by their affection and sacrifices for each other. It is typical for older siblings who have achieved some success to be responsible for nurturing younger siblings, hence David's brothers supporting him in secondary school.[1] All was going well until, "Well, I, uh, didn't pass the exams." He ducked his head sheepishly upon revealing this news: "At the time I was a small boy and the brain was not so much up for it." Lacking the maturity to succeed, he returned home to his village and buckled down to study. David intended to repeat the exam the following year, 1991. He never made it back to the examination room.

KIDNAPPED BY AN INFANT REBEL MOVEMENT

"So I was about to repeat the exam, but the timing was very bad as the war was just starting. Life was very difficult and we had to make a decision. It was just my mother and me at home, and I decided to take her out of the village and we left the district. We crossed the river, and the rebels captured me, this group headed by Mosquito."

David and his mother lived in a district bordering Liberia. It was one of the first places struck by the initial RUF cross-border raid in 1991. Not knowing that another band of RUF had entered east of Pujehun, in the diamond-rich Kenema district, David and his mother traveled in

that direction. That group was led by the rebel commander Sam Bocka-
rie, who had nicknamed himself Mosquito (*Maskita,* in Krio) because
he fancied himself an "irritant," one whose quick attacks aggravated
the government to the point of distraction, as a mosquito would. David's actual recruitment is unusual, as it combines elements of kidnapping and ideological recruitment. In the first days of the war, with no
broadcast plan and few cadres, both were likely necessary for the RUF.

"They told us that they are not attacking us, because we are poor
civilians. They were only interested in military targets. They asked us
to return to our villages, and we made to go. However, before I was allowed to accompany my mother, they called upon all the youth. They
told us that they would take us for this war. They said nobody will
hide from this war, and if anyone attempts to escape, they will kill
you." Mosquito's decision to recruit forcibly, after initially releasing
civilians, became typical of his behavior throughout the war: contradictory, violent, and remorseless. Mosquito used fear, rather than love, to
keep his cadres intact. He was fighting the war for his own benefit, not
for anyone else.

David emphasized that he stayed with the RUF out of fear, not love.
"They made an example of one of my friends, Unisa Koroma. One
night he tried to run away. They caught him and shot him, they woke
us up and forced us to watch. I was terrified from that point, as was
everyone. We were still determined to go back to our village, but just as
we made the decision and were planning our escape, I heard that some
friends who had escaped the RUF and went to the military base were
killed immediately by the army. I realized it was impossible for me to
go, now that I was associated with the rebels. So I stayed on the training
base for two months, when Foday Sankoh appeared."

David and his friends were faced with a "choiceless decision": to die
at the hands of the army or live with the RUF.[2] The RUF had not successfully indoctrinated them; they were homesick and afraid. Those who
attempted to escape from the RUF were killed as examples, and those
who reached a nearby army base were taken into custody and executed
the moment they mentioned the RUF. David, sobered by Unisa's death,
decided that, between the rebels and certain death, he would choose the
rebels. It was the same choice Captain Mansaray made with the AFRC:
adjusting to a situation, as resisting would have dire consequences.

David's life took a positive turn when Foday Sankoh arrived. David
was highly educated among his peers, which Sankoh liked. He built a
movement that endured for ten years partly by valuing people's skills

in ways the government had failed to do. By assigning David a position of responsibility, he created a reason for David to warm to the RUF. David, however, emphasized in his narrative that he was not instantly loyal.[3] "I was very fortunate that Foday Sankoh was looking for educated people to be his administrators. Sankoh said he needed radio operators, he trained me himself, and I became a radio operator for my group. I stayed with my platoon and did my job, but I was waiting, waiting for a moment where I could escape and also not encounter the army! While the fighting was going on by the border, a few of us escaped, and went to Liberia as refugees. I needed to eat, so I went to the mining area to dig diamonds."

By escaping, even with the stakes so high, David emphasized to me that he was never ideologically part of the cadres. It was 1992, less than a year into the war, when David slipped away from the RUF as they skirmished with the army near the Liberian border. He thought he would be free of his rebel identity once he left Sierra Leone, but was incorrect in thinking that rebel insurgencies respected lines drawn on maps. The RUF had been nurtured in Liberia, and many rebels roamed the borderlands, rounding up Sierra Leonean miners to bulk up RUF numbers.

"I hopped the border and escaped from the RUF, and joined some men in the mining area. Unfortunately for me, one day I was digging diamonds when I noticed some strange men staring at me. I didn't know at the time that they were part of the RUF, until I heard a rumor that they were going to send us back to Sierra Leone to fight. At that point I ran again, and went to the center of Liberia. I was with my friend Kakata, and we met up with other Sierra Leoneans who had escaped from the RUF. People knew we were strangers, because one day we were surrounded by Liberians and taken to jail. When Foday Sankoh got this information, he went to the jail and released us. We were loaded in trucks and taken back to Sierra Leone. When we were in Liberia I was made to suffer, they tortured us. And when I came back to Sierra Leone, I was just waiting to be tortured again. I knew we would be punished for running away."

Again David emphasized his nonadherence, his lack of control over his life. His torture at the hands of his RUF commanders must have been awful, because he swallowed dryly at this point in the interview, paused, and asked for water. I produced my bottle, and he drank long and deeply, set the bottle down and looked over my shoulder, off into a distant past, for several moments. There are many ways in which individuals remember, express, and come to terms with pain, but our conversation was not going to serve that purpose for David. The language of pain is rarely spoken in words, and as words were all we had at that moment, David was clear that they were not enough.[4] He knew that I had never experienced torture and could not understand viscerally what he had endured; therefore it was not a shared silence. He took his time, processing the memory on his own, and I sat with him until he continued.[5] I reproduce that here in words, filling his silence until he was ready to speak of what occurred next.

ADJUSTING TO RUF LIFE

Life improved at this point, as David was moved to Kailahun district. Kailahun is the most remote eastern district, and is surrounded almost entirely by Guinea and Liberia. The town of Kailahun, the district capital, was the RUF's headquarters until 1999. It lost administrative primacy only when Makeni, less than a hundred miles from Freetown, was occupied. In the interim, Sankoh was settling in for a protracted fight, and a contrite and penitent David was tasked with several key administrative positions.

"When they had us back from Liberia and we were feeling suitably punished, they divided us into several groups. As a communications man, I was in the operations room. We were working well, then Foday Sankoh called upon our commanders to make plans for agriculture. He said that all civilians, fighters, and commanders must start farming rice. As a socialist organization, we had to cooperate to feed ourselves. They provided seed rice for all of us, and I worked on a communal farm and my own farm for two years."

Food production amongst the cadres was key to the RUF ideology that Foday Sankoh later set forward in the booklet *Footpaths to Democracy,* as were the universal availability of education and health care.[6] David described a logical division of labor, with assignments made according to skills: teachers became adult literacy educators, farmers grew food, and store clerks distributed it. It was, in the words of one administrator, a communist cooperative in which everyone contributed their skills and everyone received what they needed: "During that war, it was compulsory for all members of the RUF to practice agriculture. The civilians living in Kailahun, we asked them to join us, and they too were involved in farming. All chiefs that we appointed, every village, they had a state farm, their own communal farm, and each member had their private farm. Anyone who is over eighteen should farm. It was a policy in the RUF . . . military policy."

This utopian commune must have been real, as David—who emphasized that he was not a fan of the RUF—had no reason to defend nonexistent policies. He described finding a quiet niche in the cadres, a calm life in Kailahun, which was what he desired. He manned the communications radio to the warfront and farmed until he was ordered to move to a bush camp commanded by Foday Sankoh himself. This was January 1996, the NPRC palace coup had just occurred, and the country was moving towards elections. Pulling the cadres out of town, literally shaking them out of the domestication of the previous two years, signaled a change in Sankoh's strategy: the RUF could not get too comfortable, could no longer consider themselves in détente with the NPRC. This was reinforced when, after the election of Tejan Kabbah, the Kamajors presented the RUF with a new enemy.

David did not describe the political developments, rather he emphasized that he suddenly felt "at war" again. For him, bad times were always manifested in his rapid decline into ill health. David was terrified of dying, and the bush was an inhuman place. "I moved from Kailahun in January 1996. I reported to Foday Sankoh and experienced serious sickness in the bush. Malaria . . . yellow fever . . . edema, etc. which were all caused by hunger, we were so hungry. We had to eat food without salt, and I would go to bed without being able to bathe. Sometimes I would use a cloth but go for a month without washing and with no medical facilities. It caused me serious illness, but thank God up until today my life has been spared. I was posted to Kangarishi, in the northern region, and soon we experienced Kamajor attacks. There was no resting. Every day we were under the gun. I slept under the gun, with hunger, without my own private family."

David's fastidious nature emerged as he relived the unhygienic conditions in the bush, and physically shivered at the recollection of not being able to bathe. He showed me his arms, scarred from insect bites, and pulled his shirt collar aside to reveal his neck, which he had gashed while stumbling through the jungle at night and nearly impaling himself on a tree branch. David resented being pulled out of Kailahun; he felt he did not deserve this barbaric life, nor did he have any talent for it. He would never have chosen a life that stripped away health, dignity, and family. He was, therefore, not a real rebel, rather one who had inhabited the role out of necessity. He was compelled to be a rebel because he planned to save his life, however depleted it was.

When David mentioned not having his private family, I asked him to clarify. He was speaking initially of his mother and siblings; he was glad that he had not tried to follow his mother, whom he had urged to go to Liberia and where she remained for the duration of the war. He last saw her when he was separated from the group returning to their village after the first encounter with the RUF. However, he had found someone else: "I did have my private wife with me in Kailahun, though we were not legally married."

This was the phenomenon of "bush marriages," a euphemism for relationships often characterized by domestic labor and sexual slavery, experienced by many girls at the hands of combatants of every faction. Human Rights Watch estimates that as many as two hundred thousand women were sexually assaulted, as more than one third of their interviewees were kidnapped and forced into sexual slavery, or "marriage."[7] The euphemism served dual purposes: ideologically aligning the RUF with a "normal" world, while enforcing the domestic nature of the relationship; marital rape is not recognized in Sierra Leone. A girl performed domestic chores for her "husband," and could only hope that her combatant's status was high enough to protect her from assault by other rebels. In essence, the best she could hope for was being forced to have sex with only one man against her will, rather than many.[8] David was matter-of-fact about the existence of his "wife," with no sense of shame or remorse.

It was not incongruous that a fastidious man, seemingly gentle and terrified of dying, was forthright about having a bush wife. He broke no taboos, as this marriage was merely a more violent version of ordinary domestic relationships in Sierra Leone.[9] However, his wife was a constant presence in his narrative, and he spoke of her gently, with a lover's caress. He fretted for her safety and sulked in his loneliness when they were apart. Her absence when he was ordered into the bush made his agony over his failing health more clear: he needed nurturing, and she was his only source of support. Isolation during war is frightening enough, but David's situation was exacerbated by the fact that it was 1997, and the AFRC was about to seize power.

JOINING THE MUTINY IN FREETOWN

In late 1996, David heard Foday Sankoh announce that he was traveling to Abuja for peace talks. "I was so happy for that, as I thought my life would come to safety now." Between peace talks and the AFRC coup, however, his narration became circular; his tale grew vague and paradoxical as he struggled to present himself as an unwitting hand-maid to what was later revealed as one of the RUF's lowest points, with cadres participating in the worst excesses of terror. He focused on his personal losses rather than describe his actions, where he might possibly reveal acts that confounded the gentle image he portrayed to me. The silence in itself was an apology to his social world.

"When we got to Matatoka, a town along the main road to Free-town, the commanders went to report in Freetown. I joined as their communications person, and my wife was so unhappy, because she had to stay behind. And when we went to Freetown, we left the others in Masiaka, along the way. We heard later that Masiaka was under at-tack, and in that battle I lost my wife and my son; he was six months old. We tried to return and hit another battle. There I lost my best friend, my brother, who was hit by an ECOMOG bomb. I lost everyone and found myself in Makeni for a time, and then we started running again, that was 1998. We had to keep running. I usually fed myself in all of these struggles by begging from people."

David slumped as he related these memories, a blur of trauma and battles that followed the coup. His cadre, including his wife and new-born son, were in Matatoka, forty miles east of Makeni, for the bulk of the coup, during which life in the provinces was quiet. When he went to Freetown, the rearguard, including his wife, stayed in Masiaka. He described arriving in Freetown just before the ECOMOG invasion that drove the AFRC into the northern region, and it was during these attacks, involving all the towns along the highway, that Nigerian jets killed everyone he loved. David would not reveal how long he was in Freetown, nor what he did there, only speaking his loss and agony.

David's reference to the death of his brother is a reminder of the emotional closeness of love. Their brotherhood was not biological, for David had been separated from his own family since he was kid-napped in 1991. It was based on their friendship, shared experiences, and shared food. Food is such a critical part of nurturing that individu-als judge the state of their lives on the number of people they eat with. David's emphasis on being reduced to begging for food reveals that the RUF stripped him of his humanity. To beg in Sierra Leone means one is friendless, utterly alone, and extremely vulnerable.

After the death of his wife, son, and brother, David spoke of no longer caring about finding good relationships within the RUF. He was tired of living in the bush, on the run, with all of his love and care for others shattered. He mourned his family, and was ill and battered. David wanted desperately to go home, and thought that the reinstatement of President Kabbah in 1998 after the fall of the AFRC would provide him the opportunity to return to his village. However, fearing repercussions from the Kamajors, who were now "covering my home area," and carrying the memories of friends murdered by the army when they escaped, he decided it was safer to remain in the north with the RUF.

The north was neither safe nor calm. David described a chaotic situation, where no one was still long enough to farm. After retreating from Makeni when ECOMOG drove them out, he returned to Kono, on the eastern border, and "started struggling fresh." They searched for food in the bush, "like animals," and as David often mentioned, retired every night without bathing. He caught a chronic illness, probably a stomach parasite, that weakened him significantly, and which he lacked money to treat. He was shot in the arm during another battle, and had to remove the bullet himself. He insisted that this, rather than a desire to seek revenge on those who had ousted the AFRC, was why he joined the ragtag march on Freetown: he needed to find a doctor.

The January 6th invasion of Freetown was one of the most devastating moments of the war. Thousands of people died in a slaughter instigated during the RUF/AFRC retreat, after government forces repelled them. David described his role as a passive one. "When we got there, we saw so much fighting going on. We encountered serious return fire from ECOMOG, so I ran away from Freetown, although some boys stayed. I ran to Waterloo [east of the city] and stayed there while others were in Freetown destroying it. We waited for help but there were no reinforcements, so we retreated back east."

David acknowledges that his faction was responsible for mass slaughter, though he insists he "ran away" and did not take part in the scorched earth campaign. This may or may not have been true, but David wanted me to believe that he was not capable of such brutality, nor did he have the strength for it. He did not, however, disagree with the concept of seizing Freetown, which was why he waited. "I wanted to get out of the bush," he explained, with no embarrassment at his desire to live a "civilized" life. He assumed that reinforcement would come from Makeni, but heard rumors of internal fighting among rebel commanders in Makeni, as leaders of RUF and *sobel* factions fought to control the town. Several commanders were killed, and Makeni was eventually taken over by seasoned RUF veteran Issa Sesay, who traveled to Makeni from Kailahun at Foday Sankoh's behest to set up an advance headquarters. David and a few others walked to Makeni to help reinforce the new RUF base. David emphasized that he was still not safe: he remained under orders and had no right to save his own life except as a member of the RUF. He repeated this point exhaustively, that RUF adherence was his only lifeline.

David's continued emphasis on the precariousness of his life signaled many things. He portrayed himself as a trapped man: why would he choose injury, dirt, exhaustion, and loneliness? He seemed embarrassed by how his situation had defined him as a depleted person. He could only improve his chances of surviving by securing nurturing relationships. Throughout the war, he seemed a willing, though distant, participant, doing what was necessary to survive, looking for love and stability.

David sought to control his own life, however his universe was circumscribed by the fact of his being a young man in Sierra Leone at the wrong time. He was cognizant of his perilous situation within the RUF, but his life had been shaped for many years by his RUF membership, which had become his only realm of social and physical safety. It would have been suicide to leave the cadres. Being a former combatant was not a safe option, especially considering rumors of the treatment given suspected rebels by Nigerian soldiers. One notorious officer, nicknamed Evil Spirit, boasted of killing anyone he believed was a rebel. During the January 6th invasion, he was responsible for the torture of a mentally handicapped boy whom he accused of being an RUF sniper.[10]

David had to be a good enough rebel to not be accused of betrayal and shot on sight. Deserting was not an option, as he would lose the safety of armed numbers. There was no possibility of good relationships, as the RUF was on the run and had little to give its members. Commanders relied on all of these fears to maintain loyalty. "You looked after yourself; you found food for yourself. And when they wanted to use you, they used you! They didn't care about you otherwise. If you needed medical help you had to treat yourself, because there was no medicine and no field hospital. I stayed . . . I was living in fear that I would be attacked by my countrymen."

The war itself had adopted a cadence that destroyed the possibility of good relationships for David. His "private family" was dead; his investment in others had come to naught, and he was alone. Without brothers among the cadres, David reduced himself in his testimony to a victim. His description of his victimhood is contextualized profoundly within love: this was his lowest point not because he was near physical death, but because he was near social death. All of his relationships were negative, based on fear and coercion, and he had nothing to give that would induce someone to love him. The only possibility lay in returning to Makeni, as stability created the potential for a good life.

BANISHING FEAR IN THE PURSUIT OF PEACE

Though David spent over a year in Makeni before the disarmament, the day-to-day activities of the occupation were worthy of no attention in his narrative. His story was an inducement to compassion and pity; the ordinary would arouse no such feelings in the listener, nor would it contribute to the project of indicting the RUF for endangering his life. Life in Makeni was still rough: food and medical supplies were scarce and, after January 2000, the gunship made frequent bombing trips to the town. Problematic for his narrative was the stasis of that time; there was little movement towards a life outside of the RUF, until the occurrence of an event in which David could place himself squarely within a larger narrative of history. This was worth telling.

David had been living in Makeni for six months when he heard rumors of peace talks, which made him "extremely happy." Under pressure from the United States, Tejan Kabbah agreed to meet Foday Sankoh in Lomé, the capital of Togo. Kabbah was reticent about talks, as Sankoh had ignored the Abidjan Accords, but knew that a good faith effort would nurture support for a UN peacekeeping force in Sierra Leone.[11] Kabbah believed that external intervention was the only way to end the war, and in July 1999, he traveled to Lomé to secure one. Only the government and the RUF were present at these talks; as occurred in Abidjan, there was no representation for the army or Kamajors.

The Lomé Peace Accords were a victory for Foday Sankoh. The Accords granted members of all factions, including Sankoh himself, total amnesty for acts committed up to the moment of signing. The international community seemed happy to bend to Sankoh's desire for authority and wealth. In lieu of being granted a political party, Sankoh was given a new position in the Sierra Leonean government, chairman of strategic mineral resources—diamonds, iron ore, and all future discoveries—and the vice presidency. Here was an agreement that ostensibly offered Sankoh everything that he wanted, short of total power, and thus remedied the fatal flaw of the Abidjan Accords: Sankoh would only agree to an accord that fed his ego. He wanted to be the cotton tree.

As injurious as this agreement was to Kabbah's sense of justice, he received a UN peacekeeping force and Sankoh's word that disarmament would proceed unobstructed. The United Nations Assistance Mission to Sierra Leone (UNAMSIL) was organized, and Kenyan peacekeepers and unarmed military observers arrived in Makeni to establish the disarmament center. Sankoh made his famous disarmament tour, the same tour where he called Makeni people rebels. David emphasized different details:

"Sankoh said that he had had his time to make a statement in Sierra Leone, and now his time was over. The war is over, he said, and nobody should again take up arms to fight anyone else. He said they had agreed to a political solution to Sierra Leone's problems, and now the UN was in charge. That was the message that he delivered to us in Makeni. He stressed that nobody would fight again. Immediately after that order was passed, men started disarming. He spread this message to everybody: that he was the one who had called them to arms, and now he was ordering them to surrender."

Major Phil Ashby, a British Marine, was posted to Makeni as a military observer. He was thoughtful on the state of the town after the Lomé Accords: "The RUF leadership could be reasoned with and, for the most part, seemed to agree in principal to the end of the war. It seemed the leaders knew the war would end soon and they wanted to make a good impression. Issa Sesay, the local RUF commander, wanted to be a politician, so he turned Makeni into his personal show town. He instituted laws and consequences, he brought in food for the traders to sell, he tried to keep the hospital running, and the people were pretty pacified."

The one person of whom Ashby was extremely wary, however, was David's own commander, RUF big man Augustine Gbao. "Gbao ran the RUF's security division, the police force. On a day-to-day basis he was a very powerful guy, because Makeni was largely peaceful and the police had primacy over the foot soldiers. Gbao wanted people to know how powerful he was, so he always had some police function going on. The RUF had its security force at the police station, and that was always where he had us meet him. Gbao would always have twenty armed guys with him, so when he was sitting down looking at documents, guys would sit there in their ragtag rebel uniforms. This freaked me out because they were wearing the uniforms of people they killed, and some of them had UN uniforms. He did this deliberately, and he would have small kids smoking massive reefers and playing with their AKs. In the middle of the meeting some rabble-rouser would start chanting the 'Hungry Lion' song, which was their battle cry, and dancing around like a Zulu, waving his gun. This was the middle of a meeting that was otherwise mundane. I was always really edgy."

Gbao was the "bad cop" in Makeni, in direct contrast to Issa Sesay's "good cop" image. Gbao was furious that Sankoh had signed the Lomé Accords without consulting RUF commanders, and took every opportunity to inform Ashby that the RUF writ large was not ready to cooperate with disarmament. Gbao was suspicious that President Kabbah was using the United Nations to wipe out the RUF, and that Sankoh was sacrificing them to his own greed. Gbao was not ready to disarm before the other factions. However, the UN bosses believed that it was an acceptable risk because Foday Sankoh was in Freetown, and could thus be held directly accountable for the actions of his cadres.

The disarmament center in Makeni opened on May 1, 2000, guarded by peacekeepers and staffed by military observers. The first day it received ten frightened and reluctant rebels, who, having been disarmed, were offered gestures of good faith: food, drink, a bath, personal supplies, and a small cash allowance. Once a rebel disarmed, he was to remain in the center under the United Nations' care. Gbao was told that the British had kidnapped ten of his cadres, and he was incensed. Several hundred RUF fighters marched to the center that evening, pounding drums and singing "The Hungry Lion," and demanded of the Kenyan platoon guarding the center that the cadres be released. The commander refused, and the RUF attacked. The Kenyans radioed Ashby over the UN frequency, "We are being overrun."[12]

Here David linked his narrative to historical events. He had joined Issa Sesay on a trip to Kono to monitor the RUF's diamond mining, and was not in Makeni at the time of this confrontation. He described hearing communiqués between commanders on his own RUF radio, in which Gbao admitted that his forces had attacked. Bitter over the RUF using him and preventing him living a good life, David broke ranks and attempted to block RUF command from relaying misinformation over the radio, which he assumed would prolong the war.

"After the UN set up the disarmament centers, I heard there was some grumbling. Gbao was always on the radio, telling us that Foday Sankoh is not properly preparing everyone for the peace process, and that could make the peace scatter. But I didn't think anything about it because I didn't believe him. I believed that there would be no more fighting again, only peace. Later, I heard that Gbao, leading our soldiers, had attacked the UN! Then I monitored on my radio the report that was given officially, which was sent to Sankoh in Freetown, that the UN attacked us, which was false information! We attacked them. It was Issa, over this radio, he was covering himself for leaving Makeni."

David, as radio operator, relayed all messages between commanders, and his bitterness over his victimization by the RUF came through in his attempt to rectify the misinformation that was being passed. David had access to the communication in which Gbao and his number two, Maurice Kallon, discussed possibly attacking the United Nations to punish Sankoh for not including them in the spoils of the Lomé Accords. In Sierra Leonean practice, this is clearly a breach of love on Sankoh's part, and therefore grounds for commanders to pull down their big man. If all the RUF commanders were not going to get dividends from the Lomé Accords, then Sankoh would not either. Sankoh had fatally underestimated the anger of loyal commanders who felt their leader was slighting them because he wanted to eat on his own. They attacked, and David found out.

"It was the RUF that attacked the UN. As a radioman, I knew this was true. I continued monitoring the messages. Maurice Kallon sent a message to Issa that they had decided to attack, but to tell Sankoh specifically that the UN fired first! So I relayed this message to Issa, that we had attacked, and Issa prepared a message for Sankoh. I relayed the message to Sankoh, and Sankoh ordered Issa to return to Makeni and stop the men fighting." He smiled. "When I relayed the message to Sankoh, I was not clear on who had attacked. I left it open for him to think maybe Gbao had betrayed him."

David used this episode in his narrative to align himself with a peace agenda, rather than RUF warmongering and eating, thus placing himself on the right side of history and Sierra Leonean love. Whether or not this story of radio communications is factual—and whether or not the radio operator was David—Sankoh did order Sesay to stop the fighting. If Sankoh believed the RUF had attacked, it endangered the vice presidency. Sesay's reaction to this command reveals that he, like Gbao and Kallon, had no interest in disarming under terms that were only favorable to Sankoh. Sankoh was outnumbered and, as he was in Freetown under UN watch, extremely vulnerable. By assuming that having Sankoh with them as they launched the peace process would guarantee success, the United Nations displayed fatal ignorance of the precariousness of big men. Not only could Sankoh's commanders carry on without him, doing so was their best option if he refused to include them in the spoils.

David watched the Accords break before his eyes. "Issa did not stop his men fighting. Instead, he had reinforcements come to Makeni to keep attacking the UN. I decided to go back to Makeni, even though there was no way to enter town on that morning because of the fighting. When I finally entered Makeni, everything was upside down. Everything the commanders wanted, their radio equipment, the vehicles, the food, they took for themselves. They demolished the camps. Everything was looted. The peace had scattered."

With the Accords shattered, individual RUF commanders pursued their own routes. David's unit was ordered to Freetown to protect Foday Sankoh, who was under house arrest, and the West Side Boys ambushed them as they attempted to pass through the Okro Hills. This was the same band of rogues later annihilated by the British; they had nothing to gain from peace accords that catered only to Foday Sankoh. David's story continued: "I was severely injured when we battled the West Side Boys, a few of them jumped in a truck and tried to run me over. They knocked me into the bush and I thought my life was ending. I received a gash that bled and bled." He lifted up his shirt and revealed an ugly scar running under his ribs. The Boys refused to allow the cadres who were attempting to aid Sankoh to pass. David's unit retreated to Makeni. Times were bad once again: "In all these months I was running up and down, no food, no medical. . . . I was struggling until we saw the peace again."

David maintained his post as radio operator. He was part of the RUF contingent that met with UN commanders in 2001, when UNAMSIL brought the full force of its power down on Sierra Leone. With seventeen thousand troops, at the time it was the largest UN peacekeeping deployment in history. Meetings in Abuja, Nigeria, ended in ceasefire agreements, Abuja 1 and Abuja 2, during which the final transition plan was put in place. It officially took effect on May 17, 2001.

"The ceasefire came, and so did the UN general. He came to Makput where they delivered the UN equipment to all the camps, like the armored cars and other weapons. Maurice Kallon was invited to meet him, and he took a contingent. I was on the scene as a communications man. The general came with helicopters, lots of troops. Security was high, guarding everyone. After that, we came back to Makeni. Now, the peace started coming a little bit at a time. We agreed to disarm, we handed over our weapons and whatever military equipment we had, and we were taken to the disarmament camp."

David's time as an RUF rebel had ended, but the absence of fighting did not quiet the hearts of now "ex"-combatants. They did not know if disarmament would proceed undisturbed; David was more vulnerable without a weapon and had to trust himself to an invisible accord rather than to flesh-and-blood people. Former combatants feared mass trials and crowded jails, and so were reticent about being counted within the Disarmament, Demobilization, and Reintegration (DDR) camps. After ten years of fighting, most former combatants had their closest relationships with each other. The greatest danger of disarmament was not that the RUF would break it, but that it would break the RUF.

TO BECOME AN EX-COMBATANT, YOU MUST LEAVE YOUR RUF RELATIONSHIPS BEHIND

As an ex-combatant, David was not privy to the meaning behind reintegration as posited by the United Nations. Conceptually, the disarmament process seems straightforward. As long as you have something valuable to give someone with a gun, something more valuable than the ability to live by the gun, you can turn a combatant into a civilian. What occurred in Sierra Leone proved to be much more complicated than a cash for arms transfer, or a program to counsel former combatants and return them to the community. Several analysts believe that the United Nation's primary goal with reintegration was to break up the fighting factions past the point of reformation, rather than actually "reintegrating" ex-combatants.[13] The cadres were kept occupied with skills training and transition allowances while the gerontocracy reasserted itself. David focused instead on the logistics of DDR:

"We went to the camp and we were treated well by DDR. They gave me three hundred thousand leones [about $150 in 2002], and I received a bucket, drinking cup and spoon, a small plate, and a sleeping mat. So they asked us to stand and they took our pictures and gave us our identity cards, which had four letters on it: A, B, C, and D. It was a punch card, and they punched the A when they gave you your transition allowance. They told us to go home and wait for a bit while they processed everyone, and then the training would start. I visited my mother, and then came back when they announced over the radio that phase two was starting. I came and received three hundred thousand leones, and they asked me what I wanted to do. They said that they will provide places in programs, and then after you learn they will give you toolkits and something to start life with. They also promised to provide job facilities for us, and the promise was all there with the identity card. So I went to the DDR camp and asked for my program. My plan was to go back to school."

The ID card was the primary symbol by which ex-combatants understood their transition to civilian life, the promises the United Nations was making with respect to their futures as represented in the letters A through D. The card symbolized the need for patience; reintegration would unfold slowly and no one should be frustrated with the process. David received his ID card the day he handed in his weapon, and the A was punched. As long as he kept hold of an otherwise intact ID card, he was entitled to UN benefits. The second stage and payment, marked by the B, signified registration for retraining, which ex-combatants usually had to wait months to begin. These built-in delays bought the United Nations time; they could continually monitor the activities of the RUF as they drew down their peacekeeping forces.

The beginning of disarmament did not proceed smoothly, as rumor circulated that the DDR program was merely a front for collecting data with which to prosecute combatants. David feared that, in spite of the amnesty offered by the Lomé Accords, the newer Abuja Accords held no such provisions for the average fighter. All RUF members were potentially at risk. "We heard rumors that made us panic! People were saying that after DDR they would arrest all of the RUF. We knew our leader was in detention. And we knew the commanders had really made mistakes when they formed our political party. Due to their immaturity we lost the election, and now we had no political power either. Information was floating around . . . now that we were vulnerable, they would arrest us. I decided that I didn't want to spend years in the UN system, because they would know where to find me! So I went for skills training instead. They promised that when you were trained they would give you toolkits, you would be employed, and they would give you something to start your life."

David summarized the panic of promises made and broken by the international community in its dealings with the RUF in an outpouring of emotion. He knew, in the wake of the disastrous end to the first disarmament attempt in Makeni, that Foday Sankoh was under house arrest in Freetown. Only a few days after the debacle in Makeni, an RUF cadre in Kailahun surrounded, disarmed, and held hostage over seven hundred Nigerian peacekeepers. The events had spurred a huge demonstration outside of Sankoh's house. His bodyguards fired on the crowd and killed twenty protesters. Sankoh went into hiding, but was soon discovered, arrested, and jailed.

Issa Sesay was one of the few remaining RUF leaders still at liberty, and he wanted political power. Sankoh had forfeited his claim to the vice presidency after the shooting, and had also nullified the amnesty he had been granted from being charged with war crimes. His arrest did not, however, invalidate the RUF's sanctioned transformation into the Revolutionary United Front Party, or RUFP. It was the RUFP's failure to garner even 2 percent of the electoral vote in the 2002 elections—with Sesay running for a position as a member of parliament—that prompted David to blame the RUF's disintegration on "immature leaders." Sesay had campaigned confidently around Makeni—"his" town for three years—and was furious with the betrayal by his cadres, who defected en masse to the SLPP. According to a newspaper report, he ordered the dismantling of the RUFP throughout the country, and issued a statement banishing all RUF cadres from Makeni, his home.[14]

Sesay believed that his cadres loved him, and dismantled his "family" when he discovered that, now that he had no power over them, they had withdrawn their love. Sesay clearly perceived love where only fear and inertia among otherwise friendless rebels had existed. Sesay had been the *pa* in Makeni for nearly three years. He was responsible for all the food and supplies entering town, and could therefore claim that he was caring for everyone—and that they owed him love and appreciation. He believed he would be repaid in the voting booth. The fact that this did not occur was a betrayal of the highest order, and warranted him removing every protection that the RUF family, with him as head, could provide. By ordering the cadres out of Makeni, he signaled the ultimate dissolution of his family. Sesay was casting his disloyal brethren to the wind, and leaving them to the mercy of the United Nations. David emphasized in his narrative that if Sesay and other commanders had concentrated on being loving brothers and fathers to their cadres rather than arrogant big men, they would have been appreciated. Either way, the RUFP failure proved that the RUF was dissolving, whether due to UN manipulation or under its own social incoherence.

Sesay's brash announcement and his spiteful dismantling of the RUFP left the ex-combatants in a precarious position, in spite of their ostensible protection by the United Nations. Their leader had abandoned their party, their only political protection against possible retribution by other political factions. Foday Sankoh was in jail awaiting prosecution for war crimes; he had already ensured that tenets of the

Lomé Accord were in jeopardy. David's decision to undertake artisanal training illuminates perfectly the bind ex-combatants were in as they weighed up the pros and cons of each possible relationship. He panicked that long-term affiliation would make him vulnerable to prosecution, but rationalized that a six-month skills-training program would not. This logic—it had to be the United Nations, either way—highlights David's vulnerability once that the RUF was gone. He needed training to have job prospects, and he entrusted himself to that process, though he likely knew that, since he had registered with DDR, a war crimes court would know where to find him if they wanted to. David's choice of skills training was an act of faith in the DDR process. As it turned out, he had more faith in DDR than the architects of the program had in ex-combatants.

Ex-combatants in Makeni were victims of the United Nation's belief that only by offering training in dazzling prestige occupations could they entice the top RUF commanders to disarm. According to sociologist Krijn Peters, the United Nations felt DDR needed to offer high-level commanders training in high-status skills, as manual pursuits such as carpentry would not mimic the respect these commanders had possessed during the war.[15] Technology courses abounded in Makeni, and David opted for training in computer software. "I was lured by the idea that I could really make something of myself," he said.

David fell victim to the United Nations' prioritizing the actual disarmament over the long-term needs of ex-combatants and their families. He believed that in offering this training, the United Nations was promising Sierra Leone a modern future. He spoke about using his training to set himself on his feet and support his mother and siblings, and admitted that he had not thought about the fact that Makeni, like most other towns in Sierra Leone, had no electricity, let alone businesses using computers. Short-term concerns—the transition allowance, pride—dominated his thinking.

"During my computing course I was supposed to receive sixty thousand leones [thirty dollars] every month for the full six months. They paid me for six months, but after that, on graduation day, we should have received our toolkits. This was promised with the last letter on the ID card, the D. But we received nothing. I only received a certificate with a small bag to carry books in. That was all. I received no equipment to do computer work, and I found out that the training was not sufficient, as I never found a job. So I became an intelligent beggar. Moving from corner to corner, place to place, asking people to help."

David, like many ex-combatants, had placed himself "in the hands" of the United Nations, treating the organization like a big man who existed in a relationship of mutual investment and benefit. There was no reason for the United Nations to involve ex-combatants in the ethos of disarmament; in their view, it was not a long-term relationship of reintegration and development so much as a means of diverting attention from the war long enough for "peace" to take hold. The goal—as illustrated by offering computer training in a nation with only three electrified towns—was not about building a sustainable future. However, the subterfuge was deemed necessary for peace. Several of David's friends mentioned to me that they had made official complaints about DDR's inadequacies, and no action was taken. They were, in the words of one, "left languishing with nothing."

In September 2003 I spoke with one of the few UN officers left in Makeni. In his opinion, "This program was an utter failure. Our carpenters cannot hammer a nail straight, and no one is going to hire them."[16] He blamed the failure on ex-combatants being more interested in money than training, but later admitted that six months was not adequate training time for any skill set, nor would skills necessarily ensure community acceptance. I asked him, philosophically as much as analytically, what would have been the best way to perform DDR. The officer shrugged, mentioned that he had organized a few soccer matches mixing ex-combatants and civilians, and finally concluded that DDR's failure did not matter because the peace process was clearly successful and the Special Court would take care of the international concern about impunity. Everyone would just have to make do. Ex-combatants were attempting to "make do"; many went to great lengths to secure employment. Their greatest obstacle lay in the United Nation's deliberate fragmentation of the RUF as part of the peace process, breaking up interpersonal cooperation among friends as a way of preventing "criminal plotting."

REINTEGRATION BECOMES A TOOL OF RELATIONSHIP DESTRUCTION

David, now officially a trained, "reintegrated" ex-combatant, decided his future was not in Makeni. "I went to Abako, a computer training school in Freetown, and talked my way into the office of the principal. I begged him to take me on for a little more training. They allowed me to stay for one month. I felt better about my training and started looking for a job. But I was not able to succeed. So I came back to Makeni. Life was bad again. I didn't have food except what I begged from people, one hundred leones [five cents], five hundred leones [twenty-five cents], sometimes . . . and when I was fortunate to see my friends, sometimes one thousand leones [fifty cents]. So I struggled throughout that time without employment or anything else. The UN had promised that we would have successful lives, but they did nothing for us."

David felt the United Nations owed him a job; having embraced the United Nations as a new *pa* in place of his RUF commanders, he believed they had a responsibility to "place a hand under him." This was his first mention of relying on friends to get enough money to eat. His pain as the reintegration program slowly separated him physically and socially from his friends came through the narrative as his greatest agony—and another reason he was bitter towards the United Nations. The United Nations was tasked with making ex-combatants "safe" for communities, which meant easing residents' fears of renewed RUF "plotting." David went to Freetown because he had been admonished not to congregate with his friends. The RUF had hindered his will to live peaceably in stable relationships, and the United Nations replicated this unhappy situation.

DDR was designed to atomize ex-combatants rather than reintegrate them, and this was promulgated as peacebuilding. I spoke to one DDR program officer in Freetown, who stated that DDR officers did not want civilians to believe the process encouraged ex-combatants to remain attached to the RUF through continued association with other ex-combatants. There was no room within peace doctrine, designed to dissolve fighting factions, to acknowledge the positive bonds between combatants, those forged in love during war. Doctrines of disarmament rarely investigate the social qualities of rebel movements; understanding why someone would be loyal to group could be used to promote the agenda of that group. Combatants were reintegrated as isolated individuals, were instructed to leave RUF life and return home. This was in spite of the fact that their fellow ex-combatants represented for them relationships forged in a decade of tribulation.

Calvin, the teacher turned RUF commander, stated, "When we did these courses, we decided to organize ourselves as a group so we could be self-employed. This was what we were thinking, but the DDR organizers thought we were using reintegration to put the RUF back together!" He chuckled ruefully. "We weren't allowed to associate! We tried to organize our brothers who trained as tailors, and those who trained as carpenters so they could establish their own workshops, and those who had done auto mechanics and so forth. From there, they would be able to deploy their talents, continue learning, and bring new people on board with the businesses. When we brought this idea to DDR, we were discouraged, totally! So our initiative just ended up in a dust heap, and this is where we are now. For the past two years, we are here, with dreams of our own workshop."

The United Nations' notion that civilians would take exception to ex-combatants associating operated in spite of the fact that most ex-combatants used their retraining allowances to nurture romantic love, and many started families with local women.[17] Thus was there confusion among ex-combatants as to exactly how DDR was meant to sow peace. This self-conscious process of relationship destruction served only, in the eyes of ex-combatants, to damage the peace by destroying the power people had to help each other. As one of David's friends stated, "All of these ideas that we had in the RUF were scattered when the units were broken up, these ideas that people should work together to sustain each other. This was all discouraged when the peace came."

Disarmament and reintegration are not simple processes: there is no "right" way to undertake reintegration after a decade-long war. However, the concerns of the international community about ex-combatants "associating" must be weighed against cultural concerns such as the paramount importance of social networks and interpersonal relationships to a person's ability to secure an occupation, become "useful," and thus integrate into a world that fears isolated individuals much more than it fears connected people. Rather than working together, ex-combatants ended up just "floating" together.

"It is very difficult for me to float around Makeni now. I have been here for years, people know me, but I am struggling to make ends meet. It is not easy. And the worst part is when we go to offices with requests for employment, as long as they know that you are former RUF, you might as well just leave again, because they will not hire you. Employers refuse us openly! In our culture, you need to *sabi* [have personal connections with] people to work."

David built an intricate narrative of joblessness involving the destruction of RUF "brotherhood," the unwillingness of the United Nations to allow local relationship practices to govern reintegration, and poor training. This is not the place for detailed treatment of DDR failures; suffice to say that from my interviews, joblessness among ex-combatants was due to both a market already saturated with master artisans, and the UN certificate signifying that the potential employee had poor training and no one to vouch for his abilities and character. In addition, residents "grumbled" that ex-combatants had received benefits while they themselves received nothing.[18] As "ex-combatants," David and his friends were hampered from developing social—and therefore economic—relationships.

The marginalization of ex-combatants pushed them closer together, even as they had fewer resources with which to support each other. When I asked both David and Calvin one day if anyone had received toolkits to assist with their job prospects, Calvin nodded energetically that indeed, some carpentry trainees had. I asked what happened to them, and he squirmed, stared at the ground, and finally said with a devilish smile, "They sold their toolkits." I was aghast. "They sold them?" Of course, was the answer, what would you do if you had a toolkit but no job, no credibility, and no way to use it? "You have to eat," he explained, "Or when you die from hunger, they can bury you with the toolkit!"

When word got around that ex-combatants had sold their toolkits, civilians held this up as proof of their worthlessness, that they were more interested in *eating* than contributing. Their exclusion from skilled work was justified, as they were clearly ungrateful consumers with nothing to give. But, as Calvin pointed out, it is better to be alive and disdained, than dead and revered for your principles. This is a choice to save one's life, made as the structures of war and rebuilding circumscribe one's ability to care and be cared for.

WHY DID EX-COMBATANTS REMAIN IN MAKENI?

Having suffered continually from disappointment and rejection, why did David not return to his natal home in the south? His answer was simple: shame at not being able to take care of his family, and having few prospects in his rural village. "I went to visit my mother at home, and she also came to visit me one time. But I didn't see any advantage to being in my village. In fact, it would be harder for me to live there: no jobs. My father is dead; my family house was burnt, leaving my mother to sleep in the kitchen. And up till now I have no chance to take care of them. That is why I am far away from home, to find some way to take care of them in the future. For now there is no way to do that."

David needed to nurture others in order to reactivate his original bonds of love. David's position and reasoning were common among ex-combatants. They remained in Makeni because, in spite of being jobless, they figured there had to be greater scope for opportunity in a large town than in far-flung, inaccessible villages. As one of David's friends stated poignantly, "There is nothing I can do at home. I would just have to cry a lot because I cannot help my mother." For Freetonians to claim that ex-combatants remained in Makeni because they had committed too many atrocities in their home areas to return, but were welcomed by Makeni residents, illustrates their willingness to treat Makeni people—ex-combatant and civilian alike—as though they do not act within the same cultural context as everyone else; essentially that they are *not* Sierra Leonean; perhaps not even human.

Reintegration and the foregoing evaluation of Makeni were based on a false notion of war as a suspended state, with people only valuing what they had before violence erupted. Indeed this is not so. For ten years war was the background of life. Combatants matured, built relationships, and acted on their responsibilities to their loved ones. Many men had married women they met during the war or in the aftermath. Couples wanted to stay together, provided they had the means to do so. Among those who met and started families during the war, settling in Makeni offered more options for a new life than did either partner's natal village, where they had been absent for a decade. Many women—even if they had been kidnapped at gunpoint—were shunned by their families after disarmament as damaged goods, threatening to their families' social standing.[19] Living in town with their husbands was preferable to returning home stigmatized. Ex-combatants with transition allowances had the resources to start families with local women. The men themselves gained new relationships and respect in town, and their wives—as newly minted breadwinners for their natal families—were encouraged to move their new husbands into the family home.

Marriage brought the responsibility of care and nurturing, which the men did not take lightly. For a time, allowances came as promised, and DDR presented itself as a solid foundation for building a successful future. However, as the retraining ended and jobs failed to materialize, the material base on which they built their families—and thus their relationships in Makeni—dried up. A woman retained the option of leaving a husband who could not provide for her, and, in the desperation of the poverty that engulfed the town in the wake of the aid drawdown, many exercised this option. Their husbands did not blame them, as David's friend Idriss lamented when he spoke of his own wife, Fatu.

"I haven't seen any success, and one day my wife told me she was going to leave me. She went back to her own people, even after everything

I had tried to do. She went home because of hardship; she couldn't handle it with me anymore because we didn't have anything. I don't blame her, I said okay, she is gone, and I must get something for myself. After I get a job and have some money, then I will go for her again. And I will come with her back to my home. I don't want my wife to strain, let her have a better life with her family. I can see the house where she lives but I can't go there yet, until I have money." Idriss, like many ex-combatants, had fathered children and wanted to be near them even if he could not support them. Between the pull of their families and potential opportunities in town on one hand, and the unbearable shame of returning to their natal families empty-handed in spite of having taken part in DDR training on the other, most ex-combatants remained in Makeni. This was the true face of "collaboration" for which residents were stigmatized.

Shame was a critical feature in keeping men away from their natal homes. David was especially concerned that, no matter how much he explained his situation, his family would never understand how, after his training and allowances, he was unable to support them. So, after over a decade of absence, it was not the atrocities he had committed that kept him away. On the contrary, he stated that when he returned to visit his family, they were thrilled to see him alive. However, there was no possibility for mutual nurturing, as there were no resources for anyone to offer. His love for his family had not been supplanted, but put in a more sacred place: not to be activated until the now grown man could take his expected position as the head of his family. He would not return to his family as a beggar; only success and the ability to provide would prompt the journey home. Indeed, the fact that so many ex-combatants followed this logic and pattern underscores the fact that the war added additional bonds, rather than destroying existing relationships.

Ex-combatants did not suffer from *destroyed* relationships as much as *competing* ones. In order not to be torn apart by the sheer number of relationships, they had to prioritize their more immediate prospects.[20] David's greatest regret about his time with the RUF was the forced suspension of his original family. The fatigued, emotionally aged man sitting across from me lamented the loss of his father, killed by the rebels, and regretted his inability to become the chief breadwinner of his family: "The RUF let me down. I can only speak for myself when I say this, but the RUF endangered my life to the point that I cannot live a normal life with my parents. So I would like to say that I am a victim, I am a victim. I cannot take care of my mother and myself and my little brother and sister. I should take care of them, but what I have . . . I don't have the capital right now to do so. But I hope, with the help of other people, I still hope to succeed in life before I die. Yes. But would I ever join any illegal group to do anything in Sierra Leone . . . as for me, no. No, no . . . I will only join somebody who wants to bring progress for the people of Sierra Leone. That is the only group that I will volunteer myself for. Even without payment, I will do that! I know that when Sierra Leone is better, I will be better! Because when I have food, my mother will get food, my brother will survive. But when only David has food to eat, and David doesn't have food to share, then how can I expect myself to improve?"

In spite of everything, David emphasized the rightness of relationships in his narrative. If he did not have enough to share even a little, he would never see progress in his own life. Real progress in Sierra Leone *requires* love: one has to make oneself dependable and reliable, a potential provider of good as much as a consumer of it. This is why David argued that until he had food to share, he as an individual would not benefit. There is no permanence if you cannot extend beyond yourself. The true measure of a man is reflected in a grateful family, who will remember him and sing his praises.

EX-COMBATANTS INITIATE COOPERATIVE AGRICULTURE

In 2005, poverty blanketed Makeni. DDR had officially ended, and most ex-combatants were languishing, jobless. As donor interest shifted to hot conflicts elsewhere, NGOs disappeared. Life settled into an everyday grind, and the suspicion that had initially dogged ex-combatants faded. "People had to worry more about getting their own living than they had to care about us!" stated one of David's friends. The ex-combatants— now technically civilians—were associating openly once again. But how to make a living, with the route of skilled artisan all but closed? David, and many of his friends, turned to a skill they had learned as children and honed during their time with the RUF: agriculture.

The few remaining NGOs were more development-oriented than crisis-oriented, and many smaller NGOs were willing to engage with community groups proposing their own projects. David and many of his friends took advantage of the money and tools offered by one local NGO to establish a farm on a rented plot. They officially named themselves, registered as a community organization with the Ministry

of Agriculture, and set to work on their new project: cooperative agriculture, on the model they had learned in the RUF. Everyone contributed what he could, and everyone reaped the rewards at the end of
the harvest. They were successful in their first season, but the lack of
continued financial input for seed rice stalled their project. With their
remaining money, the board of the organization rented a room and
moved in together. They waited, wondering what they should do next.
If they owned their land, it would relieve them from the burden of rent-
ing. Their lack of relationships with landowners was harming them, as
the only way to get land as a nonlocal person was through marriage.
Half the men in the cooperative had initially been married, but could
not ask for land from the families of wives from whom they were separated. But at least, stated Idriss, his wife's family now had proof that
he was trying, trying to make money to earn her return. Perhaps if they
were a little bit successful, he could borrow land from someone, and
eventually be the man for his family, and hers as well.

David and his friends decided to write a grant application to restart
their cooperative agricultural project. At the end of our conversation,
David presented the proposal to me with a flourish. He was eager for
my feedback on the writing, whether they were asking for too much
with their request for tractors, and he begged me to take it to Freetown
and present it at the headquarters of half a dozen donors he knew of.
The names of five former RUF members, hailing from various parts of
the country, with disparate experiences of the war and suffering, were
typed carefully at the top of the proposal. I looked over the mission
statement, which began, "If we work together we can feed the nation."
David continued chatting:

"I will find a way to bring myself up with the development of agriculture, but it is not easy. The bulk of people who are here are really trying.
We are still around and we are not tired. We are happy any time we can
learn a bit more about farming; maybe find a new donor. And whom-
soever comes in to help us to develop agriculture, we will be happy to
join them. This group that has written this proposal, I am the leader.
I am the number one man. So you now have the proposal we want to
submit, and I hope you think it is good. Even in the war our farming
was so good that we could feed ourselves and our civilians, and also our
private families! So, so far, so good."

He smiled brightly when I glanced up from the proposal upon hearing his optimistic pronouncement. This man, who had lost his childhood and most of his chance at life success to a brutal war, thought that

so far, things had gone well. At various points in our conversation, he had recalled his torture at the hands of Liberian militias and the RUF; revealed myriad scars from his horrendous injuries; related the deaths of his father, best friend, wife, and infant son; and detailed how he was reduced to asking strangers for food in the waning days of the war, and how he now called himself an intelligent beggar. However, the friends and the narratives were what counted. He had unburdened himself to me, creating a story where he had survived and done right by his fellows, in spite of the efforts of the RUF and the United Nations to break his most treasured relationships. He was alive to have this conversation, still had the full advantage of a sound mind, and a body well enough to contemplate the agriculture that would feed his family. He was ready to work, to be useful and in good relationships, and had the proof of friends who would support him, typed at the top of the page. So far, so good. Indeed.

4

"I Held a Gun but I Did Not Fire It"

The Student

> The main problem with the notion that stories can be equated with lives is the assumption that a human life is essentially an individual life, an island in the stream, and that we can refer back to this individual life, this originary, self-contained subjectivity, to determine the truth of the narrative that is constructed out of it.
>
> —Michael Jackson

The chapters thus far have highlighted the fact that individuals deploy narratives about their lives in particular ways, fashioning history and their past selves in ways productive in the present and portentous for the future. Mohamed and David framed their stories to highlight both the importance of love to behavior and decision-making, and how they acted conscientiously within this framework. They created new "truths" out of the facts of their survival—facts that were unverifiable—in the process of telling them to me. More than relaying a factual past, such truths were nested within their social world in ways that helped them reassert good relationship with other people and the world at large. That story-telling helps people create the grounds for a viable society is, according to Jackson, the most important aspect of its "social life."[1]

Alimamy, the subject of this chapter, was a gifted storyteller. Always aware that he was producing himself for me as he narrated his story, he presented an intricate portrait of himself as a victim-hero: "just a student" pulled into unspeakable acts in order to protect his mother. He described being forced to join the rebels during the occupation of

Makeni, and trained his narrative carefully on his exemplary conduct as a youth: care for others, concern for his reputation, and above all, love of family. Equally emphasized was his rescue at fortuitous moments by people who knew his family, though they were unknown to him personally. Alimamy narrated surviving in part because people loved and respected his father, inspiring them to help him. By telling this story, he honored his father—placing himself in a world of "good" relationships with elders that contrasted with his time with the RUF—and his mother, with whom he has an intimate bond. He also explicitly challenges the official narrative of "collaboration," as by acting out of love for his primary loyalty, his family, he casts aside all questions of whether or not he has a responsibility to the government not to work with the rebels. As is common among street gangs around the world, there is no question of moral condemnation of youths' activities, if they are undertaken in defense and support of a morally good world of family.[2]

This chapter departs from the previous two in that Alimamy and I sat down several times over the course of weeks, and this narrative—perhaps disingenuously to the act of storytelling—is an amalgam of many different accounts of his survival. His narrative was often paradoxical; his stories changed slightly in their emphasis if not their facts with each retelling, as well as moving around different points during the occupation. His narrative had no chronological order; there was what I call "interpersonal" order. Individuals important to his life, and all the stories involving them, were told together, even if the events occurred months or years apart. Though this chapter has a basic chronology, Alimamy's narrative method highlights the chaos, confusion, and trauma that characterized the occupation.

THE FUTURE ACCOUNTANT

Alimamy, unlike David, never called himself a rebel. The short, fresh-faced young man who approached me one day, grinning from ear to ear as he smoothed the wrinkles out of his shirt, appeared a carefree teenager. He insisted I take down his story, the story of a "native," because he wanted to create a conscious political counter to the collaboration stigma that continued to harm the town. "I have my own story of Makeni. I was born here, a true native son, and I can tell you everything." We ducked inside his father's office, into the cooling darkness, to work out details of when we could sit down for a talk. He offered me a chair by his desk, and wrote down his address.

"Are you a student?" I asked.

He nodded. "I want to be an accountant."

We arranged to meet the following day, on one of his few days off from school and from obligations at home. He had no time for a long chat, because he was due to take a handcart into the forest with his brother and gather firewood for his mother. The work did not bother him: "If she doesn't get the wood, then she cannot cook!" The mere thought of no dinner made him shudder. "My mom is a very good cook."

Alimamy's education had been severely disrupted by the war. Though he did not look a day over sixteen, at the time of our meeting he had just turned twenty-four. He was struggling to find a school-going rhythm again after many years of not being in a classroom, but he did not mind the toil. "Though I thought my brain was spoiled for school by the war, I am finding that bit by bit I can get it back again." The way he told his story, Alimamy was always a student, no matter what happened. "From the moment I found I had a bit of talent for school, I became very serious about it."

Alimamy went into great detail about his elementary schooling, from the girls he had had crushes on, to the problems he had encountered with jealous bullies, to the exact scores he had received on national exams. All of this stopped in 1997: "I was about to take the national exam to pass to the next form when the war met us here. It was the junta guys who took over, and they closed the school. I was unable to go to school, none of us were, during the war, so I just had to sit for many years."

He was lost in thought. I lost Captain Mansaray briefly in the same way when he came to the part of his story where the Kamajors attacked his platoon. David also went missing in our conversation as he remembered being tortured at the hands of Liberian rebels and the RUF. For those who have never experienced war firsthand, there is no possibility of understanding how it feels when your world is turned upside down, when your will to give it form with words is obstructed or destroyed. Alimamy did not take long to compose himself, though his story never composed itself once the war arrived in Makeni.

FATMATA: THE FIRST IMPORTANT REBEL RELATIONSHIP

Alimamy met Fatmata when the AFRC junta ruled Sierra Leone. The chaos in Freetown was replicated on smaller scales in the towns, and Makeni was a tense and unwelcoming place. Food was scarce as traders feared traveling to villages lest they be attacked. Alimamy described welcoming an overture of friendship with a soldier/rebel as a logical way to ensure the safety of his family, though he gallantly refused her romantic love:

"I had a friend who was a rebel, a girl whose name was Fatmata, and she liked me. She also helped my family. She gave me groundnuts when she looted them. She had her husband with her and when the husband went to loot he brought things, and I gave them to my family. So I was able to give my mom rice, groundnuts, pepper, everything! And Fatmata told me that she liked me. So I said, no, you have your husband. But she kept trying to get me to be in love with her. One day she gave me a gold chain. It's a chain that is very costly, so they call it 'master' chain. She gave me that chain and it was brand new, so I kept it and put it on my neck. I should not have kept it outside my shirt!

"I was walking down the street, and another rebel came and took the chain and walked away with it. He had a gun, so what could I do? When I returned home Fatmata was there. She asked me, 'Where is the chain?' and I said that a rebel had taken it. She went wild, and said that the chain signified something else to her, and she wanted to find him and kill him, and get the chain back. And I didn't understand and I said, 'What do you mean? I don't have the chain now, so what can I do?' And she said, 'Let us go to my friends and I will collect it. You will come with me because you know who has the chain.' And I said, 'No. I am a civilian, how can I go there?' That was the rebel place, so I told her I would not go there. If they didn't kill me, I could still never come back from there because everyone would see me, with the rebels in their own place. I was begging her and she started threatening me, slapped me, took her gun and flogged me with it. She threatened me and I cried. She damaged me a lot. The next day she wanted to talk to me. I said, 'No. I don't need your company.' She said, 'If you don't need my company I will kill you.' She said she would destroy my family. There was nothing I could do, that was the issue."

Alimamy endangered his life by giving a rebel the silent treatment. She had been offering his family food, gifts, and protection while he acquiesced to her advances, however he seemed to underestimate the power of negative coercion to replace love. Alimamy was simultaneously naïve and arrogant in this narrative; possessing a "right" orientation to the world that allowed rebel interactions to occur in his space, but not in rebel places. He embraced these relationships only when his life was at stake.

"I said okay. And she gave me another chain. So after that ECO-MOG entered. It was Fatmata who told me that they were going on another looting operation the next day, and the town would be sacked again. But she said not to worry, that she would protect us. I said, 'Hmm? I don't believe you people. Because you are rebels and rebels can change at any time, I don't have confidence in you.'

"She said, 'You don't need to worry.' So before they had a chance to go on another looting operation, ECOMOG entered, and drove them away. They chased them and took their vehicles and the rebels ran away and went to the bush. So when they ran they looted everything in our house, looted the whole property. There was nothing left for us, we had to start fresh. You can see yourself when we go to my house. On that day we had tiles in our house, mats, everything. They took everything, everything."

Alimamy referred to most of his negative characters as "rebels," emphasizing his distance from them ideologically within the narrative, whatever actually occurred. Emphasizing that "a rebel can change at any time" signified that he never worked to cultivate love with Fatmata, even as she offered him resources, because that investment would have been foolish. Fatmata was used to eating through looting and violence, and forced Alimamy's loyalty by threatening to remove her care for his family. She was "worth having" in the moment as she could ensure temporary survival, but that was all.

NEIGHBOR-ON-NEIGHBOR VIOLENCE

Fatmata left when ECOMOG flushed the junta out of Makeni in early 1998. Johnny Paul Koroma was ousted and Tejan Kabbah was president once again. Kabbah attempted to impose a sense of normalcy and order on the nation, and immediately ordered teachers back to their schools. Alimamy recalled that he was trying to study, once again, for his exams as the town descended into a collective post-traumatic stress, a post-invasion dysphoria of mutual suspicion. Alimamy recalled being so troubled by this that he could not concentrate on school.

"Some of the rebels would not go. They would not leave the town and it caused our people to fear everyone. Sisters, brothers, mothers, and fathers singled other people out and then killed them. The civilians are the ones that destroyed the rebels. But then they started destroying themselves. If they did not like you they would say, 'This is a rebel.' So they would beat someone, put tires on his body, and burn the tires."

This gruesome style of public execution, called *necklacing* in South Africa where it became prominent during apartheid, was how civilians in Makeni aired grievances with each other. I suddenly realized why Alimamy had been so sensitive when I asked if his friends had become rebels, and why he snapped at me that they had merely *joined*, that is, gone looting with the rebels in order to acquire resources for their families, and to prevent their siblings from also being harassed as potential recruits by volunteering themselves. He was burdened with the memory of losing friends who had looted to feed their families, and were then killed by their neighbors and friends in flares of anger over their betrayal. The threat of imminent death in Makeni encouraged many boys who had joined in looting to go with the rebels when the latter were driven out of town. It was safer at that point to openly commit to the rebels than to attempt to regain civilian status in Makeni.

"The civilians would point fingers at anyone, but especially those who turned. This is why most of them ran away and followed the rebels. They killed a lot of people, the civilians did. I witnessed the death of a friend of mine, but in order to protect myself I couldn't save him because I would also be cornered as a rebel. They took him, flogged him. We were so terrified . . . his brother was standing there and he could not do anything. This boy's brother is a soldier. When they captured his brother he heard that they thought he was a rebel and were looking for him too, they wanted to kill him as well. So he took off his soldier uniform so they could not identify him. But this guy was standing there watching as they killed his brother, burned him alive as he was standing."

Alimamy distinguishes between rebel and soldier, and notes how the soldier had to hide his identity in order to survive. In the wake of the junta, any soldier, whether loyal to the government or a mutinous member of the AFRC, was a target. The soldier may have been part of the junta, or he may not have. It was the uniform that mattered. As for the rebel, Alimamy knew that he had simply joined to feed his family, but that did not matter. No one would be able to save this boy and remain alive; they would have been guilty by association.

Alimamy was troubled because stark framing of the terms of love and betrayal discounted the need to protect one's family. He too had been "guilty" of befriending a rebel to feed his family. However, Fatmata's willingness to bring him food, rather than forcing him to join her on looting sprees, spared him the fate of being known as a looter, a betrayer of the town. His friend's brother, however, did not try to endure the chaos in Makeni, leaving the next day for Freetown. The retribution killings subsided, and the town settled into a tense calm.

TRAUMA AND SCHOOL

"After that the rebels had gone to the bush again we were able to restart school. I sat the national exam, but my result was not good. I took it twice and both times I had bad results. The first time I went to Freetown to St. Edwards School to take the exam even though I had not been concentrating on my books at that time. I dropped off the end, my result was shameful! So I returned back to Makeni and sat it again and managed to pass all three subjects I tested in: science, math, and English."

Alimamy seemed visibly embarrassed that he had had to take the exam twice. As someone who defined his adolescent years by his success in school, failure—in spite his traumatic experiences—seemed to cause him anguish. His father had committed the family's paltry resources to send Alimamy to Freetown the first time, and the added expense of the second exam nearly broke their finances. However, with as much as his father had invested in his education to that point, the result was still not enough. Three subjects would never qualify him for a good school.

"My dad said there is no way to go to secondary school with the scores I had, even though I had passed. So I sat again with eight subjects, and I managed to pass six of them: math again, and English, science, social studies, physics, and a few others. After that I was given a place in a good secondary school where I am today."

Alimamy smiled broadly, and gave me some details about why success at school was so important. As a child he had been troublesome, "I was a real burden to my parents!" He fought with other children, started a gang, studied little, and his mother wept every night. Doing well in school became a story of early childhood redemption and growing into the responsibilities of manhood, framing all of the events that happened later. "In secondary school I changed my life and concentrated on my book learning. So now I'm almost twenty-something years and I can't be a child anymore. I have to act as a man. I'm the oldest boy so I want to help my family, I can't play anymore."

During the time of the junta, from May 1997 to January 1998, formal education stopped. Unpaid teachers and administrators drifted away, and the students languished, bored and idle. They flocked to school from the moment Kabbah returned to power, and persisted with their schooling up until the moment that the rebels returned, in December 1998. Alimamy had narrated his pre-junta schooling and early transformation to adulthood *after* telling stories about Fatmata, reframing his experiences with her from the perspective of someone who had already grown into a responsible first son, rather than an impressionable, easily flattered teenager.

THE AHISTORICAL, NONSENSICAL WAR IN MAKENI

Alimamy's story of the occupation collapsed all the violence that occurred in Makeni into a confused, conflicting account of rebels, soldiers, Nigerians, civilians, students, family, friends, love, and survival. Residents entered a state of hyperreactivity to the constant fighting, as rebels fought rebels, rebels fought soldiers, factions of soldiers and rebels emerged and fractured, and different commanders controlled little militias, each desiring control of the town. Residents described these skirmishes as *infights:* armed men fought turf battles, and civilians, though they were ignored, were often caught in the crossfire and mayhem, and suffered the rule of whoever seized power.

Alimamy had no "history" of the occupation. He remembered fragments, rife with shootings, beatings, love, and loss, and it was never clear *when* he was in his narrative, or who the "rebels" he spoke of were. What carried his narrative along were the details that were important to him: that he looked after his mother, that he used his relationships with soldiers and rebels to keep himself and his family alive, and that everyone in the town whose good opinion mattered to him recognized he would never intentionally harm anyone, especially not his loved ones. The only date he remembered was the RUF invasion: December 23, 1998.

"It was on Sunday morning that they attacked. The first time they attacked from the Binkolo area, about three miles off from Makeni. They came with a vehicle and started erecting checkpoints around the town but we didn't know that they are rebels. We thought they were soldiers because they were wearing soldier uniforms."

The *sobel* phenomenon was so widespread at this moment that it seemed impossible that citizens would not be suspicious about anyone in uniform, but Alimamy narrated thinking they were "soldiers," framing his narrative of the town as a place that was attacked, rather than complicit. Each small narrative intervention reframed the town as innocent, rather than a "place of collaborators."

"Binkolo was the first town where people knew the rebels had come and they were running away. On Saturday in the evening, around midnight to one, they caught this taxi driver and started flogging him, almost to the point of death. This rumor floated in that he had been beaten, and then we heard the gunshots coming from Binkolo and people are running. I did not lock my window because it was so hot; I had left it open. Suddenly I was awake and I heard this shouting but I didn't understand. When I woke up I peeped out the window and saw that people were passing, a lot of people! They were running with their lamps and so I called to my mom, and my parents knew. All of us gathered in the parlor. Our uncle lives in Binkolo and suddenly he came to our door. He told us that the rebels were attacking. So we lodged him here, but we did not sleep. In the morning, about six o'clock, the rebels attacked the barracks. That was on Sunday. So we knew the rebels are here, and anyone that you see was a rebel."

Alimamy's assertion that "anyone that you see was a rebel" was due to rumors floating around that the rebels had led the attack by sending children into town as vendors, who then relayed the layout of the police stations, barracks, and main roads back to their commanders. Alimamy was convinced that when the attack was in full swing, he had seen these very same children pull weapons from their vending boxes.[3] He emphasized that Makeni residents were innocent victims.

"We tried to convince my mom that we needed to run and go to her village about six miles from Makeni, where her parents were living. But she refused to go. And from six o'clock at the night we heard serious firing from the barracks. The rebels were fighting the soldiers. All we heard were gunshots, and them killing people, our friends, our sisters. They killed a lot of people and so many people ran away."

When the RUF attacked Makeni, they annihilated the Nigerian soldiers in Teko Barracks. President Kabbah had dissolved the army and turned security over to Nigerian troops under the ECOMOG banner six months earlier. Captain Mansaray, whom we met in chapter 2, was in Guinea, awaiting his fate. Nigerian troops guarded Makeni, and many refused to lose their lives in a confrontation with rebels. Those who were caught in the barracks were killed, and the rest ran away. The family remained in their home, but action was necessary, as they had no food and Alimamy's mother was pregnant.

"In the evening I had to get food. At that time my mom is pregnant, with that troublesome boy, my youngest brother. Me and my younger brother went for food, we were the strongest and could run fast. We went to the market, got food, and cooked it behind the house so no one saw the fire, but my mom did not want to eat. We tried to force her, my dad did, but she refused. Around six in the evening people started moving because the firing had cooled, and we wanted to go but we were scared for our mom. Finally Mom said, "Let us move," and so we ran.

One of the first places we hid was a primary school nearby. There were many of us hiding at that school, so many people! We stayed there for as long as we could, and then the rebels found us. They were standing there, firing at us. I think they were trying to scare us because we just froze, lying on the ground there and they fired over us. And then they ran off down the street. We listened for noise outside. We thought the firing would cool, but it wouldn't, it was continuous. We didn't know what to do."

It emerged from other narratives that the RUF leadership was deciding the fate of the town in those very hours. Several commanders were quarrelling over whether to loot Makeni and then burn it to the ground, or occupy it as a base. The argument in favor of occupation was won on the grounds that the town, merely 130 miles from Freetown, was menacingly close to the capital, thus putting the RUF in a much stronger political and military position. However, civilians did not have this knowledge, and still treated the invasion like a loot-and-burn mission. Alimamy narrated the events as they occurred, with his family running to the bush without the benefit of information.

"We decided to go to the bush. We left the school and ran. We tried to follow some other people in the morning and go to their village, but it was not good for us because we didn't know anyone there. That evening the rebels managed to capture the barracks. When they succeeded they sent out their people to round up everyone and bring them back to town. They sent someone to this village to call to us, and he told us that all of the people should come into town. He was armed, so we didn't have a choice. All of us were taken into town. But I found out that there was a problem, that the rebels are planning an operation."

Alimamy shifted uncomfortably in his seat. An "operation" referred to any act of collective violence that would be designed around a name. The name of an operation was a psychological device—initiating warfare through inculcation of paralyzing fear—that traveled through the town as a rumor before the operation began.[4] This particular operation was called *Kill*. Rumors tend to spread rapidly in times of crisis, as people scramble for any information on which to act. Circulating a rumor that a particularly gruesome operation was impending cowed people into submissive fear. Terrified of being caught and shot as "escapees," Alimamy and his family returned home. Though they had been away only two days, rebels were squatting in the house. They were given their home back rather than being murdered, illustrating the kind of event described by nonresidents as "collaboration." Alimamy narrates the event as a deeply human moment of romance, and thus a profoundly nonpolitical act: the family survived because of a blossoming relationship. A rebel in love with their neighbor spared them and returned their home to them, and this young man was one of the central people—and central relationships—around which Alimamy's narrative began to turn.

CHRISTOPHER, THE "REAL REBEL"

"A rebel named Christopher saved my life. When he took over our neighbor's house, he fell in love with the girl who was living in the room just between our house and his. She was a friend of mine. And the girl was there the day we came back from the bush, she urged him to save me even when he wanted to shoot me. She told him that she knew me, and she saved my life."

Alimamy was saved because his pretty neighbor had affection for him, which encouraged Christopher to extend affection towards him as well. Love is an expansive, systemic practice of creating and nurturing linkages between people through their other relationships, thus binding people more tightly to the social world at large. In many narratives I heard of the war, people's lives were saved not because they appealed directly to the person threatening them, but because of an intervention motivated by *sabi,* knowledge of someone's family, or by a third person. That a person is already in relationships by which others might sacrifice to save them is an indication that they are "worth having."

"Christopher was called Liberia Boy, and he was a real rebel! He was not one of those soldiers that joined the rebels later in the war, he was one of the first that joined Foday Sankoh. The incident where he saved me was on Monday, Operation Kill. The plan was to kill and destroy, burn houses, and they had already started. They burned the house of one policeman, so the rest of the police scattered and left the town. We were fortunate that when we came back to the house, Christopher told us not to leave again because the operation was ongoing. We would not believe him when he told us this because he is a rebel. They took these hard drugs, so they can change at any time. This was why we were so scared. But we stayed. On Monday after they had destroyed everything, ECOMOG came in. There was death in Makeni town. Even with the soldiers there, the rebel guys followed through on their operation. They were burning everything, even the cotton tree, and they killed a lot of people. A lot of my friends died. Some of my friends are joining them."

This was one instance where Alimamy's narrative displayed the paradoxes of memory. ECOMOG arrived to chase the AFRC junta out of Makeni after two weeks of looting and pillaging, in January 1998. The junta had been in charge of the country for over seven months, and the town's administration had ground to a halt. Though junta members generally took what they wanted, the town was, in large part, quiet. This episode was the first of many times that armed forces fought each other over the next two years. Whether it was ECOMOG soldiers or junta members in army uniforms who attacked the RUF as they sacked the town, it is impossible to tell. By calling one faction "ECOMOG," Alimamy was implicitly aligning them with the interests of the townspeople.

The burning of the cotton tree is more significant than it appears: if rebels burned the abode of ancestors, nothing was sacred. All rules of respect, civility, and honor were suspended, and therefore the proclivity of young people to join the rebels made implicit sense, if they wanted to save their lives. Alimamy understood that many of his friends would *join* the dominant force. And yet when I asked a seemingly innocuous clarification question, "You had friends who became rebels to avoid being slaughtered?" he snapped back, "They are my friends, they are not rebels!" The difference was that a rebel was a rebel by choice. One had to *join* the rebels in order to save loved ones. He explained:

"They are students, but because of this problem they joined the rebels. They joined to feed their moms and fathers. They joined because there was no other way to get food, except to be with the rebels. So the rebels came to Makeni town to loot and rape. Here, they raped our sisters, and killed, looted, danced, drank, they did all sorts of bad things in Makeni town. But I thought there were other ways for me to get food. I had a strong heart and a strong mind, yeah. When I went to the bush they followed me. They knew where I was staying. They wanted to kill me. But fortunately for me, ECOMOG came that night and chased out the rebels. So things were calm for a little bit." Alimamy feels he was singled out by rebels and junta members—and places this at the forefront of his narrative—because he had a strong heart, one that holds fast to its allegiances. This made him a threat to their recruitment, and so they hounded him further.

There was no way of knowing when this episode took place. The first attack on Makeni was in January 1998, occasioned by the junta's escape from Freetown. The junta's soldiers were chased by ECOMOG, who then moved into Teko Barracks. The second was the RUF attack on December 23, 1998, when ECOMOG was chased out, resulting in three years of *infights* between various rebel and soldier factions. Each time a faction lost, it was forced to leave Makeni and retreat to outlying villages and towns. For residents of Makeni, life was a blur of fighting factions. For Alimamy, what mattered was that in every faction, he made a friend who was willing to help his family. Every time he befriended someone, like Christopher or Fatmata, whose identity was socially problematic, he felt the need to justify his position: he *joined* them rather than becoming one of them, as a way of saving his life. Whether or not he chose to work on that relationship to make it positive would be clear in time.

JOINING THE REBELS, SAVING ONE'S LIFE

As in most places they attacked, the rebels recruited in Makeni to augment their numbers. They went after the young, who, if they did not join willingly, were tortured and threatened with death. Alimamy admitted that he joined the rebels, however, he did so with the memories of necklacing fresh in his mind. He narrated being careful to be a model citizen while in Makeni. Though joining the rebels was important to feed his family, it was also critical that he not risk future disapprobation by being too friendly with the RUF. When confronted with joining or being killed, Alimamy joined. However, he narrated composing himself in a way that would maintain his family's reputation, emphasizing his love for his family and the town, and his need for their embrace in return.

"The rebels placed so much pressure on me. I said no way; they said I must join them. I joined in a sense, but it was only after they put me through too much heartache. And I said I would not take any arms to secure myself. I have my five senses. I know that this is my land, my town. I don't have any intention to destroy my home. I just *joined* them to protect myself. On the day the rebels rounded us up and took us east to Kono, to their training camp in the bush. It all happened after terrible things happened in Makeni. Christopher was staying with us and he told us all about it. Some rebels had captured these young boys and took them to Freetown to fight. That caused me so much concern. I went to my house and was hiding, and they found me there. Christopher had no choice but to order me to join the rebels because it was in front of his friends. He later told me I should stay with him, so I did. Unfortunately I went with them. But I never used a gun. When I stayed with them it was not in Makeni town. They had us transporting ammunition and machine guns, and we were going back and forth. That is when I held a gun, but I did not fire it. There were no bullets, nothing. It was an empty gun. When I did not have that I had an RPG [rocket-propelled grenade], I held it. But that was all I did.

"I would not hold it in Makeni town because people know my dad and I am popular in town. What would they do to me if they saw me holding a gun? I decided to never have arms in my own town after a terrible thing happened. I was in my house and Christopher was there. I went to the market with my neighbor, Christopher's girlfriend. And on that day the rebel command passed an order that no civilian should enter any shop, to stop the looting. On that day a civilian entered a shop that was just lying open because the first rebels in town during the invasion had smashed up the doors. This man took a video, and the RUF came. They took him right in front of my eyes, and shot him dead. They said they don't want any civilians or soldiers going inside the shops to take anything. If you steal anything they will kill you. I did not want people to fear me that way."

Alimamy had decided that he would never influence people negatively. To even appear to threaten civilians by being armed would destroy everything his father worked for. To be "popular" was important to long-term survival, and by making this choice, Alimamy framed himself as someone who wanted to think beyond the war. This was critical at this particular time, as RUF and junta commanders were just then fighting each other for control of the town. Foday Sankoh contacted Issa Sesay in Kailahun, ordering him to take over from the squabbling factions. Sesay brought another commander, Rambo, with him even though the two of them bickered. Upon seizing command of Makeni, Sesay passed Hammurabi-type laws where death was the punishment for criminal acts, be they looting, raping, killing, or harassment of civilians. He put his personal command stamp on the town, and, to the shock of many cadres, applied the law to rebels as well as to civilians. Alimamy had witnessed the new laws in action, but interpreted the change as inspiring fear for the RUF, rather than greater order.

Alimamy later noted that when Sesay passed laws in Makeni, word got back to Freetown and President Kabbah was furious. By Kabbah's logic, if people obeyed laws passed by rebels, that meant they embraced rebel rule, rather than his own. "The president issued a statement on the radio that all Makeni people are rebels. So that's why this order came to pass that he would destroy any Makeni people who came his way." To attempt to escape Makeni for Freetown now—now that all Makeni civilians were branded and targeted as rebels—was as dangerous as staying in town.

ON THE ROAD WITH THE REBELS

When he joined, Alimamy did not know the consequences of Sesay's rule for Kabbah's treatment of the town; he had to concentrate on his own battles. He narrated being forced to join a weapons convoy, ferrying arms between RUF bases in Kono in the east and Makeni. He felt threatened on all sides: jet attacks, hostile factions, RUF commanders who "can change at any time." Alimamy consistently emphasized that though he was forced to join the rebels to save his life and save his family from harassment, he never ceased to be a caring individual.

"We were constantly on the road to Kono, with machine guns and other weapons. When we were going this jet saw us. So we jumped, and I saw the driver struggle because the door was locked. So he broke the glass and when he opened it he cut his leg very badly. It was open and you could see right inside to the bone. But the man did not feel anything until we were hiding and I said something. The man was a civilian like me, but he was a mechanic. That was one reason the rebels captured him."

Earlier, David had narrated being proud of being selected by Foday Sankoh for a communications course because he was educated. Mechanics were specifically targeted for recruitment by the RUF no matter their age. Though Alimamy noted being in constant danger because of his youth, it was skilled artisans—carpenters, mechanics, metalworkers—who were most vulnerable to RUF seizure, and most likely to be hunted down if they escaped.

"I said, 'Hey, Mohamed, you have a wound.' And he saw it, and fell down. He fainted with the pain. So I took some clothes and bound the wound. I took his leg and wrapped it carefully, and that helped him. After it was a little better he was commanded to drive again. But fortunately the rebel commander liked me, so I played on behalf of the driver and I said, 'But the man is not well, so let the other driver come and do it instead.' I took another vehicle with Mohamed back to Makeni town, and I left him at the hospital. They treated him, and he knew that the rebels would be waiting for us on the road. So he got up and said that the two of us should go. That was my first trip to Kono. We got as far as the barracks the RUF had set up in the bush, Camp Burkina Faso. After we dropped off all the guns, we came back to Makeni. On the way back to Makeni the truck that we used broke down. It was totally fucked up, no brakes, no clutch, and we struggled on one of the hills." He paused a moment and composed himself before continuing.

"I witnessed something that makes me fear again every time I think of it. When we had this problem we were not far from an RUF camp, so some of the rebels went into the bush and called all the rebels in the camp to come and help us push this truck up the hill. So we pushed this truck and climbed the hill, this was the last hill before Makeni. We pushed it and all of us climbed aboard. So after we got up the hill the man cut the engine and we were going down the hill, no brakes. The driver told us he could do it, and no one should jump out of the truck. But one rebel boy is so panicked that he keeps trying to get off the truck. And he ordered the driver to let us all climb down and the driver alone must drive the vehicle down the hill. This was while it was moving! Fortunately I was able to jump off okay but the boy who panicked was crushed by the truck. He was in the middle of the front seat and so he went over the hood, and when he jumped he landed straight and the tire went over his skull, and I was the first person there."

This was clearly a memory that affected Alimamy greatly, and one moment where he could direct my attention to how he was still a loving person. The other people on the scene had been dead for many years, and there was no way of corroborating his story. It was his narrative, and he could make this terrible event right by placing himself in it as well as possible. He articulated running back up the hill to the boy, as the first person who cared.

"I took the boy, the only life he had was in his hand and he just shook it a little bit. The vehicle ran down the hill and the only one who didn't make it was the little boy who panicked and fell down under the tire. I just raced up and found him, and I said, 'Oh, the vehicle has just taken someone's life.' We took the body, carried the boy to the place in the village where the RUF guys were. We laid him down, and the boy was dead. They left him there in the village."

In the narrative, it was "we" who laid him down, but "they" who left the dead boy. If this was a callous act, it was not Alimamy's choice. At this point, he departed from this story, and jumped to one even more fearful. Aside from the Kamajors in the south, locally organized civil militias existed in many places in the country, though under different tribal names such as Tamaboro (in the northeast) and Gbethis north and west of Makeni. All of them used magic to protect themselves, and Alimamy feared this magic, called *juju*. Though it is likely that he met the Gbethis, he referred to them as "Kamajors" in his narrative:

"We decided to rest in the bush for a while after this horrible day, but after one week these Kamajors attacked us. A friend of mine was shot in his foot, and I took him and we struggled back to the hill where the truck broke, and I did not use any guns. I'm telling the truth. It was the blessing of God that I didn't die in that place, with the Kamajors coming chop-chop. So we are fighting, fighting, fighting, and after we turned them away the leader called other rebels to come help us overcome the Kamajors. We chased them towards Makeni. We took the broken vehicle to follow them and we fell into an ambush where I used a gun, to save myself. We were only six, and they killed all five of my friends. When they fired this RPG I fell to the ground and I was the only one saved. Everyone, even the man who fired it, thought I had died. The message reached my mom that I had died in the bush and my mom starts crying, tearing her hair out. Even the man who delivered this message was crying."

Alimamy frames his survival as an act of providence; his adherence to the *social world itself* both ensured his survival, and was realized in the messenger's crying while delivering the news of his death. This is therefore not a miraculous event, but an instance that justifies both firing the gun, and joining the rebels to begin with. God wanted Alimamy to survive, and, by saving him, was telling him that he had done no wrong.

"After one week I was still in the bush. One week I was alone. I struggled onto the road and after a bit of time I saw my friends, a friend of Christopher, he was also from Liberia, and he went by the name Sewa. He was coming from Kono and he was surprised when I hailed the vehicle. He said, 'Who is that?' and I said, 'It is a friend.' He was so surprised to see me because he thought I was dead, but he took me back to Makeni. I sent something to my mom and she was so surprised because everyone had told her that I was dead, and she had to see me with her own eyes, that I was still alive."

The bond between mother and son was the node around which Alimamy's narrative turned. At every point he noted how his mother was feeling, how she was acting, and how miserable it would be if they were parted. If Alimamy's mother still loved him, then he would have the strength to continue, no matter what alliances were required.

THE LOVE BETWEEN MOTHER AND SON

"After I came back from the bush I stayed with the men at the Christian mission. I would come and speak to my parents sometimes but I couldn't stay there. When I came back I had to keep telling people that I'm not a rebel. Because when I came to stay with my mom, Christopher was so happy that he said he would go and harass people for palm wine to bring to me. And I said no, I will not help you with that. A friend of mine helped him do that. He's a civilian, but he's a very wicked boy."

Alimamy's explanation that he had joined the rebels to save his life—while never committing misdeeds—was entwined in his narrative with working to convince his neighbors that he had joined as a survival tactic, and not because he wanted to eat. Alimamy moved out of the family home and into a neutral location, a Christian mission house, to place his family in less danger of retribution as he worked to rebuild his credibility as a civilian. He did not want to be seen with people who were wicked, whether rebel or civilian, and living with monks was the ultimate symbol of his alignment with love. The wicked civilian boy, on the other hand, did not understand this.

"This boy was so wicked to steal palm wine, so I tried in front of other people to convince him to stop doing this. I said, 'This is not the time. Can't you understand that this is your town? To come and do these acts in front of all the people who know you, what will they think?' But he wouldn't listen, so I told myself to leave him and he will do these things if he wants, even though it is not the time or the place. I didn't understand, how do you destroy your own home? I was talking to him, and after that he joined the rebels at the first chance. That was his own decision."

Alimamy emphasized his difference from wicked boys in his narrative to place himself rightly in the social world. However, this backfired with respect to RUF commanders. Because he was known to them, and yet had refused to join the RUF enthusiastically, Alimamy was vulnerable. One commander made an example of him over a rare commodity in occupied Makeni: salt. Every encounter with rebels in his narrative occurred as he did something brave for his mother, and this was no exception.

"Unfortunately there is a fight going on, led by a rebel named Green Snake and the wicked one, Superman. Superman was the one who threw people off buildings. Green Snake was so named because he is very wicked, like snakes. Superman also had a conflict with Rambo, because Rambo wanted to burn Makeni town and Superman didn't want it. So they were all fighting each other. When the infight happened I was carrying some salt for my mom. I walked to a junction and two rebels were there. One was Christopher and the other was named Colonel Ray. This rebel was Liberian. Unfortunately salt was becoming scarce in Makeni town. There was also no pepper here, nothing for the soup. Colonel Ray said he had a bag of salt, so the three of us went to hide it. They carried Ray's salt to the hiding place but as for me, I didn't touch it at all. But when it went missing Ray accused me of stealing it. I only had the small amount for my mom! He said he would kill me if I didn't produce the salt. He did a lot of things to me, but I didn't know where the salt was. Before they decided my fate I went to my house and sat with my family. And the rebel came.

"The rebels came and wanted to embarrass my family, and my mom. Ray said, 'Where is Alimamy? If you don't give us the salt I will destroy your family.' I was inside the room with my nose in a book, and my mom was pregnant and they wanted to disturb her. They said that if she didn't produce me they would kill her and the rest of my family. So I came out and asked what the problem is, and to leave my mom. And she said, 'This is the boy. You should not disturb him, he is studying.' And Ray said, 'You have our salt.' And I said, 'Which salt? I have nothing.' They looked all over. There was nothing. So he used his gun, whapped me, picked me up, tied me up, and threw me into the vehicle to go to the prison. In spite of the fighting in Makeni, my mom was running up and down, crying. She was trying to save me.

"My mom had a lot of pots and pans, and she sold them all to raise the money for the salt. She got six cups of salt, and she brought it to them. And they said no, they did not want the cups of salt. They want the bag of salt. My mom tried to appease them so they would leave me. My mom sold everything because of me, because of me. So that is why I don't want anything to disturb my mom until I'm done with school. I will take care of her when the time comes, I will help her through a lot of strain."

Alimamy consistently emphasized the sacrifices that he and his mother made for each other. Alimamy did everything he could to ease her strain. He fretted that she was hungry and distressed during her pregnancy; he considered her reputation and happiness when making choices; and he stayed in school in order to take care of her when he was older. Equally clear is her commitment to him. Possessions were precious in occupied Makeni, and the symbolism of selling even her ability to cook for her family to save his life is powerful. She would sacrifice everything for her son, even as her efforts seemed futile.

"They threw me in prison and beat me every morning, giving me 150 lashes. I was beaten to the point of death. So I am stuck there, and I didn't eat anything, and I was very discouraged. I was thinking, just let me die. They even shot me, but thanks to God they mostly missed and I have only a small mark. But Ray wanted to kill me. Even Christopher couldn't save me, because Ray was a bigger man in the RUF. So Christopher went out to find my mom to apologize."

Christopher's inability to save Alimamy, and yet his insistence on seeking out his mother is indicative of just how precious good relationships were. As Alimamy leaned on Christopher to protect him from the rebels, Christopher himself was vulnerable to the hierarchy in his organization, and could not endanger himself by standing up to a higher-ranking commander on behalf of a civilian. He could only acknowledge his powerlessness; an acknowledgement that was also a plea to maintain this relationship in spite of Alimamy's torture. Relationships were becoming even more important, as the infight was ongoing between RUF big men to control the town. As life became more uncertain, people clung ever tighter to each other. Superman and Rambo had a confrontation on the highway, and Rambo was murdered. This incensed his cadres, who went on a rampage. Alimamy was still in jail, wanting to die as the town erupted around him. The moment the fighting subsided, his mother took to the streets to secure his release. She needed him to be strong and able to help the family as much as he needed her:

"My mom knew that the rebels were framing people so they could put themselves in a better position when the infight was over. So she went out to find someone who was high up who would release me. She went to find them with the salt that she bought and gave it to the man and begged him, and he came to the prison. He gave a command to Colonel Ray and said that if he didn't release me, he would have a problem with him. So they released me. Mom didn't recognize that I was Alimamy because my face had swelled up, everything looked different.

But I thank God because he gave me a strong body, so one week after they whipped me I was better.

"My mother was so sad that this had happened but I knew I had done the right thing. On the day I was captured I went out because there was nothing for my family to eat. I am the eldest, I can't sit down and watch my family suffer. I would do almost anything except become a rebel. That day this rebel man called me and said let me work with him in town. And I had to tell him, 'Look, I'm not a rebel, I'm a student. There were circumstances that forced me to do certain things, but I can't be a rebel because I'm a student in Makeni town.' I decided instead to go look for food in some abandoned villages near Makeni. When I returned I had food for my mom and family to eat. That was why I was carrying the salt."

RUNNING TO SAFETY IN FREETOWN

Chronology did occur in Alimamy's narrative when two events were clearly linked. His time in the RUF jail prompted Alimamy's mother to urge him to join his elder sister, who was a student in Freetown. In Makeni, he was a liability to the family, who had become targets of Colonel Ray and his cadre. She gave him much of what remained of the family's money and he left town.

"She gave me ten thousand [about six dollars] and I took my things. I had a friend who wanted to walk to Freetown, so we went through the villages. I didn't know anyone there, but anywhere we went people knew my dad and recognized me. My friend was so surprised, and asked me if I knew these people. And I said, 'No. I've never been through this village before and these people, I don't know them.' But anyway the two of us walked and people recognized me, and I don't mind it. People were helping us because of my dad, because I look like him. But I had these marks on my body, which I had to hide."

Alimamy frames the journey as one where people went out of their way to help because of his physical resemblance to his father, a well-liked civil servant in Makeni. Both are short and jolly looking, clearly father and son. This marked a pronounced shift in his narrative away from the boy as occasional hero and clear target for RUF aggression in Makeni. That time was linked to his mother. On the road, he wove his narrative around people's love for his father. He was vulnerable, however, because he bore the marks of his torture. RUF life was dangerous and rebels were often wounded, which would make him, having been tortured, a target of suspicion. Though Alimamy described the first militia members he encountered as Kamajors, this contingent was the northern Gbethis, who had no intention of protecting villages.

"We knew about these Gbethis, they stayed at a nearby village. We were lucky not to run into them. That day they had already destroyed one village and killed a lot of people. We arrived at the village and were hoping for water but when we heard screaming we hid in the bushes. I saw them killing people, chopping their hands, they even raped one fine lady and killed her. We saw a lot of blood, fearful things. When they left we came out of the bush, but we were warned to take a different route. An old man came from his house and told us not to pass there, these Gbethis are still hiding so let us not use that road. He had been badly wounded and we could not stop the bleeding. He saved us and then he died.

"We were so afraid that we ran away from that place. We couldn't use the same road so we got lost. We reached another village and were welcomed nicely; people helped us get food. We passed through another village and then we were really lost, in the middle of the bush. We didn't know where to go and we started crying. And I told my friend that we should return to the village so that we can find the road. And he said that the village was too far. But I reasoned with him, that before we got into the middle of the bush and involved ourselves in more fearful things, we should go back. So we returned. We found a path at nine at night, and the place was so dark. Thank God the moon was shining and we followed it. We walked fast and reached the village at eleven. It was the same village but when people saw us they ran away. They thought we were rebels, so we called to them. They were holding cutlasses, so we said we are not rebels. We reminded them that we had just come from Makeni and we needed their help to find the road. One man and one lady said they knew me because of my father, even though I didn't know them. But they said, 'Don't worry about it.' We were so hungry. They gave us rice and we ate, and we had a place to sleep. In the morning they showed us the road."

Alimamy emphasized that his journey was socially charmed, that he survived because his father's good reputation meant people with no resources, even in villages under attack, extended compassion. It is impossible to know whether this narrative, in which people in far-flung villages miraculously knew his father, is factual. The *truth* of Alimamy's words exists in his linking himself firmly to a dense web of care; that, because of the social standing of his parents, total strangers looked after him. With this he brings into life the best social world, one that transcends war, where people love because they see others not just as human, but as worth having.

"The day after that, one man named Fofanah . . . he saved my life. When we reached this village he gave us food, because he said he knows my dad and my family. He showed us the road, but the town we were heading to was ten miles off. If we walked fast we would reach it that day. He escorted us to the road, but we came to another river. The man knew how to swim, and he knew how to paddle. But the canoe is not good, it has a hole in it. So he put my friend in first and took him to the other side. He came back to take me across in the canoe. And the two of us were in it, but I was afraid because the canoe is not good. Water was coming in the boat until it was full. It turned over and I didn't know how to swim. I thought on that day I would die.

"Fofanah saved me. I was going down and swallowing lots of water. He pulled me to the surface. We were saved by a branch floating across the water, he stuck it in the ground and I grabbed it. He asked me if I was all right and could help myself. The man went to the water again and removed the canoe and took my things out, my plastic bag with all the things that I have. I had my photo album in it, but it was spoiled and all the pictures were damaged, so I threw it away. The money had also gone. I had no money, but I thanked God that Fofanah assisted me. I would not be here today without him. So I was safe on shore and he asked me if I'm alright and I said, 'Yes, I'm alright. No problems.'"

It would be overly simplistic to state that during war, people nurtured only those whom they loved directly. Fofanah went to enormous lengths to help Alimamy, based only on his knowledge of the boy's father as a good man. Even when it meant endangering themselves, people went out of their way to help those to whom they could draw some connection, as though doing so reinforced the rightness of love itself. Thus, in small ways, they fought against the possibility that the war might atomize people, isolate them from each other and hasten everyone's demise. Alimamy, however, was not safe yet.

"I was still very afraid, because of the marks that I have, that any civil militia member, if they find me they will flog me. They said that if at any time they saw men or boys who have marks on their bodies, they would flog and kill them. The Gbethis had made this announcement, and here we were about to reach them. And I told myself, well, if it is time for me to die, then it is the will of God and I will go."

Although the Gbethis' plan was designed to reveal rebels attempting to hide as civilians, it caused everyone with recent wounds to fear for their lives. Gbethis habitually stripped youth, searched for injuries, and created and executed rebels in the same moment. Thus were Gbethis and their home communities performing a sense of mastery over the war, weeding out possible rebels before they had a chance to reveal themselves. The fear that governed initial interactions between people who did not know each other—especially if one was suspected as a fighter—meant that personal relationships, even those built only on the recognition that the individual was related to someone known and trusted, became paramount as individuals like Alimamy negotiated their survival.[5]

"I used my clothes to cover the marks so that people won't see them, and the man took us to the village. We said, 'Thank you and thank God for you,' and he said, 'No problem.' Then he walked back to the river to go to his village. So we followed the people, and we reached the town. There was a man there, by the name of Mr. Sisay. He was a civil militia commander, a Makeni man who had taken charge of Port Loko. He had orders for ECOMOG that anyone who comes from Makeni must come and see him. And if he doesn't know that person, he will kill him. Mr. Sisay is a friend of my dad, but I don't know him."

In the information vacuum operating during the war, personal relationships became the only way to manage fear and uncertainty. More than dividing friend from foe, rebel from civilian, these confrontations were relationship reckonings. Mr. Sisay, rather than divining rebel status through injuries, reached beyond the war into the person's past. He determined if he knew them—by however many degrees of separation—in prewar Makeni, and if they had been good people in good relationships. This expressed faith that the prewar social world could illuminate who was wicked and thus likely a rebel. If no good relationships could be discerned, the social world would not miss that person anyway.

"My target was to go to Port Loko. From that village you could pay six thousand leones for transport on a bus to Port Loko. I didn't have it because I had lost all of my money in the river. My friend had money, and he didn't want to wait so he paid his six thousand and went to Freetown, and he left me there. What do I do? A friend of mine who lived there saw me, and he called me and I said, 'Thank God I see you, but I have a problem!' And he said, 'Well, come and eat first.' I was so hungry! As we were eating I told him I want to go to Port Loko.

"So I talked to my friend, telling him that I need money to go to Port Loko and I don't want to sleep here. He said, 'No problem, but I don't have money for you.' And I said, 'Please help me, if you give the money now, when I reach my destination I will send the money back.' And he insisted that he had no money even though he did. Then he looked at me and said, 'Give me your *crib* [plastic school shoes] and I will give you six thousand leones.' And I said, 'These are the only *crib* that I have. I don't have too many things, I have only the one pair of trousers and my shirt, and that is all I have. And I have put on the trousers and I don't have anything in my hands or my pockets, only the *crib*.' He didn't care. He said, 'Give me the *crib* and I will give you the money.' After we finished eating I removed them and he gave me the money." Alimamy was hurt by this recollection; the friendship was clearly not as strong as he had thought, even as his friend had just fed him.

"So now I have six thousand leones. And I know that when I get to Port Loko, I will be out of money, and it costs fifteen thousand leones to go down to Freetown. So I told myself that if I pray, when I get to Port Loko I will see someone else I know that can help me. I had to be strategic. I asked myself, 'What can I do with the six thousand? When I get to Port Loko, what if I don't know anyone there?' So I divided the money, I split it three thousand for using and three thousand to keep. I went to the driver's apprentice and I begged him to let me on the truck for only three thousand. I begged until he agreed. I gave him the three thousand and we went to Port Loko."

As Alimamy moved further into his story, he warmed to his theme of leaning on others in order to survive. He gave his father influence and respect all the way to Freetown, finding a natural narrative rhythm that seemed to give him strength as he told it. Every word took him further from the RUF and Makeni. Gone was the frenetic confusion surrounding Fatmata and Christopher; Alimamy outlined a sense of control over his life.

"When I arrived in Port Loko, I only have my three thousand leones left, so I decided that I had to find this man, Mr. Sisay. If my father knew him, then maybe he would help me. I asked around for him and the Nigerian soldiers took me there. I saw the man, and he said, 'I know you.' I said, 'Yes, but I don't know you.' He said, 'What is your name?' I said, 'My name is Alimamy,' and he said he knew my father. I mentioned the office my father worked in and he agreed it was the same man. I explained everything and he said no problem."

When Alimamy went to Port Loko, he went on faith that his father's reputation would save him. He had managed to scrape together survival to that point on his father's reputation alone, but it would not provide him boat fare. Resources were scarce, and finding such a large sum of money proved no easy task.

"I stayed there for one week. And I started grumbling that I wanted to go and Mr. Sisay asked what was wrong. And I said, 'I want to travel but I don't have money, I have only three thousand with me. It is not enough to travel.' I told him that I needed to see my sister and I didn't know what to do. Mr. Sisay gave me a note. He told me that I should go to the raft, this boat that travels from Port Loko to Freetown, because he knows the people who run the boats. I went to the Oga [Nigerian] commander in charge of the place. I gave him the note, he read it, and he didn't believe that Mr. Sisay would 'pull favor' for me. I went to find Mr. Sisay and the two of us went together. He told the commander to load me on the boat. In the evening we took off."

It was unusual for Mr. Sisay to go out of his way for a youth with no personal ability to return the favor. For Alimamy to tell this episode this way sheds even more honor on his father; one man's social position could literally carry his son to safety through seemingly insurmountable obstacles. In whatever ways Mr. Sisay helped Makeni residents, he fought his own battles to save his country from the ravages of war. He reached out in care to people he knew of, with these small acts repairing the world of his hometown, and reaffirming that this world would exist again for these favors to be repaid. He was actively creating the future, and stating that the social world itself is a thing of value.

PAYING IT FORWARD

"We were going slowly, slowly, and after dark I could see that there was an island in the middle that had a village on it! I was surprised, but the Oga in the boat knew that their brothers had a checkpoint on this island. They said that after half past seven no boats would cross there, because the place is so tense. The Oga stopped the boat, and I see that there is a pregnant lady in the boat. I don't know her but I can see that she is sick, and she asked for my help. The two of us were sitting together, so I decided to help her. I removed my shirt and dipped it in the water and put it on her face so she would cool off, because she almost fainted. She asked my name and I told her, and I asked her the same and she told me, though I have forgotten her first name. But her family name resembled the man that assisted me in Makeni, that rebel Christopher. I asked her if she knew Christopher because I assumed she was Liberian, and she said yes, and I asked if she was related to him and she explained herself. I said, 'I know your brother, he is there in Makeni and he is the one who saved me.' And she said, 'Well, that is good.'

"I decided to help her. We reached the village and she wanted to drink. So I crossed the water and I bought some cake for her, and I came with it. I gave it to her and something to drink, and she started feeling better. We needed to sleep but I needed to help the lady, find her a place to rest. I didn't know the place where we stopped, but I wanted to help the lady first. So I helped her find a place to sleep. As for me, I just sat down where I was. In the morning at half past seven we took off."

At the moment his own ability to reach Freetown seemed assured, Alimamy transformed himself in his narrative from recipient of care to provider. Having been saved multiple times by generous strangers, he was then in a position to help someone more vulnerable, related to someone he respected. By helping Christopher's sister, he reinforced the rightness of Christopher's kind actions in Makeni, buttressing the social world.

"When we reached Freetown I helped this lady. I said, 'Let me take you to where you stay.' I walked with her to her mom's house. I explained that her son is in Makeni town. I described him and the mom took a picture down from a shelf and showed me and I said, 'Yes, that is the man, he is there in Makeni.' She said okay, but according to the lady's story, her son was not willing to join the rebels. She said that her son is a schoolboy, and the RUF met him in Liberia. She said he was not a rebel because he was a student; it was this horrible war that forced him to join the rebels. She said that they lived on the border of Sierra Leone, and Foday Sankoh and his troops came to the school to force them all to join. When they got to Christopher, he said no. So they found his younger brother and killed him. They killed him to force Christopher. And then they raped his sister in front of him and killed her. They wanted to rape the next one and kill her to make him join. They said they would do that and then find and kill his mother and he said okay, you win. So that's why he joined the rebel force."

The terrible logic of the RUF, especially with respect to conscription, was to force children to join by destroying their relationships. Young people's love for their families *overcame* their resistance to being conscripted only as they were threatened with destruction. The RUF replaced their natal families with commanders who looked after these children, thus imitating and reinforcing familial love. Christopher's mother insisted that her son—like Alimamy—was a student rather than a rebel. Like Alimamy, he was forced to join the rebels upon pain of losing his family. Neither one saw himself as a *real rebel,* as Alimamy had thought of Christopher. They were both students, boys who were loved, had a sense of responsibility towards their families and who made new friends on positive grounds, traits that no *real rebel* would display.

To be a real rebel was to embrace eating, to discount the needs and importance of other people as one consumed resources in the quest for power. To be a student who joined was to be a boy whose world was based on love and investment, a boy who sacrificed himself to save his family. Perhaps Christopher's willingness to fall in love, to embrace his girlfriend's friends, to forge new relationships, were all signs that his authentic self was still intact under his *real rebel* façade. Perhaps Alimamy's own alliance with Christopher was just one of two battered students recognizing each other in terrible times.

STABLE TIME PASSES QUICKLY IN A STORY ABOUT WAR

"When I left Christopher's mother and sister, I did not ask them for anything. I think they were too sad to learn what happened to the boy. I had only one goal, which was to get to my sister's house, but I didn't have any money. I was walking when I passed this lady. She called my name, so I turned. She greeted me, and went into her bag and gave me cake and drink. I didn't say anything because I was so hungry! I just ate, and she waited for me to finish, then she said she knew that I was Eme's brother. I said yes. I said, 'How did you know me? What is your name?' The lady would not give me her name. I told her that I wanted to go to my sister but I don't have money. The lady removed five thousand leones from her bag and gave it to me. Five thousand. So I said thank you, and she smiled and turned, and walked away. I found a taxi and I went to my sister. When I arrived I explained everything that happened and she took me to the hospital."

Aside from inserting a stable thread about the social position of his family into his narrative, the consistency with which Alimamy received assistance from others is a particularly Sierra Leonean way of drawing emphasis to one's imbrication in loving relationships. It is a source of pride to receive assistance from others: rather than proof of being weak or needy, it is proof of one's standing. Wicked people are shunned; their isolation is both cause and effect of their unwillingness to love.

Alimamy, on the other hand, is literally carried along by his relationships. They reveal him as a good person.

"They treated me, gave me food and ointments. I was there with my elder sister and I was so tired! She asked about our family and I said they are all right. I stayed in Freetown for a while. When the road finally opened my mom and dad came to Freetown with my younger sister and the baby; they left my younger brother in Makeni with my aunt. My father needed to report to his boss in Freetown. There was an incident in Makeni so he needed to come down and file the paperwork. He gave me money because he knew I wanted to go back to Makeni because the schools were opening up again! But transport was costly, twenty thousand leones! That was why I had stayed with my sister for so long. But when my dad came, he gave me money to go back to school. My mom had already decided to go back because she was worried about my brother. She left a few days before I did, before my dad came to my sister's house with all the money that he had in the bank in Freetown. And he gave it to me to take back to Makeni."

Alimamy remained with his sister for almost a year before his parents came to Freetown. Its lack of extraordinary activity truncated this time to a single paragraph of narrative; stories of war were only worth telling as they brought new people into being, and outlined and reaffirmed the contours of the social world. Thus was Alimamy's war over. In his narrative, he fought the war by investing in and reaping the benefits of his relationships; he resisted the atomization that threatened to divide people from each other, which would have allowed wickedness, and thus the evil of war itself, to triumph. It was 2001 and the danger had largely passed in Makeni, the principal sign being the fact that the schools were open again. After three years of instability, Alimamy's only wish was to return to school. His father agreed, and trusted his oldest son to return to Makeni with the family's savings. Alimamy chose to disguise himself and walk to Makeni rather than risk being in a vehicle that would likely be stopped at an RUF checkpoint, where passengers were often relieved of their possessions. Walking, however, also posed problems.

"On the day I decided to go, there were some problems with rebels on the road! If you are walking and they catch you they will beat you up and remove all your money. So I kept my money somewhere that no one knows, except me and my God. I placed the money in these shoes here. I cut the sole and put the money inside, and then I glued it together again. I went with this to Makeni, I had 250,000 leones, and no one knows, except me. I dressed like a crazy person, because even the rebels don't disturb a crazy person, and they never have any money. So when I came with the money my mom was so surprised! She thought I had stolen it. And I said no, this was dad's money. She said, 'How much?' and I said, '250,000.' She said, 'Wow!' I was the only person who had money in Makeni town and she said, 'How did you do it?' And I told her, and she laughed and clapped her hands."

JEALOUSY, WICKEDNESS, AND THE END OF CHRISTOPHER

In spite of his joy at being back in Makeni, Alimamy was sobered by news of Christopher's death. During the year Alimamy spent in Freetown, Christopher had been promoted to the exalted position of Issa Sesay's personal bodyguard. He was liked and respected in the town because of his kindness and generosity, and as Alimamy imagined, spoke of his desire to return to school in Liberia once the war was over. However, Christopher's social success made him a target of jealousy among other rebels.

"I was in Freetown when everything when wrong for Christopher. There was a small conflict among the rebels. A man . . . I have forgotten the name of this rebel. He had soldiers working for him. They went to loot and disturb civilians, and they came to our neighborhood. Christopher was still staying in the place where these soldiers, these rebels, went to loot. And Christopher told him that he could not loot in town, especially not in Christopher's own area. Well, the man who wanted to loot was junior to Christopher. Christopher had a better post than him, which is why he had a grudge and was jealous of him. So many of these boys wanted to take the things that Christopher had."

Alimamy became very emotional at this point in our conversation. Though he wanted to continue, we stopped for several minutes. He composed himself, and told me that it was important for the world to know what happened to Christopher. He reiterated that Christopher was a good man who would have lived a good life had it not been for this terrible war. He wondered out loud why the other rebels couldn't see that real status came with making friends. Christopher did not want them to loot in his own area because it undermined his position, and, as many people say in Sierra Leone, produced *wam hat den* among others. "Warm hearts" are bad feelings between people, which literally open the space for violence. If feelings cannot become "cool," conflict occurs.

"These soldiers went to his house and called to him to come down. Christopher was taking his bath. After his bath he went downstairs, and he calmly met these boys and asked what was going on. They talked and talked, and Christopher told them that they could not talk while anyone was armed, and he ordered them to hand over their weapons. So he took the guns from their hands and placed them on the floor. The guys were shouting, shouting, and a crowd of bad rebels started to gather. One of them was RUF police and he told Christopher's woman to go tell the command that he had been arrested, because of this and that and some other things. So this junior boy finally showed up to confront Christopher. He was standing there, and said, 'Well, Christopher . . .' so Christopher tried to talk sense to the man. He said, 'Our leaders have said that we must stop disturbing civilians. Now we have peace, stop that!' The man said Christopher had no right to talk to him like that. He was leading his own life so he did what he wanted. Christopher tried to stop him . . . and the man removed his pistol and he shot Christopher. After that he remained in the room, he wanted everyone to see. According to his own statement, he wanted to kill Christopher for a long time. That happened when I was in Freetown, I just heard the information."

That Alimamy was not in Makeni to witness these events gave the story, acquired secondhand, the aura of a Sergio Leone western. A long-standing grudge from a junior man who lacked the social success that came easily to Christopher decided to kill Christopher, and finally *pull down* the big man of whom he was so jealous. This was Christopher's own failing as a big man; clearly here was a rebel whose love and loyalty he should have courted, even if this man was worth having only in his capacity to destroy. This junior man had no real intention of looting Christopher's neighborhood; he just wanted an excuse for a confrontation. What was extraordinary was the civilian reaction.

"Christopher was so popular here that when he was killed, the civilians gathered. They swore they would kill the man who killed Christopher. They wanted to fight for Christopher! Christopher was . . . he was a rebel, but when I knew that man he was the only rebel that did not disturb civilians. He loved to meet people, talk to them . . . he didn't have any reason to menace them. And if he went on a mission, he would go far, in his own vehicle, and not harass Makeni people. When he came with some goods, he would give them to civilians that didn't have anything. That is why they loved him, even though the man was a real rebel!"

Alimamy struggled to reconcile the notion that Christopher was a "real rebel" with his knowledge that Christopher had once been a student, and now seemed a kind of Robin Hood. He grappled with someone who simultaneously loved and ate, inspired loyalty and inspired fear, though clearly Christopher was capable of all these things. A "mission" was a looting mission, done at a distance so as not to ruin his reputation in Makeni, but a violent act of theft all the same. Christopher stage-managed his identity just as Alimamy had done, cultivating relationships in town that he hoped would protect him in other circumstances, and also create a foundation for a postwar life. Rather than displaying callousness, the fact that Christopher looted in distant villages was proof of his love for Makeni and how he wanted people to feel about him. Life, like narrative itself, is about perception.

"He had killed people before he came to Makeni, many people. It was in Makeni that he lost his rebel eyes, and he gained some new eyesight."

"Eyesight" is not the same as losing one's taste for war. Christopher could see the world through rose-tinted glasses because he had fallen in love, and was thus capable of acting from love rather than wickedness. He was rejoining the social world.

"It was only when he met her that he was not interested in the war. He saw she was very beautiful, very fair in complexion. He was so kind because the lady talked to him. But part of that . . . the man said that he was a rebel before, he killed many people. But now he has arrived at the fact that killing is not his whole life. So he stopped. He was reading his Bible and Koran. People knew that he was becoming good again, and they were kind to him. When my mom saw him on the street and he didn't have anything, she gave him three thousand leones, that was after he tried to save me from Colonel Ray. So even when he had nothing, people in Makeni would pull something from nowhere and give it to him. When the man killed Christopher he went to the UN and surrendered. The UN came into town with him, and the civilians were there. Everyone—civilians, other rebels—wanted to kill him. So the UN stopped the people from getting to him. That was the story."

Christopher had involved himself so completely in the town that he *became* his friendships with civilians. In low periods, especially during the UN blockade of supplies, he fared better than other rebels because he had the townspeople. The jealousy of rebels who lacked his social success was his undoing, but at the same time, his enemies risked their lives by incurring the wrath of the town. Christopher's murderer gave himself up to UN reintegration custody the moment the center's doors opened. The occupation had gone on for so long, so many new relationships had been cultivated, that a rebel now needed UN protection from angry residents. For President Kabbah to argue "collaboration" from an episode like this was not difficult.

GOD WILL TAKE CARE OF OTHERS, BUT ALIMAMY HELPS HIS FAMILY FIRST

"I came back in 2002; rebels were still here so I was one of the few people in Freetown who risked it, but I was able to stay in our house. I would go to school, eat, and at the end of the day I would come back, go to my house and go to sleep. I did this every day until my dad came back, which he did once he could open the office again. When he came he brought all his government business with him and he threw open the doors. People didn't believe that they could come back, but he told them to come and see, and they came back. Even the Catholic bishop was here and he was encouraging people to come back, encouraging the rebels to disarm. And Makeni became fine again. Now everything is okay, and my family is here except for my sisters, who are in Freetown. They visited and then they went back.

"I started attending school again, thank God, and we are here with peace in Makeni town. We pray to Almighty God that everything will be all right. We don't want any more accidents to happen here. People are already dead in that incident, the rebel war. We pray that God will give them a good way to heaven. And we pray that God will have mercy on the rebels, whatever they are doing. We pray that God will assist them and all the people in Makeni town. As for me, if I don't go to school, no money, no job, how can I develop Makeni when I don't develop my family? You must help your family first, when you consider it, that's what the town really needs. And this is it, if you ask me."

Alimamy sleeps deeply every night; his mother often joked that he struggled to start the day with everyone else. He clearly harbors no regrets over his actions during the occupation, in spite of the stigmatizations that accompany accusations of collaboration. Alimamy undertook his "collaboration" in defense of the social world—his family—rather than as a handmaiden of its destruction. In doing so every day in the aftermath, he maintains his identity as loving son, and one day, as respectable man.

"The Government Brought Death, the Rebels Allowed Us to Live"

The Trader

The mercurial weather of the rainy season has little effect on the bustle in Makeni's marketplace. In between rain showers, traders throw tarps off their wares and quickly bargain with passersby before the next squall, when goods are covered once again. One day in June 2005, I made my way through the bustle and into the lorry park. This is the center of transport and wholesale marketing in the town. The lorry park is chaotically busy day and night; as the transport center it is also a node of short- and long-distance trade. Taxis arrive from around the country and their conductors shout out the next destination, bargaining with passengers over fares and exactly how many bags of rice will fit in the trunk, arguing over the effect of rising fuel costs on basic commodities. Residents boast that Makeni is the crossroads of the country, with roads leading to every possible destination. The lorry park is the central node of that crossroads. Traders think of it as the place where one can know everything about the Sierra Leonean economic situation. In order to discover why prices are rising, you go to the lorry park.

That afternoon I headed to one corner of the park, which is demarcated by the stalls of individual traders. Most of them deal in wholesale goods—rice, palm oil, and paraffin—that they sell to itinerant traders heading further inland. I was here to meet Kadiatu, a *big woman* in the world of Makeni trading, one who maintained her stall throughout the occupation. She did so with the blessing and assistance of the RUF, and rationalized her "collaboration" through her assessment of trading as a synecdoche for the state of the world. If trading is bad, everyone starves.

Her trading neighbors pointed me toward a spacious corner stall, where I found an imposing middle-aged woman sitting on a bench. Kadiatu was all angles and energy. She waved her hands around when she spoke, and was slightly distracted from conversation by her bustling business. She had a cadre of loyal customers who plied regular routes between Makeni and smaller surrounding towns, and she kept track of their accounts in a large ledger. Many times during our conversation someone poked his head into the stall requesting goods, and out came the ledger. Part of her success, she stated, she owed to her education and thus her ability to keep written accounts. No one dared to question her rendering of her customers' debt, as there was no chance of her forgetting. Slippage was possible if she kept accounts in her head, as do most traders.

Kadiatu was known as a formidable trader before the war, but her efforts, along with those of other respected women, to sell food in Makeni during the occupation solidified her reputation as a big woman, a leader of traders. Though many residents spoke haltingly of how they owed something of their survival to Issa Sesay, the RUF commander, Kadiatu was forceful in her defense of rebel command. She was a steadfast supporter of a man she claimed cared more about the people of Makeni than did the government. He enabled the traders to revive the market during the occupation; by contrast, the government sent a helicopter gunship to bomb the town. Bringing in food and allowing a market to exist, she believed, were the actions of a true big man, one who realized that his power was predicated entirely on his legitimacy with inhabitants, a legitimacy based on his willingness to facilitate them meeting their own needs, if he could not meet them himself. Kadiatu's interactions with him took place through the rubric of her trading, which was also the rubric by which she judged if life was good and people happy. Kadiatu believed that trade itself is a nurturing activity and therefore honorable, and that a government that taxes trade without investing in the town is merely eating resources.

THE TRADER'S VIEW OF THE WORLD

Kadiatu was not the daughter of a trader, nor did she grow up in the marketplace, which is unusual for women who are successful traders in Makeni. Most I spoke to remember going to the market every day as small girls, being given tasks from the time they could walk and eventually taking over their mothers' businesses. Kadiatu was the child of farmers, born in a rural chiefdom north of Makeni. When I asked her about her childhood, she responded, "I remember all the good things that were coming with development." She was clear that although her parents were farmers, they had no objection to her taking a different route. Unlike most women her age, Kadiatu attended school for nine years. Only the first six years were possible in her chiefdom, so her parents sent her to stay with her aunt in Bo. This was a typical educational fostering arrangement in Sierra Leone, where young children are moved between relatives to strengthen family ties as they struggle for success. They work for their foster parents as part of accumulating the "blessings" of their elders that will ensure their achievement.[1] Kadiatu, however, failed the national exam that would have admitted her to senior secondary school, so she began trading instead.

"At the time I was helping to sustain myself by selling things in the market, helping my aunt to sell as she was also a trader. She sold palm oil and groundnuts. She would send me to the village to buy as much as I could from the village women, then I would bring it back to town for her. If I was able to get a big load I would arrange a car to bring me back, otherwise I would walk and carry it on my head. When I became a bit successful, I paid manpower, someone with a wheelbarrow, to bring it back for me."

Kadiatu was soon shrewd enough to trade on her own. "Even after my aunt died, I was able to continue with the business. I got married and was in Bo with my husband until 1991. I stayed there for over twenty years, when I finally decided to return to Makeni. I decided to come back, this was after my father died, because my mother was in the village on her own and she was too old to be on her own. Most of my siblings were in Makeni and did not want to go back to the village, but because I was one of the oldest ones, I came back for her. I took her to Makeni town because she wanted to be closer to town, and also closer to her children. So she bought a house and I moved there with her."

Rather than running from rumors of war, which were rampant in Bo, Kadiatu returned to the north to fulfill a positive duty. Her mother had cared for her throughout her childhood, and Kadiatu owed her a great deal for supporting her education at a time when it was not common. Though her siblings were nearby, Kadiatu took it upon herself to move her aging mother into Makeni. Moving in with her mother was both a natural outgrowth of the act of caring for her, and a means for her mother to provide her with a solid foundation from which to begin her business anew.

Kadiatu immediately established a new trade of wholesale items purchased in surrounding villages. The hardest part was nurturing *padi*, loyal "friends" on whom she could rely to make regular purchases. Traders transform occasional customers into habitual ones by offering them low prices and quality stock. Although the income may be lower, it is more reliable because *padi* come to "their" traders first. Makeni, however, was a more difficult business environment than Bo. "It was a big difference! I was not happy with the changes. We didn't have any problems trading in Bo, but Makeni . . . well, Makeni was a big problem. In Bo, everything we sold we got profits from, and this was because the town was wealthy. They had diamonds, they had cocoa, they had all of these things. And here we don't have any of that, there is nothing good for people to buy in the market, and because there is no big business, no one has any money. We just depend on agriculture. We plant rice, cassava, potato, pepper, and none of these are worth much money. People on the farms don't have money to buy things with, so it is always hand to mouth. In Bo and Kenema people come to town to buy supplies, and they go back to the mines with them."

From Kadiatu's perspective, trade is indexical of nurturing. The world is fine if trading is lively. This requires a circulation of value: goods for people to buy and sell, and profits to save and invest. Kadiatu's critique of Makeni both before and after the war stemmed from the fact that impoverished parents cannot feed their children, and the government was not being a proper *pa* and "placing a hand" under farmers. Farmers needed the government to build roads and rice mills, and provide tools and seed stocks, in order to keep food prices low. Farmers were poor before the war, and afterward were faced with starting their farms without tools or seed, which had been decimated by hungry rebels and civilians. Without government help, most were unable to restart farming, and those who could farm often withheld their meager outputs from traders for home consumption. Kadiatu's narrative, whenever she mentioned trading, immediately returned to postwar problems. Kabbah was still in power, which made her entire narrative an explicit commentary on the government's lack of love for Makeni:

"From the year 2003 until now, everything is so expensive and no one has any money. The palm oil is so costly, and I have to charge small increments so that I can feed my children, and people are buying less and less because they can't afford it. When there is less oil and less rice, the children suffer. The small, small children are there and their mom and dad have to feed them. All day they will sit down in the market for ten thousand leones (about three dollars) and when they get it they go home to feed their children. You buy things for them and feed your children, you can't hold on to any of the money. You see women with their children and they are just feeding them directly with the money."

For Kadiatu, the world is fine—and its leaders equally fine—if goods are affordable, if there is money for trading, for feeding, for saving, and for investing. Lively, profitable trade is a nurturing practice; people can think about their loved ones now and in the future without sacrificing one for the other. For people to love the government, the government must enable this nurturing, and any market taxation must result in aids to that nurturing: repairing leaky stalls, waste disposal, even paving the lorry park. Kadiatu interprets the occupation of Makeni from this perspective. For her, times are good if people come by their needs cheaply, and everyone has money to spend and save. If there is little competition, if profits can be made and turned back into a business to replenish stock, if taxation has visible results that assist traders in circulating goods, this is the best possible social world. If competition is stiff, if need is great but money is scarce (leading people to haggle more and chip away at already small profit margins), if the government takes advantage of traders by taxing them without developing the market, then trade is not fulfilling everyone's needs and the situation is bad.

Kadiatu evokes her personal history, including the occupation of Makeni, through the lens of trading. Her interpretation of the RUF is largely positive. She frames the way the RUF catered to people's basic needs, those of traders especially, in direct contrast to the government taking advantage of people by eating through taxation. She survived the initial invasion similarly to others: in a haphazard manner, a chaotic and reactive movement, without solid information. "When the invasion came we all ran away, but I thank God that they left most of us alone. We could run to the bush because we were all strong. My mother had already died and I only had to carry the small one. I was here with my husband and three children, and we spent a few nights in the bush, but then the RUF called us back out again, and said that they would not harm us if we agreed to live nicely with them in the town. I didn't have anything to feed my children in the bush, so I agreed to do this. We moved back into our home and were able to sleep in our own beds again."

The RUF settled in as an occupying force, and it soon became clear to Kadiatu that the government had no intention of liberating the town.

Though the RUF had invaded, in Kadiatu's mind, the RUF had no reason to nurture the town; this was the president's responsibility as *pa*. It was Kabbah's decision to abandon Makeni, therefore Kadiatu blamed him for all her misfortunes, including her sickly, malnourished children. One deathly ill child became a metaphor for the government's will to punish the town for disloyalty. Kadiatu believed the government should sympathize with people rallying around their families, rather than demanding they sacrifice their children to nationalism.

CASSAVA DEATH IS THE GOVERNMENT'S FAULT

Most people in Makeni ate cassava during the occupation, for reasons of both ease and safety from rebels. Rice is the preferred staple, which made anyone carrying or storing rice a target of RUF aggression. "We knew it was not fine for our bodies to eat just cassava," stated one man, "but by that time there was no more farming because it was too dangerous, so we ate cassava. If you eat rice the rebels will find you and wonder why you are eating rice, they think you are keeping it and they want some. But that never happened with cassava, so we ate it. *Garri* [dried processed cassava], we called it 'rough rice,' we turned that into a soup. At times children would die because that cassava doesn't give them the things that they need to grow. So their bellies would swell, swell past how we could save them and then their lives ended."

Kadiatu was more concerned about bulk than nutrition: "Cassava . . . we thanked God for it during the war. Now there is less cassava than we had then, and people charge too much for it! How could life have been normal during the war? Now most people can only afford cassava, so it is just like war, but more expensive. During the war it was all we could get easily, we could always go to the edges of town and dig cassava and potatoes when we needed them, so this is what I fed my children. We had no way to process it so I just boiled it, and we had to eat it without salt. Everything was okay until one day my little one's belly began to swell."

Kadiatu did not have to face the everyday danger encountered by the student Alimamy and the rebel David. Her life revolved around feeding her children and keeping them safe. As a mother in her thirties, she held little interest for rebels or soldiers. She was not a target of harassment for recruitment, as the youth were, nor was she a target of sexual advances. Kadiatu was one of the invisible occupants of Makeni; one who could not leave for lack of a safe place and people to travel to. Her relatives in Bo were under constant threat from RUF attacks. Her parents had both died, and as her siblings were also in Makeni, there was no one outside of town with whom to seek safe haven. Though she tried to care for her children, the lack of diverse foodstuffs and medicine—both shortages for which she held the government responsible—were killing her child.

"I had no one to ask for help because by that point my mother had already died. If she was alive I would have asked her if there is anything I can do about it. He started refusing his food and his hair turned light brown. There was no medicine; there was nothing I could do to save him. The belly swelled, the feet swelled, and then he died."

Though Kadiatu framed the death of her youngest child as a medical situation; her description of his death is indicative of malnutrition caused by eating only cassava.[2] A cassava-only diet is almost totally bereft of protein, vitamins, and minerals. As much as Kadiatu attempted to keep her children's bellies full by cooking cassava for them, she could not provide the essential nutrients to sustain small children. That would have been possible with nutritious local rice, but rice was unavailable because, according to Kadiatu, the government was not interested in bringing real food to Makeni.

"There was no way to get rice for my children because the roads were blocked. The RUF had checkpoints out on the roads and the government convinced the traders coming from Freetown that they would be killed if they entered RUF territory, so no one came with food. There was nothing to buy in the market that would sustain us. The traders hid their goods at first because they did not know if some soldier rebel would come steal it. There were little things, if you knew who to ask, but they were so expensive! Because of government discouragement, one cup of rice was one thousand leones. Palm oil was five thousand leones. Salt was not there, no fish, no medicine. No food, nothing."

The prices Kadiatu quotes are astronomical. With adjustment for currency fluctuation, a cup of rice was the equivalent of one dollar, with palm oil at five dollars per cup, ten times the prewar prices. Civilians in Makeni had no access to cash except what rebels brought and spent, and what they could scrape together from selling small items. Kadiatu described starting her business again as impossible. "I had nothing to sell! But even if I had things to sell there was no medicine to buy! Even food was too much. To have one thousand leones . . . well . . . that would have taken several days of selling cigarettes to the RUF. If I bought a packet of cigarettes for one thousand leones, I could sell them individually, each cigarette for seventy, maybe eighty leones. I would need to push most of my profit on buying another packet of cigarettes, and after two packets would have one thousand leones to spend on rice. There is no way to feed your children from this. It is impossible. This is what the government forced us to do."

Kadiatu viewed the occupation as the government's fault rather than the RUF's fault. Only the former had an explicit responsibility to love residents, as they had been elected. Instead they betrayed and abandoned the town, acts which were only continuations of the APC's policies. "The SLPP is not a good party. They aren't talking about us the right way. They say that it was the war that came and spoiled Makeni, but it wasn't the war. Things were finished in Makeni before the war. There were no lights in Makeni, the water was poor, we had to get it out of the wells, and Bo and Kenema still had piped water! But the water here had already been cut off before the war. The water pump was just left like that, to break, and the government didn't do anything after that time."

Kadiatu framed the RUF occupation as a continuation of longstanding administrative neglect of the township, which justified her constant disparagement of the government, her bitterness at abandonment, and her right to take her loyalty elsewhere, to someone who proved himself as "worth having." She chalked up the poor roads, lack of water and electricity, and a profitless trading environment to the government consistently neglecting to love the town, and then betraying it completely by refusing to liberate it from RUF occupation. It was the government, not the RUF, which had the power to bring food and medicine, and yet it never arrived. All the stalls in the lorry park were looted in the initial rebel invasion, for which Kadiatu blamed the government, rather than the rebels. If Sierra Leoneans had been protecting the town, rather than Nigerians, the town would never have been occupied. In her narrative, the government left her no choice but to cut her losses with her loyalty to the nation, and find other cultivable relationships with which to feed her children, her primary love.

Be that as it may, she was left without anything to sell except cigarettes. Every woman in the lorry park was in the same position, save those whose personal relationships with rebels gave them occasional access to bags of rice.[3] These "girlfriends" were often the only support for their families, and were in positions of relative power during the occupation. Kadiatu, however, had nothing to bargain with and no wish to bargain, which made her as vulnerable and poor as most traders.

In desperation, Kadiatu gathered in a meeting with other women to discuss bringing in food for their children and easing local living conditions. The only people they could turn to were the RUF commanders.

"The women gathered to talk about what we could do to help our children. We had meetings and then we had a delegation." Kadiatu had little to say on the content of the meeting; it was not her place to do so because she did not chair it. Though a big woman in the market, there were other women who were better socially positioned to lead the group that approached Issa Sesay about reviving the lorry park market. A woman of formidable social credentials marched at the front. She was the highly educated widow of a powerful chief, and I call her Kati. She used the park to frame her own story of the war, as she could see it from her front porch. Like Kadiatu, she narrated her actions during the occupation through her need to feed her children. She described her decision to lead the delegation as made out of sheer desperation.

CONFRONTING ISSUES OF STARVING CHILDREN, NURTURING, AND POWER

Kati, like Kadiatu, narrated the cause of suffering during the occupation as government neglect and punishment. "The town was not good at that time: no food, no medicine, we were struggling, you see? No one was here to help me, and people were afraid, they were afraid to come here and see what was wrong. Or they would bring more wrong, you see?"

Kati framed the occupation in terms of the government not wanting to know the real issues of residents, and instead treating them like enemies. MPs were "afraid to come see what was wrong," which would involve visiting the town and speaking with residents. That "visitors" who did come brought "more wrong" was a thinly veiled reference to the government's failure to negotiate with the RUF, instead implementing road blockades to prevent supplies reaching the town, and then bombing it. The government's only interactions with residents during the occupation were attempts to kill people, whether slowly or quickly. The first step to surviving the occupation was acquiescing well enough to give the rebels no reason to go on murderous rampages. This lack of resistance was one of the first acts of "collaboration" cited by Kabbah when he later announced he would bomb the town.

"The RUF were here with us in Makeni. I was with all the women, and we held meetings to talk to our people: that the rebels had come here and we will not challenge them, so they will not burn this place or kill anybody. We thought that if we just accepted their demands they would have no reason to slaughter anybody. Then the RUF leader announced that the RUF did not want to kill us, they are also Sierra Leoneans. Once we realized that they would treat us as brothers and sisters, we were not so afraid of them."

The "RUF leader" Kati is speaking of here is Issa Sesay. Neither she nor Kadiatu spoke about the occupation before the appearance of Sesay, the leader with whom they could negotiate. The two women both marked this time as the beginning of life becoming more "normal," as dialogue and care replaced the chaotic eating of the initial looting sprees. Even after Sesay's arrival, the food situation was dire. The women had reached a breaking point, and decided it would do no further harm to approach Sesay about restarting trade. Kati was nervous the day they acted. "My stomach was dancing when the women walked to the headquarters! I called to Issa from outside the office, to show our respect for him, and he emerged. I explained on behalf of the women that we needed food and medicine for our children, and we had no way of getting these things. We did not want trouble, we just wanted to find a way to take care. He listened to me and said that he would find a way to bring food into the town, to help us sustain our needs. The women were rejoicing."

Once the ice had been broken, the women worked with Issa Sesay to transform the occupation into a situation that could be endured for an unknowable long-term. Kati cited the government blockade as a sign that no legitimately sourced food would be forthcoming. Because the government had betrayed residents, refusing to feed them, they had the right to sever that relationship and seek sustenance elsewhere. Kati's sentiment was similar to Kadiatu's: the RUF "lived nicely" with people in Makeni because, unlike the government, the RUF was responsive to transforming proximity, power, and fear into nurturing. The women approached Sesay as mothers, as this reinforced their will to love rather than eat, which would have been a direct challenge to RUF supremacy.

"After that first day we could speak to them about any problem that arose, there was nothing we couldn't tell them about! We would talk to Issa. I would say, 'Issa! So-and-so has been harassing such and such a man about cassava!' I would tell him when soldiers were doing things. And other soldiers would solve the problem. They went to the place, they saw what was going on, and they were really helping us here, in terms of equipment, medical supplies, food to eat, they gave us rice, you see? Without them we would have been in a very bad situation. We weren't having food or medicine. Medicine was our greatest problem, and we had to do something about it."

Though Kati frames the situation as a functional social safety net for the women, the benefits that accrued to RUF command were immense. They had a new set of enforcers in town, women with no loyalties to low-level cadres, who helped them implement the new rule of law that Sesay hoped would pave the way for his transformation into a legitimate politician after the war was over. Whether or not the women thought they were "collaborating" with the RUF, from the command's perspective, the situation allowed Sesay to nurture trust and care among his new constituents.

"I was one of the people who could talk to Issa directly. He was nice to me because, well, he looked up to women. He respected his mother. Anything we told him, he would accept it. Even when we told him something that was against his own men, he would support us. He talked to the women, and we told him that there should be peace. Any time they went to the bush to fight, we told him, if it is true that peace may come, let them disarm so that we will have peace in Makeni. And he did. We saw it, because he proved it to us. So we are very grateful for Issa because he made it possible for us to be a little bit easy during the war, you see? Even the rebels were aware that it is a good thing for the doctors to come in and save our people. So they accepted them in the township."

Kati frames the relationship between women and the RUF as one based on respect for motherhood. More than any other person, a man owes his mother what she requests of him because she loved him from birth. To be big in town, Sesay concentrated on treating the visible contingent of mothers with appreciation, which translated into their and their families' support. Kati, like Kadiatu, was effusive with praise for Sesay, though he is serving a fifty-one-year sentence for war crimes for which he was brought to trial in Sierra Leone's Special Court in 2008. They feel he was better to them—more caring—than a government that blockaded, abandoned, and bombed them. They frame their defense with respect to Sesay honoring their needs as mothers. His respect for women was embedded in his implicit understanding of the reverberation of care: by responding to women, the support he provided their families enhanced his status as a big man.

The traders were granted access to foodstuffs to sell in the market, and Kadiatu started her business again, "a little bit at a time." Though she would not talk about the source of the food she sold, other interviews revealed that most of the food Sesay brought arrived from looting raids conducted on nearby villages. Sesay sent his cadres out whenever supplies dwindled, and after the RUF commanders took a cut, the rest was divided among the traders. The purpose of selling the food was twofold: Sesay solidified his reputation as a leader interested in promoting "normal" life (after all, Makeni was a market town), and he limited the propensity of hungry youth, rebel and otherwise, to loot food within the township, by making it available cheaply. Sesay lost face every time an RUF cadre was accused of looting. As he wanted to be seen as legitimate, the market thrived.

Kadiatu prospered under RUF protection, which is why she offered Sesay her unqualified support: "Things were better during the war because the RUF didn't bother us, we weren't paying any taxes so we could make a good profit." There were few active traders in town at the time, and by cooperating with rebels, she could sell, untaxed, in a near monopoly. Kadiatu was able to acquire goods for next to nothing, sell them on cheaply, and make a decent profit. She set aside rice and palm oil for her children, and her two surviving daughters put on weight: "There was no more worry about my children, no more swelling bellies. We still had trouble acquiring medicine, but the children got enough palm oil to be okay. I was happy."

There is tremendous moral ambivalence in trading in looted goods. Kadiatu had blood on her hands by trading in foodstuffs stolen in village raids, but in her narrative she took for herself what the government refused to give. The traders and mothers had been betrayed, they were forced to fend for themselves, therefore she had no reason to care about the government's other people. She blamed Kabbah for the death of her child, so Kabbah could worry about children in other villages.[4] The town became a trading oasis in an otherwise decimated landscape, a testament to residents' will to survive under Issa Sesay's command. The presence of the market is one of the main reasons that citizens around the country, even those living just outside the township, assert that the inhabitants of Makeni collaborated with the RUF. From Kadiatu's narrative, the market was a reaction to the government having left residents with no other choice.

Both Kadiatu and Kati emphasized that Issa Sesay never let the women down. Kadiatu asserted, "We thank god for the RUF and the nice way that they were here with us. We didn't have much before we talked with them but when they came to an agreement they brought food and supported us." This was in direct contrast to the government, which, rather than attempting to liberate the town, decided to destroy it. The presence of the market was a key aspect of Tejan Kabbah's outright condemnation of the town; he saw civilians choosing to love the RUF rather than Sierra Leone. Traders and mothers viewed Kabbah as betraying them first by allowing their children to die. Kabbah decided to punish the town for its disloyalty by bombing the town. Each party expected the other to love them first, and both were bitterly disappointed.

CIVILIANS TURN TO THE RUF TO SAVE THEM
FROM GOVERNMENT BOMBS

Kadiatu's hatred of the government became more powerful and vitriolic as her narrative continued. When speaking of the later years of the occupation, a trying time with minimal food, no medicine, and many children dying per week, the only "problem" she noted was the government gunship. "The only problem occurred in 2000. The president announced on the radio that all people in Makeni were rebel collaborators, and he was going to bomb the town down to the last chicken and ant. And when he was finished, he would come and rule the chickens. We did not believe him. I was in my stall listening to the radio, and the women all gathered and we talked, 'Oh Kabbah, you would come and rule the chickens?' We did not know what would happen, but when we heard the helicopter we were not afraid. When the gunship was in Freetown it brought food and medicine over from Lungi [the airport]. But it didn't bring the same things here. The gunship came to kill us all, not help us. It only dropped paper the first time. No food, no medicine, no future. People were curious so they came out of their houses to pick up all the paper. And it didn't bring anything! No food, no education, no medicine, no future. We realized that when it came back and dropped bombs."

She showed me her leaflets, the third or fourth set I had seen. Many people ran outside at the sound of propellers, hoping the gunship was dropping medical supplies. They gathered the papers that drifted down from the skies. Kadiatu kept hers as a reminder that the government promised death: "RUF: this time we've dropped leaflets," stated the first one, "next time it will be: a half inch Gatling machine gun or 57mm rockets or 23mm guns or 30mm grenades or ALL OF THEM!" A picture of the gunship accompanied the text. The reverse side showed a pile of mutilated corpses with, "Members of the RUF: government forces are advancing and are strong. If you fight you will DIE!" She shook her head at the images, and said, tapping the paper, "The only people we saw in Makeni after those papers dropped that looked like this were the ones the gunship hit."

She was speaking in particular of her friend Rugiatu, the iconic gunship victim. "That day, my friend was killed. She was nine months pregnant. She was in front of me at the market. The year 2000, it was a Monday. I was sitting here in my stall. When I heard the sounds of the helicopter I ran to my mother's house, where the children were staying, and I didn't leave again until the place was silent. I heard the wailing from the lorry park, and when I got back I saw that she was killed by the gunship. It was so bad. The gunship had split her in two, and her baby was there, lying dead on the road."

Kadiatu was not the first to tell me about the death of Rugiatu Kanu, which became the flagship story told by residents about the occupation. Rugiatu has become a martyr, an innocent victim of the government's bloodlust. As one man said, "The gunship and the jets didn't look for anyone in particular. They didn't care if they were targeting a rebel or a civilian. They just took out everyone they saw." The gunship deaths were an opening for residents to narrate their own stories, to give battlefield tours of government betrayal. This particular man's tour started with our visit to the home next to his own, where his elder brother had lived and died:

"The Nigerian jets came at the same time as the helicopter. When they passed over this street they saw my brother's three sons playing football. The boys saw the jet and they ran inside the house and hid under the bed, and when the jet made another pass it dropped cluster bombs right on the house. My brother was also inside; the whole family was killed." We toured the wreckage of the house, roofless, with walls and floors scarred by the bombing. The four victims were buried outside, under a tree that marked the front of the property. He wanted me to take pictures. He then guided me to Rugiatu's grave.

Rugiatu, her baby, and three other victims of the bomb were buried thirty feet from where they were killed, under a tree across the street from the lorry park. The area had served as a graveyard during the colonial era; Rugiatu was buried next to Arthur Charles Carless, a British administrator who died in Makeni in 1946, aged forty-six. As I wandered around the graves a man emerged from a nearby house. He was Rugiatu's widower, and he handed me a picture that had clearly been handled hundreds of times before, worn, torn, and water damaged. It was his wife, posing jauntily with a friend. I commented on

FIGURE 3. Rugiatu Kanu (right) and a friend before the occupation and bombing of Makeni. Photo by author.

her beauty, and her husband smiled. "She left behind three children when she died. I had to take them and run after their mom was killed. And now we are back, and I am caring for them in this place near to where she died."

Everyone I spoke to in Makeni told the story of Rugiatu's death, whether or not they witnessed it, defending the town against collaboration with stories of government barbarity. Of those who finally ran, facing the perils involved in a fifty-mile journey to safety, most left after this incident. The newspaper articles detailing the "pathetic human chain" leaving Makeni testify to the horror and fear caused by the "Lion News" leaflet drops and the death of Rugiatu. If a pregnant woman can be lined up in the crosshairs of a bomb attack, then absolutely no one is safe from government rage. Neither Kadiatu, nor Kati, nor anyone else I spoke to blamed the RUF for these attacks.

Kadiatu remembered these as the worst days. "I didn't want to leave because I had lost one child and I knew the other two would not survive if we tried to go to Mile 91 [a town fifty miles to the southwest; at the time it was not held by the RUF]. So we stayed through the bombings. The RUF never fought back when they saw the gunship. They gathered us together and instructed us: if you hear a helicopter, it is not bringing food. It is coming to destroy us so you must take cover before the pilot sees you! And so I was always on edge. It targeted the market because there were always people here in search of their daily needs. If I heard anything strange I would close the stall, run to my mother's house and try to cook and keep my mind off it. They sent it to kill, and they did not care if you were a mother or a child or a rebel. They wanted to kill everyone. This is why I say, 'Bless the RUF. Bless Issa Sesay. Bless Foday Sankoh.' The government is supposed to be for all people, but it just made everyone afraid and we all scattered."

Kadiatu narrated her pronouncements passionately, capping off a story of government hatred with near-religious worship of RUF command. In her story's crescendo from losing a child due to government callousness, to Issa Sesay's positive intervention, the glorious freedom of an untaxed market, and government bombing, enemy and friend were crystal clear. Kadiatu endured the hardship of occupation, she witnessed the suffering of her friends and neighbors, and she heard the stories emerging from the south, where the RUF was responsible for amputations, mutilations, and other atrocities. However, she buttressed her pro-RUF position by describing the government's encouragement of collateral damage in order to destroy the RUF ethos as well as its command. The RUF was, in her eyes, in favor of people surviving the occupation, while the government was not.

"The government didn't care about the people, they just wanted to flush the RUF out and scatter them so they weren't organized. So they did wrong by us. The RUF was not going to kill us. They saved our lives by telling us to run away from the gunship. And when people went to the bush because they were so afraid of the gunship, some of them had nothing and died there. And the government did that to them."

In Kadiatu's reckoning, the government's main failure was its unwillingness to consider why civilians would attempt to live comfortably in occupied Makeni. Rebel-civilian coexistence was the government's own fault because it had left the occupation to persist for so long that residents, no matter their sympathies, were forced to turn to each other and to the rebels to survive. With more children dying of malnutrition, the women were moved to speak with the RUF command because they refused to let, as they saw it, the government kill them by abandoning the town. They found the commanders amenable to easing the situation by encouraging trade.

Kadiatu argued that the government had a responsibility to nurture the town because the president is the biggest of all big men. Like any other big man, if he betrays his people, they have a right to desert him or pull him down. By making the residents of Makeni mere collateral damage in the fight against the rebels, the government cast them out of the nation, punishing them for disloyalty. Therefore, they had the right to take what they needed from elsewhere. The government neglected the town before the war, abandoned it to foreign troops, stood by idly as it was seized and occupied, refused to liberate it, and then bombed it when residents did what they could to survive. The excuse was towns-people's willingness to coexist with rebels. For Kadiatu, the only thing the townspeople proved themselves willing to do was search elsewhere for nurturing after government betrayal. Kadiatu survived with the only resource she had at her disposal: her skill as a trader. This put her in the spotlight of condemnation, but she was only one of many who brought their families through the war by making other alliances. David was condemned for staying with the rebels, but all he had were his friendships. Captain Mansaray served with the AFRC to avoid being targeted for execution. Alimamy had only his charm, his father's good name, and the friendship of a rebel. Kadiatu did what she did best in order to avoid losing her other two children. She traded.

THE GOVERNMENT STATES THAT NO ONE IS INNOCENT

My interviews with Kadiatu, Kati, and several other big women in the town signal a need to reframe the relationship between town and government, rather than merely pointing fingers at "collaborators." These women did not have unusual experiences; they were not alone in defending the RUF leadership in my presence. From conversations with Alimamy, David, and many others, it was clear to me that the lives of these women and their families had been improved by their work with the RUF, their aiding it to maintain an ideological grip on the town, thus their collaboration with it. But what does "collaboration" really mean?

I was mulling this over as I traveled to Freetown for a long weekend, and stopped first at a café to have lunch with my husband, who worked in the city. As I sat down at our table, his eyes slid to an individual sitting a few tables over; an innocuous looking, bespectacled, and slightly paunchy middle-aged white man, who was lunching with a few youths. I was confused. "Who is that?"

"Neall Ellis."

I caught my breath. Neall Ellis was well known in Sierra Leone. A pilot for the defunct South African mercenary outfit Executive Outcomes, he had been hired by Tejan Kabbah to fly the helicopter gunship. He had told several journalists that "war is a game," and admitted that the adrenaline rush of piloting the gunship was one reason he did it.[5] My husband had been speaking to Ellis before my arrival, and had anticipated my questions:

"Neall doesn't lose any sleep over the accusations that the strafing bombings he did in Makeni in 2000 were wrong. He just sees this as his job, that he was following the president's orders to flush the rebels out of their stronghold so that the war would end sooner. And in a way, he was right. The bombings did force the issue to a head."

"But what about all the civilians he killed?" I had chosen a side for the moment.

"Well, I think he gives this answer to everyone: 'If they were innocent, why were they just standing around chatting like everything was normal? Innocent people in an occupied town are afraid of their own shadows. If they were really civilians, they would have run when they heard the gunship approaching. In fact, they would hardly be seen out on the streets.' I think he sleeps at night because in his mind, there is a clear distinction between victims and perpetrators."

For Ellis, collaboration exists in postures of ease. His rebel enemy was anyone who lived in Makeni as though they had a right to be there: confidently, as though in no danger. The beaten-down, subjugated, starving, and miserable civilian, on the other hand, would jump at the mere mention of a gunship. A civilian carrying food openly, walking without fear of being robbed, must be collaborating with rebels. Collaboration, in this perspective, is marked by the existence of a relationship of mutual understanding, which is predicated on conversation and agreement. For Ellis, the scene that presented itself in Makeni was obvious.

When approached from the framework of love—especially in light of Kabbah's initial betrayal—the issue of collaboration is no longer a sensible notion. From the perspective of residents, Kabbah had betrayed the town first, by refusing to liberate it immediately after the attack. Residents were therefore right to search for succor elsewhere, and after a rocky first year as rebels and soldiers fought over the town, they came to an agreement with the RUF that saved their families. The argument over collaboration and betrayal began because Kabbah and Makeni residents had different ideas about who owed the other their primary loyalty. Kabbah expected loyalty from an occupied town, and residents expected a loyal president to free them. It was impossible for residents to "collaborate" with rebels if Kabbah was the reason the rebels were there. It was up to residents to transform a negative, draining relationship into a positive, nurturing one.

This presents troubling questions for postwar justice. Are the only truly innocent people those who died—the small children, the elderly, the ill—or does the rubric of love destroy the meaningfulness of such categorizations as innocent and guilty? Kadiatu does not care whether people think she was innocent or a collaborator who profited from her association with the RUF. "Everyone bears their own burdens. Mine was my children and I carried them through this war. The government doesn't care about us, so I have to care for my daughters and me. I am the only one doing it." Her position, from the perspective of love, cannot be argued against.

THE GOVERNMENT IS PUNISHING US BY TAKING WITHOUT GIVING

Kadiatu's reckoning on the RUF occupation occurred from the perspective of a postwar world where a new town council was targeting the market for taxation to fill its nearly empty coffers. She was bitter that, once again, a government was taking without giving, as there had been no improvements made to the lorry park or the transportation system that would inspire her gratitude. Though traders in West Africa have historically had tumultuous relationships with the state, Kadiatu was firm in her belief that, rather than controlling trade, government should do everything in its power to promote it.[6] She believed the government was eating once again without nurturing.

"Development in Makeni isn't fine! There is food in other places in the country, but not here. We don't have any help from the government to get it here from the villages. The government doesn't care about us, so development is poor. I want to expand my business but the money isn't there. I want small things, like a place where my children can sleep but I don't have a house. I lost the right to live in my mother's house after the war because the title was lost. I could live there peacefully during the war because the rebels did not ask for pieces of paper! What are my children going to eat? What kinds of times are these? The government controls everything but they don't think about what people need. And we need a lot! No one can depend on their family anymore. The war scattered people, they lost everything and need to cope up with supporting their own children. My sisters and brothers cannot worry about my children. All people carry their own burdens."

Kadiatu states that all people carry their own burdens and yet the government is responsible for caring for everyone. Though this seems contradictory, other Makeni residents state a similar sentiment, brushing off the "collaborator" label, and insisting that the president, as *pa* to the nation, bears the responsibility to act first. Kadiatu blames the government for refusing to be big in the traditional sense of providing a safety net for people. Instead, it preyed on people. No one among the RUF command questioned her right to live in her deceased mother's house, but the postwar government evicted her because she had lost the title. Though bureaucratically fair, Kadiatu insisted that this was wrong because her president and government are big men, and must act that way to maintain her support. It reinforced the resentment she already harbored over the occupation and the gunship.

Her insistence that no one can depend on their family and that everyone must carry their own load was tinged with the bitterness of a failed marriage. It emerged at the end of our conversation that she and her husband had become estranged, and that this was why she banded together with other women. They approached the RUF command as sole breadwinners for their families. It was an unenviable position for mothers, but evoked sympathy from Issa Sesay, who saw neither threat nor potential recruits in the form of husbands. When Kadiatu's relative monopoly on rice during the occupation came to a crashing halt, insult was added to injury. The local government's first act was to seize administrative control of the lorry park and tax all the traders. The end of the war also brought stiff competition in the form of other traders. Kadiatu ticked off on her fingers the products that were now nearly too expensive to trade as a result of these developments:

"Groundnuts weren't easy to find during the war so if you got your hands on some it was easy to sell them, but in the last two or three years everyone tries to sell them and the market has gone so stiff! It is so difficult to sell things for any profit. During the war, things were reasonable.

The palm oil, for one pint, you could get one for 15,000, or 10,000. But now, from the year 2003 until now, palm oil is so dear! And there is also the situation of the government. They have brought many, many processes. They have brought local tax. We pay for market licenses, this and that, and it eats away at income. Right now rice is almost seventy thousand leones for one bag. When you buy this bag, it doesn't even last a month and then it is finished. The palm oil is now forty-six thousand [leones] for the bottle [a five-gallon jerry can]. You go buy it for forty thousand in the village, you pay for transport, you pay ten thousand for market dues, and this state of the country means that you only get small profits coming. If you don't have money then you have to sit down without doing business, because you need money to start it. You have to just sit all day and wait to do business!"

Kadiatu's rage and despair stem from two circumstances: other traders flooding the market with foodstuffs that were precious during the war and are now common, eating away at profits; and taxes that cut into profits without tangible rewards. Between trading competition, a market flooded with goods that no one can afford (which forces the price down to wholesale), an excessive tax burden, and no assistance from the government to improve farming (which would make goods cheaper to purchase), profit margins are at an all-time low, and she struggles to take care of her children. Kadiatu is still a big woman in the market, but she feels diminished by the increased burden of competition and tax. The health of her children is the barometer by which she assesses the state of the world, and it was easiest to feed them in the two years that Issa Sesay controlled the market. Therefore, that was the time when love, enabling survival, was the strongest.

6

"It Was the Lord Who Wanted Me to Stay"

The Evangelist

Every day on my walk into town, I left the dust, bustle, and danger of the highway and diverted onto a crumbling street that was too potholed for vehicles. I picked my way carefully and took in my damaged surroundings. This road appeared particularly hard hit by the occupation, with many homes mere shells of ruined concrete, tin roofs held up by flimsy wooden poles and laundry strung up between exposed walls to dry in the sun. The sole exception was the house at the end of the road, which was freshly painted a rich green, the yard swept clean. There was no activity in the compound, and when I first began my daily walks the front door was always shut. This is unusual in Makeni, where life habitually spills out onto the street in a noisy cascade of children, chickens, cooking fires, and conversation.

One day the door was open, and an elderly lady emerged and called to me, "You are a stranger here too! Come greet me." I walked through the yard to meet the lady I would come to know as Miss Adama. Her first words were, "I would offer you a place to sit but the rebels took everything!" I motioned to the wooden bench propped against the wall behind her, and was rebuffed with, "I mean a proper place to sit, with padding and covered in fabric. I used to have easy chairs. This," and she waved with a disparaging flourish, "is not fit to sit on." As if to prove a point, she settled her considerable bulk awkwardly on the rickety wood. It took on a decided lean. "See how uncomfortable it is?"

I dropped my backpack and propped myself against the railing, which satisfied her as an acceptable compromise. She sighed. "You wouldn't believe that I used to have a lovely waterbed! When the rebels destroyed my house, they burst it so that it flooded my bedroom. They did it just to be malicious!" I must have registered shock, though not in precisely the way Miss Adama interpreted. "A waterbed in Makeni?" I thought. She nodded, "They knew they couldn't transport it because it was too heavy, so they just decided to destroy it!" As I soon learned, Miss Adama had a higher standard of living than most, and this was, socially, her biggest problem. If one's life is too comfortable compared to those of one's neighbors, it implies selfishness, wickedness, and perhaps witchcraft.

"I like finding other strangers," she continued in English that was tinged with a British accent, "because I do not like the people of this town! All I have are my animals, they are my friends." As if on cue, a marmalade kitten jumped into her lap, curled up, and started purring. She scratched it under the chin and it kneaded her dress appreciatively. This situation, an elderly woman alone with her pets, was very unusual. Adama's solitary lifestyle aside, in the aftermath of war, domestic animals were not indulged. People strained to feed their families, and so dogs were fed grudgingly and left on the verandas at night to guard the house. Cats were kept for their ratting abilities, and were rarely a source of companionship. Adama, on the other hand, loved her animals and feared the people around her. What prompted this unusual state of affairs?

Our conversation revealed that Adama was most certainly *not* from Makeni. She was a Freetown native, and came to Makeni because it was her husband's hometown. As the oldest male he had inherited the house upon his father's passing and needed to be closer to his family. She presented the move as one that she had made grudgingly, as it required her to be away from her hometown and her people. But there were some consolations: "I brought my animals with me." She smiled and the kitten flopped on its back, paws in the air, and fell asleep.

Adama appreciated that I craved a little furry company myself. She gave me a kitten, which went missing a few weeks later. As I was in Freetown when the kitten disappeared, my caretaker, assuming responsibility for the incident, supplied two more kittens. Though sad at the loss of the first one, I thought nothing of it. Adama took a different view. When I walked past her house the next day she rushed out to greet me. "How is the kitten?" Chagrined, I related the story of his disappearance, adding that he must have escaped through a hole under the wall. She was furious. "Is your houseboy a Muslim?" Confused as to the relevance of this question, I answered affirmatively. "Hmm," she sniffed, "Muslims eat cats. I don't trust them. The girl I have come cook for me is a good Christian, and a Limba, not a Temne. I selected her from church one day after service, because she was quiet and didn't talk back. I asked her mother to have her come here every day. She leaves the kittens alone. Temnes are usually Muslim."

The girl, Beatrice, squatted by the pot of cassava leaf sauce, stirring silently, never acknowledging us. Beatrice and Adama were not warm towards each other, and the lack of conversation in a social environment that normally rings with laughter was discomfiting. Beatrice never looked up, intent on finishing her task expediently. When the food was finished, she poured the rice in one pot and the sauce in the other. She covered both pots and took them inside, then took her leave with a formal, "I am going, madam." Adama paid her weekly, and she and Beatrice never ate together.

Adama seemed lonely and afraid. She insisted I stop by every day. As a woman and a stranger to Makeni, I had something in common with her, and this made us good company. "I know you must be a Christian woman to come here and care about people's problems," she said one day. "And you have been to England, yes?" I nodded, and she smiled. "My daughter lives in England, and I was there during the war. I thank God every day that I was able to go, because I would not have survived long during this rebel war. I came back afterward and I had only this, my husband's house, to return to! There was no one in Freetown, nowhere for me to live there so I came back here." Two men emerged from the house across the street, shot us hard, penetrating looks, and struck up a conversation as they walked away. Adama shuddered. "I think these men are going to break into the house one night and kill me. All these Temne men are thieves!"

I queried her about her neighbors. "These men want my food. They have demanded it before, and I won't share with them because they are Muslims and they are not nice to me. I have this food because my daughter sends me money. They have their own families. Why should I share with them? I count on our Lord Jesus to protect me from them."

Adama was devoted to her evangelical Christian faith, and in conversation framed her interaction with others through their spiritual proximity to, or distance from her. This placed her in a precarious position in the aftermath of the war, as it circumscribed the relationships she was willing to forge. Thus was bred the mutual hostility with her neighbors, who were not Christian. Her suspicions prevented us having a long interview on her porch, as I explained I would use a tape recorder and take notes as we chatted. That suspicion was not directed at me: "If those boys see the tape recorder, they will think that I am reporting them to the Special Court, and they will come after me!"

Adama proposed an alternative solution. "Give me your tape recorder," she said one day, as I stopped on my way home from a town council meeting. "I will keep it for the weekend and I will give you my testimony. I will let Jesus tell me when is the right time to do this, not when you say we should do it." I agreed, and Adama poured out her heart one night before bed, after she prayed by lamplight. From the recording emerged the story of a woman who interpreted the war through her faith, who cultivated friendships because it was God's will that she provide salvation. Adama pursued relationships with rebels because God wanted her to transform them, to save them. She perceived her spiritual life as incompatible with the social world, which she had left to become God's instrument. However in the chaos of war, the social and spiritual resonated and ensured her survival. Whether through faith or love, she reached out to others. However, just as chaos compelled her to embrace others to save them, so did ordinary times of aftermath hasten her retreat from them, as she derived her nurturing from elsewhere.

SINGING PRAISE TO THE BUILDER OF THE HUMAN WORLD

Adama did not want me to ask her questions to answer later in her solitary recording. She wanted to testify; in essence, she would tell her story the way she wanted to tell it, without clarification or interruption, as a complete self-portrait. In taking this approach, Adama emphasized that the *truth* of her personhood and experiences would not be revealed in a dialogue about her life during the war—perhaps she anticipated that I would ask questions about facts, which are quite different from truth. Rather, this was her construction of those experiences vis-à-vis her faith; from that foundation she cultivated relationships that kept her alive.

"Praise the Lord, Hallelujah. Before saying anything, I must first give thanks to the Lord by singing a song." Her voice rang true and strong:

Goodbye world, I am no longer with you.
Goodbye pleasures of sin, I am no longer with you.
In my life, I have gone God's way, the light of my life.

I have made up my mind, to go God's way, the light of my life.
Goodbye world, I am no longer with you.
Goodbye pleasures of sin, I am no longer with you.
I have made up my mind, to go God's way, the rest of my life.
I have made up my mind, to go God's way, the rest of my life.
Free! Free! Free! In God I am free.
I have met a man, a man from Galilee.
He took away my mood, my whole world of sin.
And now I am singing hallelujah.
Free! Free! Free! Thank God I am free.
I have met a man, a man from Galilee.
He took away my mood, my heavy load of sin.
And now I am singing hallelujah.
I will never be the same again, no, no.
I will never be the same again.
Since I joined the way of the Lord.
I will never be the same, again.

This hymn is striking in its emphasis on the separation between the social world and faith. Her decision to make her faith an alternative to the social world was made immediately clear by her life before her conversion. Adama was raised Catholic, her mother having converted from Islam upon her marriage. She articulated that her mother had chosen "the way of God," had "learned" to turn away from a heathen religion. She held her mother in high esteem, and had a low opinion of Muslims even while she herself lived what she later viewed as a debauched and unfulfilled life. Adama married well and was a wealthy bar owner in Freetown, where she and her husband enjoyed "the things of the world," splurging on pleasantries like weekly trips to the cinema. She had begun her adult life eating, indulging herself, and in 1970 experienced a conversion that changed everything.

She told her story: "In Kenema, when we were transferred with my husband's job, the Lord called me. I went out early in the morning to pray, I didn't know anything about the Holy Ghost then because I was a Catholic, but the Lord taught me and told me to go out, and said that my former life was finished. The bar I had was enough, I had had enough pleasure. Go out now and preach the gospel to every creature. At first I was reluctant because I didn't know anything about preaching the gospel. But the Lord was with me. That very day I started. The Holy Ghost came upon me, and I was prone before my master. And I started to do the work. I started to go out early in the morning, around 3:30 in the morning, oh, to preach what the Lord Jesus Christ has done for me. That was in Kenema, and I continued until my husband was sent to Bo."

Adama joined a British missionary church upon arriving in Bo, and preached on behalf of the missionaries, for whom she worked to gain converts. Adama's religious orientation began framing her understanding of the social world and her position within it. Instead of the casual relationships of the bar, she nurtured others by sacrificing her own pleasure to convert them and save their souls. Adama narrated learning through personal contact with her God, taking that lesson to others, and then moving on to new places. The constant movement is unusual in Sierra Leone, as moving prevents one from investing long-term energy in relationships with others. Considering the luxury of Adama's house compared to those of her neighbors—the upholstered furniture, the waterbed—her husband's job clearly provided for them, lessening the necessity for Adama to need anything in return for her efforts. She was instead recouping on years of eating and selfish pleasure.

"I was there with my husband until he retired, and we went to Nigeria and came back with a new church which is still in Sierra Leone. And then we came to Makeni and I started the work again. Preaching in the morning, preaching in the evening, going from house to house. The Lord taught me how to preach. I went to the hospital to preach to sick people, and then to the prison, which I am doing up to this very moment. I thank the Lord for his goodness and his mercies, which I have enjoyed forever. I thank him for what he has done for me . . . in my married life I have two children, one boy and one girl. She is in England, and she is a doctor. I praise God for all God has done for that child."

Adama had so structured her understanding of the world around the will of God that she attributed her own and her husband's personal nurturing of their children to God. By creating her world around God, she humbly submitted that she was merely an instrument. Her daughter's success is due to the intervention of God. The focus of this worldview did not alter significantly even as war engulfed Makeni. Adama viewed the war as God's will, and her survival was predicated on the fact that she was one of his servants. Thus, it was fated that she stay in Makeni, despite being elderly, without her children, and now, without her husband.

"IT WAS THE LORD WHO WANTED ME TO STAY"

"During the war we Sierra Leoneans were driven out of our country. We were afraid to stay with the rebels, and many people left to save their own lives. But when they entered Makeni, I couldn't go anywhere, because I don't know any village in this place. I don't have anybody of my own blood in Makeni. And others don't help, with their dogs and cats and little children and everything that they have! But I was staying here, in my place. I think it was the Lord who wanted me to stay."

Adama was vulnerable, and clearly without her husband and his family. She mentioned him only to note that he was originally from Makeni, that they met and married in Freetown, that he was Catholic, and that she was widowed. She emphasized that she lacked her own blood relations, which made her life difficult but not theoretically impossible. David too was without blood relations as he navigated the war, and he transformed his relationships within the RUF to create a family, acknowledging how difficult it would have been to survive on his own. Adama framed herself as unworthy of other people's care, stating that they were too busy with their own lives and problems to reach out to her. She stayed because she had nowhere else to go, and interpreted that as God's will.

"When the rebels came at night they opened my door, took me outside and shouted at me, asking if I had money. There was no money, there was nothing! And they pushed me back inside. They left me sleeping in a dark room, without light, no water to drink, without any food to eat. But the Lord was sustaining me, and at least I could praise His holy name. After that fearful night when they broke so many houses, early in the morning I got up. I packed my bag, put it on my head, went out to my garden, and off I went. By the afternoon the rebels were looking for me, and they forced me to return to my house. But still I was determined to find a peaceful way out. I couldn't go at once because the Lord wanted me to stay in Makeni to preach to the soldiers who are coming. Because when they went to Freetown, there was no God among them, and the ECOMOG . . . the Nigerian people came to help us. There was no sense here, the people were fighting themselves."

As is common when recalling trauma, Adama's timeframe stretched and condensed like a concertina. The immediacy of the rebels bursting into her house and demanding money from her was terrifying, and after a frightening night she tried to escape. This event occurred during the 1998 invasion, when the RUF and *sobels* who seized Makeni followed their attack with a manhunt in the bush, during which they forced people to return to town. Adama, thinking Nigerian soldiers were still protecting the town, waited for them to liberate it. She interpreted being forced to return to Makeni, which was now under rebel control, as a sign that the missing Nigerian soldiers were godless, and would need her when they returned. The Nigerian battalion that came with the

United Nations in 2001 marked the end of the occupation, and also the end of confusion, infights, bombings, and devastation. Adama restored order to her social and spiritual world by taking action inspired by God. By exercising her faith, she exerted control over the chaos.

"They used to bring the mortally injured people to Makeni from the villages: boys without arms, girls without legs, people who had been mutilated, everything! And the Lord said to me: go to the hospital and see what you can do. So I got up early in the morning and crossed town to go to the hospital. The rebels sent people there from the villages; they even sent other rebels if they were injured, and I went there to tell them about the Lord Jesus Christ, that they should give their lives to the Lord before they die.

"And the nurses cried out to me, 'Help us! We are trying to give assistance to the dying.' I preached to them, and some of them accepted Jesus because they were dying and they were very afraid. So I told them: if they believe in the Lord Jesus, even though they are rebels, they will find their savior when they die. God will give them eternal life. If they did that I could bring them to peace even though there was nothing: no water to wash the bandages, no medicine for the pain, no food. I couldn't bear it, so I came back to the house and picked mangos for them, boiled the mangos and brought them something to eat, and water for them to drink. Some of them would die late at night, some in the early morning. The beds were always full of the dying, because they were bringing them in every day. And I couldn't stay too long there. I couldn't bear the crying."

Among the ill and injured, the mutilated and dying, Adama created a world of compassion and peace. These rebels were far from home, alone and afraid, and facing troubling questions about their choices as they lay dying. They had left family behind, their uninjured brothers were busy elsewhere, and they risked dying alone and uncared for, which is every Sierra Leonean's nightmare. There was only Adama. She spoke to them kindly and offered them spiritual salvation, and they accepted hungrily. They needed her, and as a lonely and frightened elderly woman, she needed them.

The preaching had a significant effect on Adama's ability to live securely in town, though in her testimony she seemed unaware that her spiritual life had positive social connotations. In her mind, the two were now separate. Though she followed through on her work in the hospital because she interpreted it as God's will, she made friends there with nurses and commanders, who appreciated the care and calm she brought to the dying. As an old woman she posed no threat to RUF power; however, her presence in the hospital exposed her to many rebels. They respected her, thus giving her some security from being targeted for her wealth. Adama's spiritual life resonated within the social world, though she perceived the two as antagonistic domains and interpreted her work as purely spiritual.

The work itself, however, drained her energy and frayed her emotions. "Every time I came home telling myself I would never go back, I always got up and went back again the next morning. Because it was not my decision, I had been called by the Lord. One day I was feeling the burden too much, and some of the nurses came to my house. And they begged me, 'Mrs. K, please come and help us!' And I said, 'No, I am not a pastor, I am not going to come and bury people. I cannot.' But they called me to pray for people, for the dead and those who buried them. And I continued to do that for three or four months. I was there working for the Lord. Even when a rebel was discharged and sent home, I went to his house and continued to pray for him. And so many accepted the Lord Jesus, and many were afraid. And I praise the Lord for that. I thank God because the Holy Spirit was using me, it was not my own power. I have no power! I don't know anything about the Bible, but the Lord Jesus Christ sent the Holy Spirit to come and teach me."

Attending to the dying was traumatizing and emotionally draining, and it was only faith that sustained Adama. She was modest about the impact of her preaching, but it had a profound effect on the people with whom she worked at the hospital. That injured rebels were afraid of dying alone Adama interpreted as conversion, while hospital workers saw suffering rebels cling to what remained of their social worlds by being with her; she steadfastly reproduced something good in the world with every deathbed conversion. The most satisfying and the most painful aspect of her work was their need for her, as she became an instrument of constructing, if only for a fleeting moment before death, a nurturing world. Though I cannot interpret the feelings of the dying, their desire for her company meant these were moments when the social and spiritual became one.

ADAMA INVITES REBELS INTO HER HOME

As well as performing deathbed conversions, Adama preached sobriety to the healthy rebels with whom she came into contact. Bolstered by her success at the hospital, she felt compelled by God to transform rebels who were addicted to alcohol and drugs, once again reaching out spiritually and receiving a social response. She was targeted for possessing medication early in the occupation; as a wealthy elderly person, the RUF members assumed that she had pharmaceuticals. This was her impetus to work on them.

"They came into my house, and they said they wanted pills. And I said no, I would never touch pills!" She suddenly burst into a diatribe on violence, drugs, and politics: "I used to lecture them: 'You came wanting pills? I thought you RUF wanted power! If you did not know what you want why did you come to destroy us in Makeni? Why did you come to burn our houses and kill our people?' The Holy Spirit was giving me the power to talk to them. After a while they would come and beg me to give them rooms. And I said, 'Okay, I know that you are sober now. I will give you two rooms but you are not to enter here unless your wife and your children are with you. I am the only one in the house.' So I stood on my Bible with my faith, and Lord help me, they listened to me! So I gave them two rooms and they brought in their wives and their children, and they were here together."

By turning her home into a sober boarding house for rebels, Adama once again merged faith and the social world. Every rebel was an opportunity to work on someone, even as it sometimes put her in danger. That too she saw as God's will. "In the morning they would do all these things for me, but even then they were not living right. Those rebels, they would shoot their wives in the feet if they were having an argument, because they were jealous thinking their wives were seeing other men and they didn't want them to leave the house. After that they would take them to the hospital for treatment. And I told them not to do that. They used to have quarrels because they would drink in the house, they would smoke at times, they would do everything! I realized that they were not sober; they had broken their promise to God. I was just in my room praying that God will protect me. And I thank the Lord; he provided for me.

"I praise the Lord for my pastor, Pastor T. When things were too heavy at my house, I ran to his house. Most of the church members were there with him and his wife. And that man hasn't got anything but he planted cassava, God bless him. That man went out with the youth early in the morning and brought cassava, and then he prepared it for us to eat. We would sleep on the floor . . . but I thank God he prepared a room for me. You see, God provides for me! He prepared a room for me, and whatever we had we ate in common. I was with them for one or two weeks."

Adama consistently attributed her good fortune to the will of God, interpreting her overtly social decisions so they resonated with her spiritual life. Her lack of attribution of good fortune to her own work meant she was equally unable to understand the effect of her antisocial decisions, whether or not they were made upon spiritual meditation. In Adama's perception of the world, being given her own room was down to her standing with God, rather than her pastor's feelings for her. She discovered when she attempted escape from Makeni that to do so endangered her social position. She betrayed the friendships she had nurtured by walking away, and this was problematic.

"I decided to go, to leave Makeni. So I walked with my dog . . . I left the cat in my home. We walked about six to eight, ten miles, I don't know, to a village. When we arrived there, they said we should turn back to Makeni. They said I could not live in the village. So I came back with my dog and he ran away because the house was in chaos now! The dog was lost and I had no home. It was so hard on me. My flowers . . . they had uprooted my flowers for fun. But one day the little boy, my dog, was there again! He was jumping and cry-ing and shouting . . . you know, some creatures are very grateful. So I thank God for having my dog back. But before I came back they had eaten the cat and they had taken my bedroom. I had to sleep in the storage room." Adama's house had been trashed. Though she inter-preted this as the rebels callously having fun, in the framework of love and betrayal, *she* had deserted *them*. Angry and vengeful, they in turn lashed out at her.

"I decided to continue my work and I continued to go out, I didn't stop. At times I didn't have food to eat. Because rebels on the street, if they saw it in your hand, they would ask you where you got that cassava. And if you didn't tell them there was more and where to get it, they would take it from you. But the Lord was using those people who were staying in my home, he had shown them what they must do. After they took everything from me, they went out to the villages, and caught people's chickens, and stole their rice, palm oil, groundnuts, ev-erything, and came home and gave it to me, so I could eat a little bit." These sudden transformations between violence and nurturing emerge from Adama's desertion causing "warm hearts" among her boarders: anger, which opens the world to violence. Their hearts became "cool" upon her return, and they initiated rebuilding the relationship. Her faith initially prevented her from accepting the food, even though within the social world she was right to do so:

"At first I was afraid to touch it, but I went and enquired with my pastor whether I should. The pastor said, 'Mrs. K, you don't have food to eat or anybody to prepare it for you. If God sends these people to give you food, can't you take it? Are you the one who went and stole the food?' I said, 'No!' So he said it was okay. They cooked and they gave me food. And the ladies were Temne." Adama sighed audibly into the tape recorder. "But still I am out every morning, every evening, to visit these people! Nothing happened to me, and I know it was the hand of God Almighty to save me from the hands of these people. They have killed so many, they have raped so many girls, they have broken houses, they have done everything that is against the will of God, but they didn't touch me. Praise His holy name! They didn't touch me!"

Adama never realized that her unruly houseguests were trying to be her friends; it was God's will that prompted them to feed her. Adama's own beloved pastor understood this, and convinced Adama of the rightness of accepting looted food, as long as she had no blood on her hands. This prompted a reinterpretation of every event that followed: now that it was God's will that she should survive, looting was morally necessary, rather than problematic, and the rebels were servants of God, rather than his enemies. God sent the rebels to the villages on her behalf, therefore it was acceptable that she consume their food, even though the women preparing it were Temne, and thus likely to be Muslim. The social and spiritual melded once again.

Though Adama lacked family in Makeni, she had blood relations in Freetown. She was unclear on how many months passed between the invasion and her nurturing by rebel wives, but she had made peace with it, until God told her it was time to leave. "God put fear of them for me. They were afraid of me because of what I have done; I have been working this hard for the Lord. I would meet with them and we used to pray, and I was praying for deliverance, so the Lord delivered me from them. I was tired, I was weak, I was thin when the Lord's messenger came! I could not have waited much longer. One blessed day, as I was lying on a mat in the sitting room in the early morning, I received a knock at the door. And I said, 'Who is that?' It was my cousin, who came from Freetown!

"He came all the way from Freetown through the dangers to collect me. And he said, 'Get up, get up! What has happened here?' I was afraid to open the door at first because I did not know who it was. And then he called my name: 'Ada, Ada, get up, I have come for you.' And I said, 'Thank you Jesus, you have saved my life.' I told my cousin, 'I am not happy to leave these rebels who don't know you. I want both of them to know you before I go.' Then I opened the door, and he said, 'Okay, let's go.' And I said 'No.' I said, 'Please, three days now I have not eaten. Let us go to the market.'"

"We went to the market, and we came home and cooked and ate. After that I went to say goodbye at the hospital, to the rebel nurses, and to the rebel doctor, and they said, 'Mommy, will you come back?' And I said, 'I will come back if it is the will of God.' When I went to say goodbye to the pastor and the church, they prayed for me. Finally I was ready to go, and I went with my cousin to the lorry park. It was the rebels' vehicle that took us. They gave me a letter, these rebel people gave me a letter that nobody should harm me along the way. My God is good to me."

Adama survived the occupation through the gregarious nature of her faith, which put her in constant contact with others.[1] As the chaos unfolded, her mission of salvation intensified to match it. These relationships were the key to her survival; her spiritual work and her social needs inadvertently merged. She acted on God's purposes, and reaped the benefits of social love in return. Whatever their motives, rebels reciprocated her care, which Adama accepted by reinterpreting care as God's will. She wanted to create God's community, and found success in the commitment her boarders had to nurturing an instrument of a Christian God's love, in spite of their adherence to Islam.

BETRAYAL WITHIN THE FAMILY

"We went up to Port Loko to spend the night in ECOMOG territory. We were told to sleep in an ECOMOG mosque. I told them that I am not going to the mosque; I am a Christian. The Nigerian man started to argue with me. He said, 'Are you going to stay here or not?' I did not want to stay there because the mosquitoes are too much! I don't know whether I will be able to sleep. And he said, 'You people must stay here. There is nowhere else.' And I said okay. I couldn't sleep because of the mosquitoes. The door was open and there were no windows. I had a tired body. I wanted to cry because of what had happened to me. In the morning God made us to wake up, then we went and bought food. We cooked, and ate, and I was so bodily tired! I was thinking that I would not be able to bear it. But still the Lord saved my life. He gave me the strength to cope with the situation. We went to Freetown, took the car, because they sent the car to collect me."

Compare this brief story of a journey to Freetown with Alimamy's month-long journey of walking, nearly drowning, narrowly missing civil militias, and selling his last possessions for transport fees. Though his relationships saved him in small ways at critical moments—a friend with food, admirers of his father providing safety—nothing compared to the resources clearly available to Adama and her family. She produced her own path out of Makeni with an RUF vehicle and letter, and, once she arrived at Port Loko, her Freetown family did the rest. As Alimamy was just at the start of his transition to adulthood and Adama was an elder in a gerontocracy, it was socially right—even during war—that her journey be eased.

"When we arrived in Freetown everybody was crying, my people were crying. They were so happy that I was still alive that the tears couldn't stop. I went to my sister and her husband. They took me in, gave me food, and I lay down for some time. Then I couldn't sleep. I thought about my son, because he was in Freetown the whole time. I was so afraid in my house with those rebels, and he just left me there in Makeni. It was my cousin who came to save me, and my sister who took me in! And so I went to the British embassy looking for a visa. I was not going to stay there."

Adama's family bonds were much weaker than those of most other families. It took months for someone from Freetown to rescue her, and it was a cousin, and not her son. He was now a source of insomnia and ill feelings, as he had breached his responsibility to his mother, his primary nurturer during his childhood. Adama never spoke of whether or not there was a rift between them, but she did not want to encounter the boy who refused to return the care she had given him. She decided instead to join her daughter in England. Now in a place with telephones, Adama could communicate with her daughter, who encouraged her to apply for a visa.

"I traveled all over West Africa to find a visa to go to London. I couldn't get it. Whenever I went somewhere they would say, 'No, British officials in London said that we should not give visas to Sierra Leoneans because they are pouring into the country. This is why we cannot allow them to enter.' It did not matter to them that my daughter was there! I used to ring my daughter in England to tell her which country I am in. Every month on the 28th she would send money for me so that I will not travel in another country as a beggar. She used to speak to the ambassadors: 'Please take care of my mother, she is the only one I have.' And God saved my life until I came back home to Sierra Leone, and I went to Freetown because I could not get a travel visa from any other country.

"My daughter decided to apply for a dependent visa. They gave me some forms to send to her. And within three days she received a phone call from the embassy: 'The question is, do you have a place to lodge your mother? Are you able to take care of her? Are you not going to leave the responsibility in the hands of the government in England? If anything happens, are you able to send her back home? Will you please tell us where you are working and how much tax you are paying the government?' You know, all of these questions, they demanded answers before they gave the visa."

Adama had been trying to secure a standard visa to the United Kingdom, an effort which failed because the country was trying to stem the flow of war refugees requesting asylum with no way of supporting themselves. When her daughter realized this, she applied for a dependent visa, taking a different bureaucratic path and assuring the British government that she would assume total responsibility for her mother. This was a more expensive path, but unlike her brother, Adama's daughter was happy to care for their mother. The dependent visa resonated with the Sierra Leonean ethos of care, and her daughter's answers were so satisfactory that the visa was issued immediately.

"Within two or three days, she rang me and said, 'All the documents are done. I have signed all the papers.' My daughter and her husband signed that they have a home of their own. They have five rooms, and have prepared one for me. They are able to take care of me. They will not allow me to go out and work because I am traumatized; I am coming from war. And when they received these forms at the embassy, they started to look for me in Freetown. I couldn't go out, because I was sick from malaria. My body was hurting me. But they found me, and they said, 'Your daughter has sent everything for you. She has sent money for your ticket and the airport tax.' Everything, money for me to use on the way, she sent it all, and I said, 'Praise the Lord!' I just thank him for his goodness and his mercy that I am able to spare my life. But I was so sick and weak. I was short of blood, and all of these things. I was so thin. But I pulled myself together and we took off from Banjul, in the Gambia. I had to survive a boat trip there from the beach."

Adama's transition from isolated elder in Makeni to legal dependent of a British resident illuminates the strength of her relationship with her daughter. Adama was alone in Makeni, developing new relationships to survive, only because she could not reach her daughter. With this lifeline finally reestablished, Adama was tapped of the adrenaline that had sustained her through terrifying and traumatic months in Makeni, and she collapsed, exhausted and ill, finally able to let down her guard and be cared for. Though Adama interpreted her asylum as God's will, it required tremendous persistence from a loving daughter to perform this kind of rescue.

"I went to Banjul and spent two nights there before we traveled all night to Amsterdam. We arrived early in the morning, and it was a difficult journey for me. They asked for tax at the airport, and I had to walk so far, and my foot was hurting me from walking in the bush. And at last, I took the plane to England, and she had sent enough money to buy my ticket all the way to her town. I had to wait overnight in the Amsterdam airport, and then I took the plane to England. And my family was there. My daughter and son-in-law were there, waiting for me."

THE MYSTERY OF THE MISSING HUSBAND

"Oh, you could not imagine the happiness, the joy it was for me to be with my family! They collected me from the airport and took me home. I was with them for four and a half years. They were so happy with me to go to church with them, the Anglican Church, and they allowed me to give my testimony about what the Lord has done for me."

During her four years in England, Adama became a dependent in her daughter's home. The restrictions on her activities were tremendous; as a dependent she could not look for work, and could only undertake activities in the company of her daughter. The four years comprised an "everyday" worth no elaboration in her testimony, save a single development that came to me, the listener, as a surprise:

"After three years of me being with her, she was thinking that she should send for Saidu [Adama's husband] to come and meet us in Britain. But unfortunately for him, God took his life, and he had died. One day when I came from church with the pastor I was expecting to hear news of whether or not he was coming. We arrived home and my daughter . . . she dropped to her knees and kissed my hand, and I said, 'Daughter, is everything all right?' She was so sad. And I asked her, 'What happened? Is he delayed?' And she said, 'No, mommy, come in.' And I said, 'What is wrong?' And she said, 'Saidu has died.' Her daddy died, and I knew in my heart already because God showed me. I knew

that he would die before I made it home. And she said, 'Yes mommy.'
I was very sad."

Adama had presented herself as a widow, widowed even when she
lived in Makeni during the occupation, and this was not technically the
case. Her husband had been living in Sierra Leone while she was alone
in his house in Makeni. Adama had framed her residence there as a
sacrifice that she made for him, as she was a stranger in Makeni, but
never mentioned that she and her husband had separated. His absence
during the occupation implies that he was not living in Makeni, though
it was his hometown and not hers. This memory revealed and partially
clarified the relationship troubles she suffered. She had been alone, a
stranger, in her husband's hometown; he was elsewhere; and her own
family—including her son—lived in Freetown.

Adama's relationships confounded Sierra Leonean standards: she
developed friendships with rebels, and yet was estranged from her
husband and son. In this light, her will to interpret her relationships
through the rubric of God's will is logical. Divine will makes it possible
to accept that dedicating one's life to saving others adversely affects
one's own closest relationships. To embrace God as a framework for
love and a good life enabled Adama to attribute to him reasons why
evangelism caused rifts in her own family; it was God's will she not be
with her husband. Socially, she *was* a widow during the occupation—
that relationship was dead, and God "showed her" that this would be
the way. Her bond with her daughter, however, transcended religion:

"My daughter cried, the family sympathized with me. I cried a lot.
Then she said, 'Mommy, please go and bury my daddy. I will send all
of your things.' I had a container of things that I wanted to bring home
because my house in Makeni was empty. It was a very long way to
Freetown, but she said, 'Just tell me where you will settle, in Freetown
or in Makeni, and I will send the things to you.' And the Lord help her,
she gave me one thousand pounds. And there was other money that
the church presented to me. I came to see them, everybody was there
waiting for me. Oh, I could see people who wanted to be with me, who
wanted to give me courage to be without my husband. I thank God for
all of their work to bring me home, though it took over a year. I thank
God for his goodness and the things he endured. When I finally made it
back, I came home to Makeni, where I am now, giving this testimony."

Up to this point, Saidu existed in her narrative only in his conspicu-
ous absence once they had moved to his home in Makeni. As this was
her testimony, and not a place where I could ask the obvious questions,

it was clear that, narratively, she framed her life during the occupation as a relationship she had with God, during which she was otherwise alone. As she narrated the RUF attack, she noted that it was God's will that she stay, and the occupation thus became a metaphor for the strength of her faith, and of God's love for her. In death, Saidu drew her back to Sierra Leone, where the war had ended months before. Given the choice of where to settle, Adama decided, for reasons she did not reveal, to live once again in Makeni. Though she had family in Freetown, her son's abandonment was a bitter pill in her testimony, a moment that provided her the resolve to go to England. In contrast, she had survived terrible tribulations in the Makeni house, had nurtured relationships there that saved her life, and she drew strength from it. Whether those reasons were social or religious—if it was God who wanted Adama to live in the house where he saved her life—did not matter, for emotionally she had the will to live only where she had proven she could survive.

EVANGELICAL FAITH AS A SOCIALLY UNCOMFORTABLE POSTWAR PRACTICE

"When I came back to Makeni, I found out that my house was spoiled. The lights were shattered! Everything has gone, not even broom, not even tiles in the floor . . . they have taken them away. The rebels took away my freezer, my fridge. They took away everything in the house. And all of my beds and wardrobes, cupboards and kitchen things, were all gone. Nothing was left in the house. But I didn't cry. I just praised the Lord. I thanked him for getting me to my daughter in England, so she would support me. And she bears it."

Adama had been through much worse than the mere stripping of her house. It was still shocking to see her lovely house spoiled, in spite of her expectation—symbolized by all the furnishings her daughter was sending her—that this would come to pass, considering what the RUF did to her home the first time she left. The container symbolized her daughter's will to support her, to "bear" God's will. The care that her daughter lavished on her was certainly magnified by the enormity of the task of refurbishing the house:

"She sends me money every month so that I can fix the house. She sent money for a generator. Because there is no light in Makeni, there is no water, except if you have a well. But I couldn't fix it! In fact, I am afraid to fix it, because I am the only one in the house! If I fix it, my neighbors would see that I have light and maybe they will come and kill me. And I have people who have threatened my life because they say I have money. I haven't got anything except what I should eat. And although I haven't got money to fix my home completely, God is helping me. The wooden chairs I have now are old, but the church is making new ones for me. But still I am afraid. I know that the Lord will cover me, he will provide for me, he will protect me, he will help me to fix my house again! And I just want to praise him. I am not yet able to dedicate the house back to God because of the situation in Makeni. Things are so hard, the cost of living is so high! My daughter is still taking care of me because I don't have anyone here to take care of me. And I thank God for it."

Adama's wealth and isolation were precisely her problem, as they signify the antithesis of good social practices. She had enough money coming to her from her daughter to contemplate rebuilding her former life, but she was terrified of revealing her wealth to her neighbors, for fear that they would rob and kill her. Their jealousy was likely compounded by suspicion. The facts that she ate alone, could pay Beatrice, and was not working led to only one conclusion in Sierra Leone. Only witches—individuals who fly by night and consume the organs of innocent people—have inexplicable wealth and live in solitude. They are selfish, uncaring, and secretive; all things that are anathema to proper sociality. The condemnation is such a tremendous social sanction—in rural areas the penalty for suspected witchcraft is death—that it forces even the shy and retiring into a public social life.[2] To all appearances, Adama was a witch. It might have been her personal disbelief in witches—as believing in witches totally contravenes Christianity—or her personal beliefs about Muslims that prevented her addressing the issue. Either way, she never made an attempt to reach out to her neighbors.

Adama wanted to "dedicate the house back to God," which I discovered a few months later meant being able to host traveling evangelical pastors. However, because she lived alone, she could not muster the courage to decorate the house in what she felt was a suitable manner to host properly. Decorating would have served only to reveal her wealth to already suspicious neighbors. Adama was in a serious bind. The exigencies of living through the war, which had stripped her of her property, made her the economic equal of others and pushed her to connect with others outside her religious circle. In the aftermath, this connectivity had been replaced by support from her daughter, which allowed her to reassert the primacy of her personal religious practices. Adama wanted people in her life, but just as peace had given her more control over who that would be, so had it stripped her of the courage to transcend those boundaries in her personal life as she transcended them in her work.

"God of heaven! He is there in my life, there in my soul. He sends people to help me, help me to clean the house, to do my laundry, to help me mop. When I came back I had to just sit down, I couldn't walk for nearly three months. But the Lord has healed me, and now I can walk a little to do his work. Presently, I am an evangelist. I still go to the hospital, I still go to the prison, I still go to the police station. And I know that the Lord will keep me until the time he wants me. I have got no one. My mother died before the war, my brother died during the war. My husband died. I don't know how he died. But I am telling you my dear brothers and sisters, if you believe in the Lord Jesus Christ, everything will be right with you. If you put your hope and trust in him, he will see you through, and that is what God has done for me. Presently I need someone to be with me in the house, to be with me, to encourage me, to help me because of what has passed. I offered that prayer up to God and God has sent somebody: a pastor and his wife. We are praying together, worshipping God together, going to church together, and I have a nanny. A young girl, who is taking care of me in the home and making sure that I have everything I need. And I still have, every month, my daughter sending the payments."

The evangelical faith sustained Adama through the war by providing her spiritual comfort, but it also provided what she truly needed to survive: relationships. The war effaced the ideological and physical differences between Adama and everyone else, and the relationships she crafted with rebels were acts of compassion and interpersonal need mediated by faith. Though in the aftermath she fabricated a more deliberate social world that encouraged her relative isolation through her religious orientation, her foreignness, and her wealth, she had enough sustaining relationships—her daughter, her pastor, and her evangelical network—to fulfill her everyday needs. This does not mean that she has nourished all potential relationships. She recognizes her relative isolation, and laments this fact, even as she exhorts everyone who gains access to her testimony to also follow her chosen path. Even with its shortfalls, she has found it a fulfilling life.

"Please, my brothers and sisters, accept Jesus today. Take him as your Lord and master. He will help you, he will see you through, as he has helped me in this strange land. I was not born in Makeni, I was born in Freetown, and my family is still there. But I am in Makeni, where my husband brought me, and I am staying my husband's house. My children are all older, but God sent people to encourage me, to bless me, to be with me. I haven't got anybody today in the world, I have no mother, I have no father. I have no brother and I lost my husband. My children have gone from me. But God is here, he has said that they should help me, and my daughter and my pastor help me. Bless them and bless the Holy Father. He watches over them so that they will support me. Please pray for me that God will continue to comfort me. Pray for me for my enemies. They are around, and they say, 'She is cooking every day and not working. Her children are in England and they are sending money for her! We will enter the house and kill her! And burn the house.'"

The words of her neighbors are the words of jealous, excluded individuals who feel that a big woman is eating and not sharing her gains. Pulling her down—through murder and burning her house—would level the social field to discourage others who might not share, and also cleanse the town of a witch. The ordinary world did not offer Adama the same ability to reach out as she found the strength to do during the war, when she interpreted the chaos as God's will, with herself as his instrument. Faith, combined with Adama's own instincts to be generous and reach out, became powerful instruments of survival and social thriving during the occupation. These same qualities that saved Adama during the war were less compatible with her ability to thrive in the aftermath, when her primary linkages were foreign or overtly religious. However, having chosen her path, she lived with no regrets. Adama ended her testimony as she began it, with a hymn:

I have decided
To follow Jesus.
I have decided
To follow Jesus.
No turning back,
No turning back.

The world before me,
The cross before me.
The world behind me,
The cross before me.
The world behind me,
The cross before me.
The world behind me.
No turning back,
No turning back.

Though no one joins me,
Still I will follow.
Though no one joins me,
Still I will follow.
Though no one joins me,
Still I will follow.
No turning back,
No turning back.

I have decided
To follow Jesus.
I have decided
To follow Jesus.
I have decided
To follow Jesus.
No turning back,
No turning back.

In the second stanza, Adama had both the world and the cross before her, and made a decision to put one of them—the world—at her back. She was clear on her relationship priorities: she loved God more than anyone else. The nation never came into play in her testimony, neither positively nor negatively, because Adama never answered to demands that the president—or any other mortal—should come before faith. "Collaboration" with rebels may incite government vitriol, but "collaborating" with God is another realm entirely.

"They Really Damaged Me"

The Father

Musa is not a tall man, but his bearing is dignified and his smile wide and inviting. He was always initiating conversations in the neighborhood, whether about politics or his older daughter and her progress in kindergarten. He brought her to meet me one day after school. Prim in her ironed uniform, in pigtails, she looked up at me, squinting in the sunlight, offered her hand and shook mine firmly, introducing herself slowly so that I would pronounce her name correctly. "I am Ra-MA-tu," she squeaked, "It is nice to meet you!" Musa beamed at his little girl, bursting with pride over her manners. The story he later told revolved around the risks he took and the sacrifices he made to ensure that his precious baby girl was born safely, in the middle of the occupation.

When I met him, Musa was employed by an NGO as a caretaker, and he was always happy to finish his daily duties with a soda and a chat. It seemed incongruous that such an intelligent man mopped floors and ironed shirts for a living, however the pay was steady and he would do anything to keep Ramatu in school and perhaps save for when his younger daughter, baby Isatu, was also ready to don a uniform. "It is so important to educate your children," he remarked one day, after disclosing that he spent a third of his salary on tuition at a private kindergarten. "She is the future, for my family and for the country. I would be failing as a father if I just left her there like that."

Ramatu was a metonym for Musa's life. She symbolized everything he had had as a child and everything he wanted for the future. Musa's narrative revolved around nurturing family: his own happy childhood, his schooling, then raising his own family, educating his daughters, and most importantly, putting himself in harm's way during the war. During the war Musa remained a steadfast civilian as he worked to support his aging parents and pregnant wife. He was in an awkward position vis-à-vis the RUF: the same age as many RUF commanders, he was thus often harassed by rebels wanting to assert their authority. In his narrative of being "a good father," the harassment revealed the strength of his character—a calm reasonableness and respect towards others that enhanced his chances for survival. He wanted only to take care of his family, and never wanted to eat in competition with the RUF. In framing his narrative carefully as that of the humble caretaker, he left no room to challenge his motives, no room for listeners to identify "collaboration." Musa always acted out of love because, in his story, this was his experience as a child.

A HAPPY CHILDHOOD

Musa reminisced often about his own childhood in Makeni. The town was yet to enter its period of extended decline, and they had water and light at home. Light was important because it meant he could study at night. Musa attended a prominent secondary school, though at first he did not study as much as he should. He was not aware of the sacrifices his parents made to keep him in school, and the time when they could no longer pay was a shock. "During secondary school I was an arts student. I did history, government, art, literature, and biology. I really liked government; that and history were my favorite subjects. I never did badly in those subjects. But I was not so good with the other ones, I did not pay as much attention." He frowned at the memory. "I just thought that as long as I wanted to stay in school it would be fine, but then came my O-level exams, and I was not clever enough to pass. I wanted to take them again but you had to pay the full fee, and the money was not there. My parents could not do anything more for me!"

Musa was disappointed, and resolved to amend his mistake. "I decided that I was not going to fail just because I could not earn a place at university, so I enrolled myself in a vocational institute. They only teach pure science at the vocational institute so I had to change my course of study. I started a diploma course in agriculture: physics, chemistry, statistics, biology, animal science, soil science, engineering, methods, most of the science subjects. It was a big change."

Musa started his three-year course in 1996, and married the love of his life a year later. "Elizabeth was so beautiful! And she was very *strong* [feisty]. My parents thought it was a good match so they approved of us being together. We were living with my parents while I attended the institute." He was one semester away from completion when things fell apart. "Things were very easy, things were going very normal until this war came to Makeni. The war made everything very difficult for us."

KEEPING A FAMILY TOGETHER IN CHAOS

Musa was young, strong, and capable, and was not forced by poverty or disability to endure the occupation of Makeni. He became mired in the war—like Calvin—because of his unwillingness to abandon infirm family members. "It was a very, very bad time for us when the rebels entered Makeni town, this was December 23, 1998. I was with my family and I didn't have a way to move them, so we stayed in Makeni. My parents were very frightened that I would leave them, and they had to depend on me only because most of my brothers and sisters were in Freetown. My elder brother was still here but he was looking after his wife's family, and they were on the other side of town. Things were too dangerous for us to meet! I stayed in my parents' home in Makeni because I was the youngest and I was still in school. I was the only one who could take care of them, and they were very old. My father the tailor . . . his eyes were not good after so many years of work and he did not want to leave. My mother . . . she was not strong walking, so there was no way for her to run! There was no way to leave. Things were very hard." It was not as though his other siblings did not love or appreciate his parents; he was the only one in a position to act. Though many people framed their narratives heroically—like Alimamy always being there for his mother—much of the time, as with Calvin, the burden of caring for parents falls not to a specific child, but to the one who happens to be nearby. That son or daughter must choose whether or not to flee when trouble arises; of everyone I spoke to, no one did.

Musa did not blame the Nigerian troops stationed in town for fleeing when the rebels attacked Makeni: "So they attacked the Nigerians in the barracks and removed them, and killed a lot of their troops. The rebels removed them, and those of us who did not know that the rebels had attacked the barracks stood and watched as all these Nigerian soldiers came running. One of them asked me to show him the highway because they were going to Mile 91. I directed him there, because it was no good wanting them to stay. The rebels would only kill them all, so it was better to let them save their lives. During that time there were also no government troops. We alone lived through the rebels. They controlled us. Unless you abide by their rules it is a big problem for you, a big problem."

During the initial invasion, the "rules" boiled down to one: might makes right. Musa narrated being powerless, having his dignity stripped away as he did his best to take care of his parents in a town run by the most vicious members of the mutinous army and their rebel brethren. It was a narrative of explicit noncollaboration, of victimhood. "It was too much hassle that we took from them! Every day the rebels visited different homes and even our house. They would choose a house, go there, take whatever property they wanted, and there was no way for you to resist because they were armed. There was no way for you to say 'No, don't go with this.' They took what they wanted to take. It was such a fearful time when you heard them on the street, and wonder if they were going to burst the door and enter your house! You could not keep anything for your family, even if your parents were old. The rebels had no mercy for our parents, and it made me to wonder if they had parents. They even took the foam [mattresses] off the beds and carried them away. I was just staring at the boy who did this, but he would not meet my eyes. He just threw his weapon over his shoulder and went off with the foams on his head. So we were just left to sleep on mats on the floor!"

Musa describes the first months as the near destruction of the social world, the gerontocracy mutilated by youth who harassed the elderly regularly. This was his first contact with rebels—though these were mostly mutinous soldiers—and he described them as inhuman. Musa did not know the recent history of soldiers being cast out of government employ, using the RUF to extract revenge for years of disrespect, neglect, and lack of appreciation at the hands of the president. The soldier who took the mattress had not been paid since the Kamajors became preeminent. His rice ration was given to an upstart with no training, and no pledge to give his life for his country. Perhaps he had been loyal to the government until the moment that a group of civilians, seeking revenge on the *sobels* they assumed were attacking their village, came after him. Perhaps he had lost a brother, or father, or cousin this way. Musa's parents, and respect for elders, were not in his purview.

I argue that during the war, what appeared as sheer opportunism stemmed from a will to do more than just survive: cadres needed to invest in others and transform their own relationships. Only the commanders had the luxury of not needing to loot for themselves. Many young men were high on marijuana and *brown-brown,* a mixture of cocaine and gunpowder that distracted their minds and kept hunger at bay. This youth may not have eaten for days before the attack, when the meager findings from the last looting spree had been shared around. He likely had not slept on a mattress for months, or even years. The moment he seized it and took it back to where he slept, it became a mattress for many people. Even in ordinary times, it is common for two or three youths to share a mattress. Perhaps he traded it for some rice. Musa could not know these things; he saw only his own powerlessness.

"We just gave them what they wanted because once they had it they didn't bother us again. We could only keep what we could hide. The only thing we could ever hide was a little bit of money. Sometimes I would put it in my slippers or we would hide it in back of the house. It was the only thing we had. But I don't know what we were keeping it for because there was nothing to buy in the town, the rebels had looted it all! We had to go searching for our food."

I asked naïvely, "What about farming, was there any way to grow food at the time?"

Musa did not find this a curious question. "They were not preventing us from farming, but if you farmed a rebel would find you and you would just have to farm for him, not for yourself. Because they would collect everything when the produce is at the range to be harvested. They would go there and harvest for themselves. So we abandoned this farming idea, because we never got anything out of it." What was curious was that rebels did not let their civilian laborers keep any of the proceeds, by which they could survive and continue farming. The shortsightedness meant the rebels were not thinking about long-term occupation, merely immediate survival.

"And when people left the villages with the rebel attacks, they left their fields. We were hungry so it tempted us into the bush, to go and dig the cassava that was left in the ground. That brought troubles. Sometimes when my parents groaned with hunger, I went to the bush to find cassava. I would come with it, grate it, and produce *garri* [dried cassava meal]. I would sell it, because you cannot eat only *garri* or you will be sick. We would eat some and then sell the rest and save the money. I thought if another kind of food became available, we would buy it. But that never happened. We just kept the money we had because there was no food! *Garri* and cassava was all we had, just small foods. So we ate them and saved money, maybe to pay for transport to Freetown if the time came where the vehicles would pass again. But before that, you had to get the cassava back from the bush."

THE SMALL BOYS UNIT AND THE INVERSION OF THE SOCIAL WORLD

It was risky leaving Makeni, locating abandoned cassava fields, digging up the tubers, and bringing them back. The rebels had surrounded Makeni with checkpoints, and it was a foregone conclusion that one would encounter rebels while bringing cassava from the villages. "On our way back from the bush usually they would take the cassava . . . unless sometimes we stood against them!"

I had to ask him to clarify: "You stood up to armed rebels?"

"Yes, we were fed up! We were hungry, and I had myself, and Elizabeth, and my parents to think about. They were all depending on me and it was just cassava, it was not like I was carrying gold. I had to find the courage to go to the bush so we could feed ourselves, and I was not going to make all that effort just to have a small boy take it from me. It only happened to me one time, but that was enough. I went to collect cassava, and on my way coming back, I met these guys from the SBU. Do you know the SBU?"

"Do you mean the 'Small Boys Unit'?"

"Yes, those small boys."

The international human rights community documented the use of child combatants in Sierra Leone extensively, and most analysts construed child soldiering as a loss of the innocence and security of childhood.[1] From this perspective, child soldiers are a symptom of a militia's depravity, their willingness to destroy the fabric of society. To reconcile families in the aftermath, the children must be rehabilitated within a "discourse of abdicated responsibility." This involved absolving children of responsibility for their actions, therefore creating a new childhood free of guilt or confusion over violent actions.[2]

From a Sierra Leonean perspective, the full horror of child combatants was realized in the inversion of the social order, because children are "unfinished" and can normalize violence, thus rendering impossible their "good training." There could be no greater insult, no greater social problem, than a small boy giving orders to an adult. Every time I interviewed a former RUF combatant, I asked the same question: "Did you have small boys under your control?" Every one answered in the negative. This was obviously the politically correct answer, as I am a

Westerner. But their explanations never stemmed from a place of, "I would not do it because it is wrong." In fact most of these combatants were kidnapped at a young age and chose to stay with the RUF, making them former "small boys" themselves. Their answers came from how problematic and potentially dangerous it is to create the space for children to eat.[3]

"Seriously speaking," said one former RUF commander I call Charlie, "I would never take on these small boys because they are so difficult to put under control. I had my own reputation as a commander to think about in this town, and using small boys . . . you invite people to hate you. Small children don't have any sense. If I annoyed a boy because he wanted something and I would not give it to him, would he just pick up his weapon and shoot me? You have to use hard discipline to lead an SBU, you cannot have any fears." He paused, and mentioned that it was only the "really crazy" commanders who enjoyed using children in combat. These people—Superman (nicknamed for his love of throwing people off buildings) and Mosquito (whom many war historians suspect was a sociopath)—were both killed. Some commanders around Makeni liked to rule through fear, and allowing small boys to man the checkpoints surrounding the town was an effective way of both policing the roads and limiting the traffic, as only the boldest civilians would dare confront the unpredictable children who staffed them.[4]

Musa narrated being emboldened by his hunger and the demands of his family to overcome his fear of the SBU. His was a story of the courage of resistance: an overtly political act of defiance against the RUF that countered all government claims of "collaboration." He would never cooperate, nor would he cower. He tried to act casual as he passed two small boys manning the checkpoint between Makeni and a nearby village, a bag of cassava on his shoulder.

"I could see two boys at this checkpoint as I was walking. I acted like I was going to ignore them, but they called me, and asked me to put the bag down. The moment I put it down one of the boys collected the bag and put it inside a house. I objected. I said to myself, 'Hey, this is the living of my own family. If this food leaves me in this particular place it means my family and I will suffer. Let me follow this food.' So I too entered inside the house. The boys had started loosening the bag to take the cassava out, so I grabbed the bag and started to tussle with them. I called them names and it was a lot of noise. One of their commanders was outside. He yelled out, 'What is causing the noise inside there?' So I said, 'Please sir, it's me and your security.' So he said, 'Stop fighting and everyone come out of the house.' The boy grabbed the bag, I too grabbed the bag and both of us came out."

A story of such boldness when faced with child soldiers was singular. No other civilians I spoke to risked discovering through confrontation if a child was armed or drugged. Motivated by hunger and his love for his family, Musa told of being willing to sacrifice his life to keep the cassava.

"The commander looks at us and says to the boy, 'My friend, don't disturb that man.' I must have looked very hungry for him to react this way! But the boys were not finished with me. During this time a very young fellow, let me say eight or nine, started beating me with a stick. Every way I turned to try to escape the blows he hit me, and he damaged my arm. So when the commander told them to leave me, they asked me, peacefully, to give them some of the cassava. I said, 'Okay, remove what you want. This was the thing that you were supposed to do, but you decided to violence me. Now, what you are supposed to do comes last.' I said, 'Take what you want to take now.' So they took what they wanted to take, and they left the balance inside the bag."

This commander controlled his small boys by speaking to them and treating them as adults. Once the boys had put Musa in place at the bottom of the social order, they asked him "peacefully" for some cassava. There was a perverse logic to their relationship with their commander, wherein he gave them orders in order to keep them nominally under control, while still allowing them to assert themselves as rebels. The result was a badly beaten Musa, with half a bag of cassava.

"From that place to the time I reached my home I was in terrible pain. This hand . . . I could not lift it at all. It was heavy and it swelled up. My wife cried for me. She prepared hot water and ointments to treat me. So much of the money we had saved from making *garri* was used to heal my arm. But she was successful and that pain passed after a while. And it was okay for me to go back through that path and get cassava again, because the boys knew that I would give them some if they asked for it nicely, rather than snatching it. If their companions tried to violence me, others who were aware of this would say, "Leave this particular man. He's a young man and a gentleman. See him going to the bush to get cassava; he is doing it just because he needs survival for his family. He has a family."

Musa initiated a potentially dangerous confrontation, which, by his account, ended peacefully because he was respectful of RUF authority. He called the commander "sir" and the boys "your security," refused to fight back as the boys beat him, and gave them half the cassava he had gathered. Like Kati initiating the conversations with Issa Sesay that opened the market, Musa's boldness, inspired by his love for his family, was recognized and respected by rebels, who saw that his purpose was not to challenge authority, but to sustain his family.

DEATH OF THE FATHER, WAIT FOR THE DAUGHTER

Five months into the occupation, Musa had a steady rhythm of activities to support himself, his wife, and his parents. He dug cassava in the bush, lost some of it to the boys at the checkpoint, and brought the rest home. What was not eaten immediately was turned into garri to either save or sell. However, like Kadiatu, Musa encountered the problem of sustaining weaker people on a cassava-based diet.

"My father was old and he was not strong. His heart could not stand losing everything in the house; he was too frail to sleep on just a mat without his foam. And the cassava . . . it was not good for him. Everyday he ate some, but it got to be less and less. He was too tired. He died in April of 1999." The death turned Musa from de facto head of the household into the eldest male bearing the burden of care. He was now only responsible for his wife and his mother, but the weight felt heavier, rather than lighter, with the death of his father. He felt vulnerable without his father's calm authority. "Sometimes we three stayed alone in the house, and sometimes I would collect one or two friends to stay with us. People did what they could for their family's survival."

Musa was especially concerned about his wife, as Elizabeth was pregnant. He had been relieved of the burden of finding food for his father, but it was replaced by the concern about feeding Elizabeth enough to sustain the pregnancy. He knew that she needed more than just cassava. They needed money, having spent their last leones on medicines for his shoulder. Musa was in a bind. He had made enemies in town through the boldness of his food-finding missions, and they came back to haunt him.

"I had problems with one SLA soldier who was a rebel. He was the first one that threatened me in this town, that he will kill me because he could, because I was going to the bush and coming with cassava. He became annoyed that I was allowed to do this. When I got money I decided to buy cigarettes. During that time my wife was pregnant with my first child. I decided to give these cigarettes to my wife to sell so that she could get some things for the baby that will come. Elizabeth is a good trader, and also I thought that because she was pregnant she would not get so much hassle from the soldiers and rebels around town."

Musa defended his decision as strategic rather than callous endangerment of his wife's life. As a woman and an expectant mother, she posed no threat to RUF authority, and would be able to get a better price for individual cigarettes because of Sierra Leonean men's respect for mothers. In a move that resonates with Kadiatu and Kati's interaction with the rebels, Musa was using the undercurrent of normal social relations—respect for nurturing—that influenced behavior during the occupation. However, in his eagerness to promote Elizabeth's business, Musa got himself in trouble.

"I was with a friend one day sitting on the veranda. We saw across the street an SLA soldier in the house he had confiscated and he was sitting there doing nothing. He had some small boys around him, acting as bodyguards. A few minutes later another soldier came and asked him, 'Say my friend, I want to smoke cigarettes. Do you have any?' I heard this discussion, and decided to join it. I said, 'Please, I know where they sell cigarettes. Let me help you.' I thought I would go inside to find Elizabeth. Oh, that particular fellow! He was suddenly annoyed. He said, 'My friend, I don't need your talk. This day I will kill you.' I said, 'Hey, what have I done to you? I only want to assist you, what have I done to make you want to kill me?' I decided to move quickly, and told myself, 'Let me go and find your bosses.' If I found a commander I could explain to him that I had done nothing to annoy this man. When I started to move this the man and his wife and their small bodyguards crossed the street. I was in trouble." Musa had broken his own rule and initiated an unwelcome interaction with rebels, thus challenging their authority.

"Other people came out of the house with knives and cutlass. My wife heard the commotion from inside the house. She was having a *strong* pregnancy, and she felt bold! She came out and held my hand. She said in my ear, 'Don't stand here and wait for those people. Move!' Because I was tense over the situation, it had caused me to become paralyzed. My wife brought me inside, put me inside one room and locked the door. Those people began shouting for me. I could hear them calling through the windows, looking for me. My mother took control at that moment. She came out of the house and said politely, 'What's wrong?' So they replied to her, 'Your son. We want to lay his blood down on the ground today. We will kill your son.' My mother fell to the ground in front of them and said, 'Please, don't do that! He's my son, please don't do that.' She was begging them, begging them . . . she removed a small amount of money from the knot in her *lappah* [skirt] and gave it to them, and they decided to move."

Musa narrated knowing that he had overstepped his bounds. As a civilian, he had to be consistently passive and submissive with rebels, while simultaneously encouraging them to purchase his goods. Musa leaned on his mother's ability to elicit their compassion and feed their vanity with begging and a bribe, which returned the rebels to their rightful place of gaining his compliance through fear. Musa gives credit to the fact that his wife was vigorous in her pregnancy with saving him before he was murdered on his doorstep.

This would be the last time that his mother was able to intervene on his behalf. "My mother was grieving for my father. But now that he was gone and things were getting even worse with the infighting, we had an idea that she could join my brothers and sisters in Freetown. When I asked her one night, she would not agree. I had to persuade her. I said, 'Mother, this place is not convenient for you. Life here is too hard; soon the cassava will not be enough for you. We have some small money, let me find a way to move you to Freetown.' She protested that she did not want to leave her home. It was her only home since she was married and you know how old people are attached to their home! So I said, 'I will stay in the house, and secure the house and the rest of the property in it.' So finally she agreed, and I was able to walk her to the RUF checkpoint and find her transport to Freetown."

Musa was relieved to send his mother away. Her frailty reflected badly on his love as her son, and he was moved to ease the constant strain of occupation for them both by moving her out of harm's way. This left only pregnant Elizabeth to worry about. However, within a week of sending his mother away, the situation deteriorated yet again. Issa Sesay had just arrived in Makeni and was asserting his authority. Though popular with residents because of his new laws, Sesay was rapidly making himself a target of the wrath of other rebels, a situation that led to the largest of the infights.

ATTACKING NURTURING IN THE FIGHT FOR BIG MAN STATUS

"I was so relieved that my mother had gone to Freetown, though it was very tense for me in the days after, waiting for maybe a report to come down the road that a taxi had been ambushed. But these reports never came, so I was a little bit at ease over the fate of my mother. I only had to get cassava to eat, and grate, and sell the rest for me, Elizabeth, and the baby that would come. This would be fine except that this was the time of the infight, when Issa and the SLA tussled! During this time the SLA guys forcibly entered the house and looted all the *garri* I had processed!"

As David mentioned, Foday Sankoh was tired of the squabbling among commanders in Makeni. Many of these, like Superman and Green Snake, commanded mutinous soldiers, most of whom joined the RUF in Makeni after the AFRC was chased from Freetown. Sesay was tasked with seizing the town for the "pure" RUF, headed by Sankoh himself, rather than the joint command initiated by Major Johnny Paul Koroma during the 1997–1998 coup. Sesay was one of the original RUF members, having met Foday Sankoh in Cote d'Ivoire in the 1980s when he was mining gold. Sesay crossed the Liberian border with Sankoh in 1991, and disarmed only on Sankoh's command. However, he too wanted to be a big man, and attempted to muster consent to rule from both civilians and rebels. Many rebels who had initially welcomed his rule ceased to support him in confrontation with other commanders when he banned looting. By preventing them from eating—or even taking care of themselves—Sesay undermined the very status he wished to achieve.

"The rebels that Issa brought with him from Kailahun decided to forcibly remove the SLA from the town, because they were giving the RUF a bad name in this place. Issa drove them out, and then passed laws! No looting, no raping, and he made a list of many other crimes. He said anyone who does these crimes will face a death penalty, and he did that. Most of the guys that were having this habit of looting and raping were the SLAs. Anyone found guilty of any crime, he will put that man in front of a firing squad, and kill him! At that time, I can say that the SLA were the worst people, worse than the rebels, they were very wicked. They followed through on all their threats! Because of the rules and regulations that General Issa put in the town . . . they broke the law and he killed most of them! They were not expecting this, they thought he was a brother."

This idea of Issa being a brother was a reminder of the love forged among combatants, which had been critical to David as he negotiated the war. SLA soldiers felt the government had betrayed them, and that by joining the RUF they were attaching themselves to a new, more nurturing family. They expected to be fed and supported by their new boss; they ran rampant among civilians not as a function of their new relationship, but because of their idea—mistaken, according to Sesay's plans—that their betrayal by the government gave them this right. The draconian punishments authorized by Sesay bucked both their sense of revenge and their will to eat; once again their leader was betraying them. Sesay's particular brand of big man politics was anathema to their desire for vengeance on the nation, and the SLA commanders were enraged.

"Superman was not happy about Issa seizing control of the town, as Sesay was killing his men and he was losing his face as a big man. Issa was embarrassing him! So Superman and the SLA decided when the intervention took place in Freetown [the January 6 invasion], they would take advantage of the chaos to remove Issa from this place. Superman was RUF, but he collaborated with the SLA because he could be his own big man, not under Foday Sankoh's control. So he and his own rebels removed General Issa from Independence Square and drove him from town, so Issa went to Magburaka. Because of the way they removed him, it was clear they wanted to kill him. They killed one of Issa's commanders; his name was Rambo, and Issa decided to move from this place.

"Issa was gone for a few days. I don't know if he had time to get more men from Kailahun, but he came back and attacked the SLA. That infight went on for a week! The fighting was so heavy at that time! Any time they saw each other they would attack. Attack in the morning, attack in the evening. The only thing that was fortunate for us was that they never targeted civilians for death. No, all of us would just go indoors. So we were there when the infights had finished. Because all the seven attacks that Issa did, the one-week attack, the SLA soldiers would repel them. They would move them back to Magburaka. After that the SLA soldiers went around to every home and removed people's property, anything that was left."

In spite of the fact that civilians were not targeted during the infight itself, they became collateral damage to the egos and frustrations of fighters. Rebels' ability to thrive was threatened by Sesay seeking his primary legitimacy as a big man with civilians. In essence, Sesay was betraying them just as President Kabbah had done: using them until he had a better option, and then discarding them. This was socially and politically risky, as former RUF combatant Charlie explained:

"I didn't have any problems with Issa because he was my leader for the whole war. But . . . to tell you the truth, I can understand that the other guys didn't like him, because of his ways. Although I cannot give a strong statement against him that he did anything bad to me, or anyone I knew. He was a big man and he was our leader. But he used to deal with my friends and colleagues in a hard way, so for that I can say he is not good, because the majority is grumbling, so I cannot say he was a good leader. They were grumbling because of the command structure . . . due to implementation of good laws . . . or let me say discipline, you see? No looting, no raping. These guys wanted to go and get things for themselves because there was not much food in the town and they didn't have money to attract women, but if Issa's men caught you doing anything they would flog you until your last breath. You are going to pay the penalty of death because he will do it. I don't mind that he implemented these laws because the SLA was out of control. It is a good thing to implement laws in any organization. The guys who were grumbling were not thinking that they would loot just to flaunt Issa's control. They did not care about command. It was their own interest they were after. Self interest."

Charlie sees Sesay threatening his own big man status by passing laws that displeased the cadres, his underlings on whom he depended for power. If he took away too much, they might instead profess loyalty to Superman, who allowed them to loot. The infight saw many "pure" RUF rebels mutiny and join forces with the SLA/RUF in order to plunder. Sesay should have expected this; big men are vulnerable to desertion if they fail to redistribute resources, even as he made food available in the market. Many rebels saw having to purchase food from civilian women as an affront to their authority. Issa's eventual military victory forced rebels who wanted the comfort of town life—and access to the resources available in the town—to accept his policies. He banked on their will to remain in Makeni and live "easy"—as Charlie stated, their "self interest"—to gain their compliance, though at the expense of civilians. In the interim, they took what they could.

The infight exposed the precariousness of big men, as Issa failed to balance love among cadres with his will to be big with civilians. By imposing sanctions on the cadres while he wooed civilians, the unhappy rebels, no longer benefiting from that relationship, turned to "self interest" to fill their desires. The continual plundering by Superman's men revealed how cadres' loyalty was a simple matter of who provided them access to resources. Sesay believed that if he gained control of Makeni, rebels would eventually return and accept his authority in exchange for the ability to live in town. Though mutated, war was still governed by the logic of resource distribution. Musa, with Elizabeth's advancing pregnancy, was increasingly concerned with security and food availability. The infight prevented him from going to the bush for cassava, as the checkpoint continually changed hands. Another dangerous moment occurred when he was forced out of his house to find food in the wake of it being ransacked, yet again, by hungry, angry soldier/rebels.

POSSESSING NOTHING BUT THE CONFIDENCE OF BEING A CIVILIAN

"After the sixth day of the infight the SLA came to our house and took everything that was left. They took the sleeping mats, they took all the *garri*, they found most of our money, and all I had left was two thousand leones. So I asked my wife. I said, 'Elizabeth, now it is only two thousand leones left with me. Look at your condition: you are pregnant. What am I to do now? And what are you two to do now?' So I sat down and I started thinking. I said, 'Okay, with this money let me buy one or two packets of cigarettes, I will do business and we will eat.' I had to leave the house again and look for cigarettes.

"During that time my elder brother was staying at his wife's family compound on the other side of town. He was selling *poyo* [palm wine] there. All of Superman's men were drinking there. He had regular customers! So I got one packet, two packets, and I told myself that I will take them to my elder brother and he will sell them for me. I will not put anything in my particular place now, because the rebels know our place. I thought it would be too much for me to travel around with the packets, because the rebels would see them. So I decided to empty all the cigarettes and put them all in my pockets. I decided to move that way to my elder brother and hand the cigarettes over to him."

Musa, though he would never collude with rebels himself, had no ethical problems using his brother's business success to earn money to feed Elizabeth. It was a tremendous risk walking across town, but because it was motivated by the survival of his family, it was defensible. This negotiation recalls Adama finding the ability to eat rebel-looted and Muslim-cooked food, as the rebels were serving an instrument of God. Neither act required an apology to the government.

"I left the house okay and made it through the center of town. I was on the way past the petrol station and I saw the SLA guys. They called one man who was walking by. They stripped that man naked looking for money, and I knew there is no way for me to avoid the same fate. Even if I turned around they had already seen me and it was too late. I said, 'Oh, I'm in trouble!' So I started walking majestically." At this,

Musa stood and demonstrated his strut, as though he were all-powerful and had not a care in the world. He squared his shoulders, threw his head back, and took long, loping strides, swinging his arms jauntily.

"I cross the street as though I was already going to do that, and take the other way, walking majestically. They were watching me, the moment I reached their end one of them called me, 'You, soldier! Soldier!' I did not stop. 'Soldier, soldier!' I did not talk. So the other one started yelling, 'You, civilian!' So I turned and said, 'You mean me?' And he said, 'Yes, come.' I said, 'No, why should I go over to you?'"

With this performance of being a civilian, Musa was reenacting the substance of noncollaboration: proving to himself, to me as listener, and perhaps in the confrontation that had occurred that he was strongly opposed to the RUF, in spite of his continued residence in Makeni. He was not pro-government, but he was also not pro-rebel.

"He got angry because his companion laughed. He used abusing language to me, and when I turned my back, the other one came with the gun. He hit me with that gun and I fell down. I tried to stand so he hit me again. So I decided to handle the gun. I grabbed at it! At that time I had more weight because he was small, so I pushed him with the gun. Luckily one of their commanders recognized me. He said to the boy, 'My friend! Leave that man, leave that gentleman. Don't cause problems.' So the boy left me and I moved. The commander didn't want to cause trouble because if Issa won the infight, I could go straight in to the task force office and report him for harassment. He was the one who had manned the checkpoint when I got cassava. I smoothed my trousers to make sure I had not spilled the cigarettes, but to them it looked like I was taking my dignity. And then I took the cigarettes to my elder brother. He sold them and we got food for Elizabeth and the baby that was coming."

Whether it was the threat of accountability to a new commander, or loyalty to a man who had always shared his meager cassava that moved the commander to action, Musa survived. He had established a reputation as a man who would never challenge authority, but would do anything to feed his family. He did not seek status, he did not contest the rebels' right to rule the town, he simply defended his right to survive and save his wife. They were worth fighting for.

TUSSLING OVER A SHOVEL

In our conversation, Musa often mentioned his elder brother, who was doing a decent business selling palm wine to the bodyguards of two

RUF commanders. After the death of their father, he often served as Musa's lifeline when Musa was unsuccessful in his quest for food. His brother's generosity precipitated an incident that caused Musa so much distress that he emphasized how much he did not want to talk about it as he described yet another occasion when he came close to losing his life at the hands of angry, bored soldier/rebels. Musa's crime was his unwillingness to be intimidated. It had worked in previous encounters with SLA, but failed to elicit respect this time:

"The other time I was damaged, the worst one . . . I don't want to talk about it. It was again the SLA that damaged me, I'm telling you they were terrible. One time I was sitting at home. My brother was buying goods and he sold those goods at the market. The rebels knew where he got the money since most of them were drinking from him, so they did not bother him! One day he bought a shovel, and in the morning I said, 'Brother, I don't have anything to eat today. Please, help me so that I will get food.' He said, 'Presently I don't have money with me. When I go to the town I will look for someone who wants a shovel. When I sell the shovel I will provide something for you and your wife, to get food.'"

"So I said, 'Okay.' Then . . . I don't know, he changed his mind. He said, 'You take the shovel and sell it,' and he went home. He gave me that shovel, I was very grateful to him. But I too was afraid of the market and did not want to go on my own. I came to one of my friends that was living in the house with us, and I asked, 'My friend, let us go with the shovel so that we are able to provide food for ourselves.' We walked on the road towards the market and we met two SLA, they were coming and we were going. I recognized one of them. The two of us passed and we did not look at them. The one turned around and called to me, 'My friend, where are you going?' I did not talk. I told my friend, 'Don't talk to them, let's move.' And again, he called to me, 'My friend, where are you going?' And again I did not say anything. I asked my friend to go along with me. He was afraid and he wanted to run away. But I grabbed his hand and told him that if he ran they would chase him down."

The SLA addressed him as "friend," but Musa interpreted this as a challenge and threat, rather than as a warm entreaty. As another sign of the inversion of the social world, the soldier/rebel was mocking normal relationships by referring to someone over whom he had direct power as a "friend." By calling him such, this rebel invoked a relationship to ridicule Musa, as he could seize the shovel if he wanted to.

"The one that was calling to me, the moment I spoke to my friend he removed a pistol and put it right on my forehead. He said, 'When you move, I will blow you away.' I started shaking. Then his friend came, he had a very long iron rod, very sharp in front. He came close to me, the pistol was right on my forehead. He started beating me with that iron. Anywhere he hit me blood came out. He beat me. He could do anything to me because I cannot do anything, because the pistol was on my forehead, the guy had told me when I do anything he will blow me away. So I stood there and he beat me, mercilessly. After a few minutes he started hitting me on my forehead. Blood started running everywhere. I was not feeling the blows any longer, I was only in my mind and I was thinking. I said to myself, 'What will be now, let it be. If this man will kill me let him kill me now. Because I'm done, I'm tired of this issue.' I decided to speak. It was the only thing I could do. So I told the man with the pistol, 'My friend, soldier man, this is too much. See now, blood is coming all over my body.' I wept."

Once again, Musa appeals to a relationship to save his life. Even though the soldier/rebel mocked that relationship initially, Musa believed he could achieve survival by reaching out, one human to another, and reminding him that, whatever the circumstances, they were known to each other. It had no effect.

"His friend did not care, he was not listening either. He did not like the fact that I was talking with that man. So that particular man, his friend, decided to drive the iron in my stomach. So he came with it with force! He just wanted to harm me. So when he came with it luckily I turned, I could see the iron so I decided to grab the iron like this and put it down." Musa was on his feet again, reenacting the moment when he sidestepped the spear and grabbed it. "We were on the bridge so I picked it up and threw it into the water." With his friend disarmed, the soldier with the weapon saw compassion as a reasonable option.

"So I asked the one to appeal for me to his friend. Luckily that man with the pistol decided to have sympathy for me. He told his friend to stop. When he stopped, the two of them came very close to me and started touching my pockets, touching every part of my body. I said, 'I don't have anything! I'm just going to town with my friend to get food.' They didn't do anything else, only asked us to get away from them. So I told my friend, 'Let's go.' We went back to the house, because the blood was still running from my body and I could not see. There was blood in my eyes. The people I passed were so shocked, seeing that my condition was changed! My body was doing very badly. When I saw my brother I told him what had happened, and he gave me small food for me to manage at home, without going back to the market. So we managed at home, until the baby came."

A NEW BABY AND THE ANNIHILATION OF THE TOWN

A smile flitted across Musa's face when he remembered the birth of his daughter, but quickly turned to a frown when he recalled the circumstances that followed. "Ramatu was born on December 4, 1999. It was a Saturday when Elizabeth gave birth. The baby was small but she screamed a lot! She was healthy and Elizabeth had enough milk to feed her because we were still getting small help from my brother. But the calm did not last very long. After a few months the gunship started coming."

Musa related that the situation inside Makeni had been calm when Ramatu was born. Issa Sesay had established order and welcomed the presence of the UN military observers in town. He allowed the United Nations to build a disarmament camp, and food and medical aid were beginning to trickle in. The calm was shattered when the government gunship arrived. Musa did not relate that Gibril Massaquoi's men had destroyed a disarmament camp, and that this had precipitated Tejan Kabbah's furious declaration that he would bomb the town to bare ground. All he told was that the gunship was coming from Freetown. Unlike Kadiatu, he took no positive stance with the rebels and against the government. He was standing, in his story, from the perspective of a father whose family was in danger. Taking the more cautious perspective of a Sierra Leonean citizen, rather than a defiant resident of Makeni, Musa worried first about his daughter.

"When the baby was a few months old the gunship started coming from Freetown. The situation was so desperate for us! We were so afraid, and Elizabeth was having trouble keeping the baby calm. Every time the noise started Ramatu cried. It made us so afraid. So I went around the house and gathered the few things that my brother had given us and I took them to the market. I sold them and I asked Elizabeth to move to Freetown. This place was not convenient for her and the baby; they needed to leave. She agreed with me so she took all the money I gave her and she walked with the baby until she could catch transport. Transport was so expensive! After the gunboats [gunship] started coming, most people had to go on foot until Mile 91, but if you could pay then you could ride longer. It was all the money we had but I gave it to her and I stayed here in the house."

Musa was now alone. People were fleeing Makeni by the hundreds, and he found it frightening and lonely, with only his friends passing through and his brother on the other side of town. With the town under attack every day, connecting with his brother seemed a remote possibility. He was a prisoner in his home.

"I stayed, but the situation was too rough! Every day the gunship would come and kill people, every day. So I decided to leave. I told myself that this situation is not good for me. Because there is no way for me to go and get food, I decided let the others don't come and kill me, let me move from this place. So I decided to go to Freetown. I had two friends with me inside the house then and we talked one night. We agreed to all move to Freetown together. When I left the house, I did not even lock it. I knew that if rebels wanted inside, they would do it, so let me not give them a reason to break the door. In June 2000 I went to Freetown. My daughter was almost six months old, she and Elizabeth had left Makeni a month before me. I thought the situation would calm down with the gunship but then I decided, let me not leave my child without a father."

For Musa to decide to leave Makeni with no money, therefore no possibility of taking a vehicle, meant he had assessed the situation as dire indeed. The three men had to walk the fifty miles to Mile 91 over rebel-held terrain, but they must have seen it as their only option. Rugiatu had been killed already, as had the three boys playing soccer in the street. On the strength of these stories alone, most people were abandoning the town.

"It took us three days to walk to Mile 91. Normally if you have a vehicle you can do it in one day, but we were very scared, we didn't know the way and there were so many obstacles on the road! Many people were trying to leave Makeni and they were just scattering along the road, dying from hunger because there was no one to tend to them. We were so hungry we could not help them. We just kept walking. I wanted to see my family. But when I got to Mile 91, I thought, 'Let me stay and assess the situation,' because we didn't know what was happening with the rebels. The peace had been broken with the gunboat [gunship] and the rebels were fighting the government again, and we did not know if it was safe to go to Freetown. I stayed three days then made a decision to move, because there was a rumor of a threat on the town. The SLA people said that if there was an attack they would kill all the displaced people. I decided that I was not fit to stay here, so I must leave this area and find my family in Freetown."

This explanation of the threats against the people at Mile 91 was confusing, but Musa did not clarify his meaning, beyond "in the attack the displaced would all die." Had the SLA forces that were loyal to the government warned the displaced that they were the primary targets of rebel attacks on the town? Or that they themselves would kill the displaced if there was an attack on the town? Either explanation made sense with the understanding that the majority of the displaced were from Makeni. After Kabbah's announcement that all Makeni residents were rebels, the fear and suspicion they encountered at Mile 91 resulted from broken trust in the country at large. Anyone who loved the president could not love Makeni residents. As had occurred in Makeni when people used the initial invasion as an excuse to rat out their enemies, an attack on Mile 91 would have been an excuse to purge the town of its unwanted refugees.

On the other hand, there remained the question of whether attacking rebels would attempt to kill all of "their" people who had deserted them. In spite of the gunship attacks, Issa Sesay interpreted civilians running from the town as a breach of loyalty. He had instituted law and order, brought in food and supplies, and generally ruled the town as a *pa,* with the understanding that, in spite of what the government was doing, he had a right to expect the loyalty of those who stayed. The mass desertion of the town upset the social contract that Sesay assumed had been forged, a serious betrayal considering that his love of the town meant he could expect people to endure hardship to support him. According to a former UN military observer, Sesay took offense that the gunship-induced mass exodus demolished his careful crafting of political legitimacy in his "show town." He had been forced into an ideological corner, where his social world and status did not matter. This made him unpredictable. Though Musa was not clear on why the refugees were being targeted, either explanation was plausible. Musa found it prudent to leave Mile 91.

"I knew that I did not want to be in Mile 91 for the attack, so I had to do whatever I needed to leave. I had just one thing left on me, my sleeping mat. It was fortunate I had it because these things were very much in demand at the time! There were so many people who had run with nothing, and I could get whatever money I needed for my mat. I sold it for seventeen thousand leones! But that was what I needed to get transport. So I sold my last property, and very early in the morning I got transport to Freetown, where I could try to find my family. I spent a year with them in Freetown."

As with Alimamy's story, where two years in Freetown pass in a narrative instant, Musa glossed over a year of his life in one sentence. That time was unremarkable not because it was "normal" but because it was unproductive; they lived in cramped quarters with relatives and were "just waiting" to return to Makeni. Musa narrated productive time in war, the struggle to make the chaotic and outrageous functional to everyday life. By anchoring his narrative on the importance of family, Musa refused to apologize for several years of interacting with rebels in a calm, respectful, nonchallenging manner.

RETURNING TO MAKENI AND CONFRONTING HIS TORMENTORS

It was Musa's mother who decided when he would return to Makeni; she wanted him to scout the town to ensure that it was safe for the women and children to return: "We heard that disarmament was going to start again in Makeni in 2001, and the place was a bit cool. We were encouraged by this news and my mother took the decision to send me back to Makeni. She wanted me to check on the house, and make sure it was safe for her and Elizabeth to return. So she and my brothers and sisters combined their small money so that I had transport and food for one or two weeks. I loaded my bundles on a taxi and I came back. The place was so rotten when I arrived! I was sad because all of the houses were vandalized, and our house . . . there was nothing left that would make it a house. The rebels, when they left a house as we the inhabitants forced them out, would break all the properties they could not take. Even the basins in the walls were smashed. And I had to use these local mats to sleep on, not even a foam mat for sale."

The state of Musa's house was typical, a result of rebels "pulling down" civilians, angry that they could no longer enjoy the fruits of occupation, and ensuring that if they did not have access to resources, no one would. This continued emphasis on material benefit *without* relationships was cited by many residents as a reason the government could not call them collaborators: how could they collaborate with people who, clearly angry about the *lack* of the relationships with civilians that would create the possibility of sharing homes, destroyed the homes when they left?

I toured one elderly gentleman's house just after he moved back in, and he despaired over the scorched earth tactics of ousted rebels. The mirrors were smashed, the sinks were pried out of the walls, even the plug sockets and the wood from doorframes had been pilfered. Graffiti covered the walls, brashly announcing who exactly was to blame for the destruction. In one room it was "Born Naked Crew," and in another "Kill Man No Blood Crew." No amount of scrubbing removed these insults from the walls. One had to save money to repaint. Musa and his family must have lived with the brutish reminders of the war for a long time before they could afford to erase them. But Musa was not deterred. He had unfinished business.

"When the war came to Makeni, all of our schooling at the vocational institute stopped. I was just a few months short of finishing my course, and I wanted to finish it now. While I was in Makeni the first week, I heard that the institute was opening again, so I decided to start. The next day they called us back to school to finish the course. I completed in a few months. It was still very early in disarmament, but the place was cool and it was fine to bring the family back. So I called them to return home. It was really fortunate for me that I had confidence to do this because I had a new job. The UN was giving money to NGOs to start the rehabilitation program for war-affected youth. I had a diploma, and I was eligible to be a facilitator for the programs."

The first days of the postwar boom were heady ones. Money was flowing liberally in Makeni. A battalion of Nigerian troops provided security, and they spent their wages freely. NGOs quickly followed, and they scrambled for eligible civilians to employ in various reintegration programs. There was a flood of funding for reintegration, due in part to the fear created by Robert Kaplan's 1997 article, "The Coming Anarchy." Kaplan wrote the article about his three-day trip to Sierra Leone, and used the country as an example of the "new wars" in Africa, triggered by scarcity and fought by a disaffected, unemployed youth underclass, the "loose molecules" of society. The only way to prevent anarchy was by reigning in the molecules. President Clinton faxed a copy to every American embassy in Africa. The State Department tasked an American consulting firm that had developed reintegration programs in Guatemala to do the same in Sierra Leone. These programs were meant to address the needs of all "war-affected youth" in the country. They offered courses to those who, whether or not they had fought, had lost their childhood and any chance at education due to the war. The idea was to tempt young men back into the fold with promises of skills and forgiveness. Aside from the money that would take care of his family, Musa thought this was a good idea on social grounds.

"These guys were hanging around, and a lot of them did not have the weapons to do official disarmament, so they were not happy. We the civilians were concerned about what they would do if they did not get some compensation, so I decided to be active in this. I went to the NGO office and I put myself forward as a facilitator. We were trying to bring these guys to the community, and we were being tutored in how to do this. My job was to bring the ex-combatants together."

I had heard many stories from other people of the lack of success of these non-DDR reintegration programs, so I asked: "What was your experience as a facilitator?"

"I was getting a lot of problems from these guys. We were trying to sit with them, teach them things and get them to be interested in the process, and most of these guys were requesting money. We had adult education courses, literacy classes, teaching them anything they needed to know to be successful in life, it was free for them and they were not interested! They were so anxious about money, expecting money for agreeing to participate. Some of them would nearly violence us when we told them there was no money and they were here to learn, but we trained people. Over time, we trained them. There were people there who were interested, and we would not let the bad ones damage our spirits. We kept everything in a low profile, not reacting when they threatened violence. We were trained to overlook these things, that if we didn't react they would realize that the power of the gun is gone, and they have to live with us. We were trying to encourage them. Many of them did not complete the course, but the majority said thanks to us, and they appreciated it."

After Musa's myriad life-threatening experiences at the hands of combatants, he was willing to step into a classroom with them, under constant threats of violence, and attempt to coax them back into the community. There was monetary compensation for him, which certainly helped his family, but Musa was driven by other factors. He did not "feel easy" about living in Makeni with ex-combatants if there was no attempt to transform them into good neighbors. He did not want to live in a town of the dispossessed and angry—this would be essentially the same situation as the infight. His emphasis on the facilitation of DDR was another political aspect of his narrative: he was certainly *not* on terms of friendships with all ex-combatants. He was clear in citing that his willingness to work with them was not motivated by love cultivated during the occupation, but by a fear of the continuation of *bad,* acrimonious relationships.

Musa offered to show me his teaching materials. The next day he knocked on my door, arms laden with spiral-bound manuals, dozens of notebooks, folders of news articles about reintegration, and photocopied academic articles positing various theories about the psyches of ex-combatants. He hovered over my shoulder as I flipped through the pages, many of them soiled and dog-eared from repeated browsing. The manual stressed the inherent goodness of people. Musa stressed the inherent need of people to be in nurturing relationships:

"The guys who had sense saw that they really damaged us in this town, especially we the young men. They were afraid at disarmament of what would happen to them, because so many of them were far from home. They did not speak Temne and they don't have family here. So we made these programs for them so they could help us rebuild the nation, and there would be no more reason for violence. Our facilitation trainer was really sympathetic to these guys, and he wanted us to be too. He said these guys are afraid that the community does not want them because they have no skills. But if we give them skills, then the community will know they are useful and appreciate it. Many of them were accepted. They are doing different kinds of jobs. Some of them are carpenters, and some of them went into tailoring and other jobs. It is just the reluctant ones that were sick for money that are not able to do anything for themselves presently. And they are not accepted, those who were just rushing for disarmament money."[5]

For Musa, the will to be engaged and productive is the necessary buy-in to a positive world; it is the first move away from eating. The selfishness, the "thirsting for money" of those who want to eat and think only of themselves had to be undone in order for peace to prevail. Those who refused training posed the biggest threat to the social world. Their idleness, their choice to be selfish rather than to improve themselves and nurture others was the biggest hurdle to Makeni being, in Musa's words, "normal." "It was like they didn't want to come back from the bush. When they refused to go through the training everyone knew they were the wicked ones. These guys . . . once the training had finished we were encouraging them to take their graduation money and go back to their homes in the south. These guys who just wanted money . . . I think they must have caused big problems in their particular area and they can't go home. Their families would not take these guys back if they committed atrocities at home. So they stayed during disarmament, even when the government was telling them to go home. And we did not chase them out. I think that is another reason people call us collaborators."

"Because you haven't chased out the wicked ones?"

"No, it is the good ones that are still here! We don't know where the wicked ones have gone, but I do not see them, the ones who damaged me. I know them but I don't know where they have gone. They had no friends so they left. But I accept the ones who did the training and appreciate. We in Makeni . . . well I think Makeni people are a bit liberal!" He laughed. "I know I can't live peacefully if I am grudging against you, so I just decide to live peacefully, if you too live peacefully."

There are two important aspects of this explanation. The first, countering the narrative of collaboration, is that the ex-combatants the government saw in Makeni after the war, the "good" ones, comprised a nonrepresentative sample of occupation relationships. The rebels who populated Musa's story, because their relationships in Makeni were all bad, left town. This makes the scarred homes and the occupation's dead the only true revelations of noncollaboration: revelations of endurance, suffering, and violence. And these things cannot speak.

Musa's second theory, of coexistence rather than vengeance, speaks to how life is better when rooted in positive relationships. "Living peacefully" implies that one is dedicated to the things that matter—work, care, family, future—rather than to upsetting the social world and causing bad feelings, fear, and violence through selfishness and eating. Musa does not comment on whether ex-combatants ever fully integrated, just that they would be left alone if they agreed to live through love. It was up to individuals to decide if they wanted to welcome ex-combatants into their lives. Musa chose not to do so, for his own peace of mind. Instead he created new relationships that would give his daughters the best possible beginning. He leveraged his connections among NGOs to maintain steady employment after his work as a facilitator ended. Eventually he became the caretaker at a home inhabited by expatriate NGO workers, and secured a steady wage and a monthly bag of rice. It provided the stability he craved for his family.

"Presently Ramatu is in school. I want her to continue, and the little one, when she is ready. I want them to learn. I want them to do things I was unable to do, heights I was unable to reach. I want them to reach that particular level."

Musa crafted his narrative carefully around the political imperative of proving noncollaboration through actions dictated by the necessity of providing for family. The violence he suffered was evidence of his status; his scars were a physical narrative of government neglect and betrayal that spoke for themselves, even as he, wanting peace, did not accuse the government outright. However, it was his love for his family that carried his story along, like a ship on a strong tide, and anchored it securely in the end.

"The RUF Thought I Was on Their Side"

The Politician

Throughout the war in Sierra Leone, love consisted of explicit practices of sacrifice and choice, most often geared towards immediate survival. Very few were in a position to achieve permanence during the war; rebel commanders were among the few in a position to become big, however temporarily. People from David to Adama did the daily work of creating and nurturing small relationships that eased the hardships of war, but these relationships were with other "small" people, who had few resources of their own. Becoming like the cotton tree was a remote dream, unless an individual could tap into outside connections and resources.

The war destroyed most rural big men, as they lost their farms and people to looting, death, and displacement, and were left without a foundation on which to seek permanence. Simultaneously, the space emerged for different people to take advantage of the outside resources that emerge through war and postwar international connections with expatriate governmental and NGO workers and organizations. Individuals with this access leveraged themselves into positions to capitalize on wartime gains, to secure themselves and their families in the aftermath. After all, during postwar rebuilding, the greatest resource is foreign money.

At the same time, however, bigness can only be maintained with social recognition and respect. Respect requires large-scale loyalty, which requires investment. This is best illustrated in Makeni in the town council elections of 2004. This was Makeni's first postwar election, and the winning councilors were elected because they had risked themselves to support townspeople during the war. One sheltered and cared for destitute women, another reorganized the APC to contest national elections, still another brought food aid past RUF checkpoints. All had been members of the town's educated elite, the people who had a responsibility to love Makeni and fight for the town, while still maintaining a personal resource base to nurture their own families. This is the delicate balancing act of the big: one must be well positioned, calculating, and also responsive and caring.

This is the story of one such man, Michael Kamara, who moved from some social privilege as a teacher to being a town councilor, elected in 2004. His wartime actions were duplicitous and ruffled many feathers, especially those of the national government, which he spent the occupation years publicly attacking. Michael was a staunch APC member, but he was viewed by residents as having their own, and not the party's, interests at heart. His unfailing loyalty to the town, even as his hard-line opposition to the government earned him enemies, conferred the ability to be big among his people. Throughout the war he risked his reputation to stand up for the town, and in the elections, the townspeople showed their gratitude.

The problem of political office lies in the need to balance public and private responsibilities, as constituents are loyal because they receive, or expect to receive, personal care. What Sierra Leoneans and the international community often call *corruption* is more accurately described by the word *patronage:* a thread of loyalty binding people together in ways *corruption* fails to describe. Though councilors are elected through democratic means, their constituents expect to be appreciated for their loyalty, and not always through public projects. An elected individual in Sierra Leone engages constantly in the gray area of ensuring that enough people receive enough to prevent them feeling betrayed. At the same time, s/he must also maintain good relationships with donors, who operate on different standards of investment and success. There is always someone with the power to topple a big man, and many constituents who can find new patrons. It is risky, and not everyone aspires to be a political big man. Michael, however, justified his political ambitions as a safety net for a father who felt familial care was not guaranteed. Though he pursued politics to bolster his long-term survival chances, he also framed his involvement as a challenge to the SLPP government, to love Makeni as much as its own power base, or be ousted locally.

Whereas most residents' concerns during the war were limited to the security of their families, Michael Kamara used his social savvy to maneuver himself into a position of relative power and privilege. As international aid drew down, he shifted his relationships from international to local actors, and was elected to the council with promises to fight for Makeni. Though dreams of what the council could do were large, lack of funding hindered the drive to be big, even for councilors' families, and battles for resources began. When a corruption scandal erupted, Michael saw an opportunity to become chairman, *pa* for the town. This required gaining the love and trust of the townspeople and other party members. They had to believe that he would not shame them, and that he would look after their interests in return for their support.

When I met Michael in the offices of the Makeni town council, he was a force of nature: large, energetic, full of bluff and bluster, and carrying a black umbrella which he shook out and propped carefully against the table when he arrived. It was the damp and dirty depths of the rainy season, and a downpour hammered relentlessly on the tin roof, nearly drowning out our greetings. Michael mopped water from his face and attempted to smooth the dripping folds of his clothes. He finally gave up and shrugged, thrusting himself into his seat and leaning eagerly over the table. "I see you are very interested in Makeni!" he exclaimed. "And you have been getting everyone's life story! Do you want mine as well?"

I nodded and smiled, explaining that I wanted to know how it was that Makeni people had survived the war and were rebuilding their lives in the aftermath, and how his own story fit into this picture. From that, he moved straight into his earliest memories, which were not of privilege and opportunity. Michael knew grief at a tender age. He also learned about care, as the loss of his mother prompted his aunt to adopt him. By framing his story with familial sacrifice, he created the foundation for a narrative where family love is irreplaceable. His status as an educated man was proof of his aunt's love, and he judged others on their educations—were they given affection as children, did they work hard and sacrifice, and did they therefore deserve to be big as adults? For Michael, the accrued wisdom of his life justified his position, whereas the illiteracy, ignorance, and narrowness of others, Sankoh included, precluded their legitimate bids for big status.

LOSS AND CARE AS A CHILD

"I was born in Port Loko district in 1950, but my late aunt brought me over to Makeni when I was twelve because she wanted me to go to school. I had lost my mother at a very young age and was under my grandmother's control. My aunt was concerned that my grandmother would just let me have an idle mind, so she brought me to Makeni so that I would go to school and she could supervise me. I was a troublesome boy, but my aunt was very strict! She had me go to school in the morning, she had people monitor my activities in school, she was friendly with the teachers and would ask them questions. And we lived next door to my teacher! So I had no way to escape school. But I was very carefully looked after. She gave me a nice bed, nice clothes that I had to be careful with! And she gave me shoes. I had never had shoes in the village. She really cared a lot for me. So I was always in school, and thank God, I am what I am today. I believe she contributed a lot."

Michael's gratitude toward his aunt framed the importance of care in his own family. For him, she had become part of the cotton tree, an ancestor whose name is spoken with reverence. Of course, his aunt had other reasons to nurture Michael carefully: she was never able to have any children of her own. Michael was her only opportunity to ensure her comfort in old age. She loved him, but also wanted him to love her and return her care. She owned a restaurant in the middle of the lorry park, and Michael remembered that she was an excellent cook, and a famous one. "So we had a lot of customers. Nearly everyone who passes would go through our own shop to eat."

Michael thrived in secondary school, and continued his education at the Catholic mission teaching college in Makeni in the 1970s. Upon graduating he found employment at his high school alma mater as a teacher. For twenty-six years he taught the town's youth, weathering the storm of the junta in 1997, until the RUF invasion in 1998. Michael was the only member of his family who did not flee when the rebels invaded, and he was adamant that his early actions were not done explicitly to support the RUF against the SLPP. That occurred later, in spite of the fact that the government had already abandoned the town.

HEDGING BETS, GAINING TRUST, AND VOTING FOR PEACE

"Why did I stay when the RUF invaded? Well, before the rebels invaded, things were still bad. At school, the salaries stopped coming. We did not have salaries for September, October, November, and December. And I have a wife and four children. There were eight of us including my uncle and aunt, seven others depending on me, and I didn't have money. So when my uncle decided to escape with my aunt, my wife, and the children, I decided to stay. I was sure that the rebels were just passing through. I stayed to protect the house, or if it came to war then I would escape with just a few items. That was the plan; we did not know they would stay in Makeni. So on the 23rd, when we were attacked on a Wednesday night, Thursday the 24th, and then finally the 25th, on the 26th, Saturday, the RUF summoned a meeting of everyone who stayed. I went to the meeting with my vice principal so we could witness things at the town hall. We were told to go to the bush, use a megaphone, and ask people to come out. They told us that they have come to stay with us and establish their government here."

The RUF recognized Michael and the vice principal as prominent residents, and it was to their political and tactical advantage to appear to control them. Michael's voice, as a teacher, carried weight, and he in turn did as he was told. His reasons for obeying resonated with what I heard from several other prominent people who were used by the RUF to control the town: "When someone is waving a gun at you and threatening your life, you do not have the power to ask them not to do that. They sent me to the bush and I complied. If I did not come back they would kill a lot of people trying to flush me out." Michael called to other residents in the bush, and they agreed to return. He hoped by agreeing to help the RUF that they would not target him as a threat to their authority.

Though Alimamy narrated cultivating relationships with rebels in service of his family, and thus the social world, Michael's will to forge political alliances was not above reproach. He was careful with how much he revealed of his relationships, both to me and to other people. Relationships resonate, so if a person is loyal to someone who is wicked, they are wicked by association. Michael was willing to risk having his loyalties questioned in the short run to gain the trust of more powerful individuals, thereby leveraging himself into better political position. One could gain permanence by befriending influential people, rather than by simply burdening oneself with more people. Michael always went straight to big people, however, he crafted his narrative to emphasize that he sought power in the interest of Makeni people. He wanted their survival, whether or not it appeared in the best light. To do this required some unsavory alliances. Complying with the initial RUF request was just the tip of the iceberg.

From the moment of the 1998 invasion, Makeni had a leadership problem. The paramount chief, section chiefs, police officers, and judges were threats to RUF authority, which placed their lives in danger. The RUF were issuing a direct challenge to Kabbah by staging an occupation, and their first task was raiding the police station and government offices and murdering everyone inside. Makeni's leadership structure collapsed as civil servants and respected elders fled, fearing for their lives. With such a leadership gap, even a lowly teacher could suddenly become a prominent figure. Michael explained that people accepted his obsequiousness with commanders, as he did not use these relationships to exploit residents:

"People trusted me because . . . well, because I did not take advantage of them through my working relationship with the RUF. There were some who did take advantage. When the paramount chief left there were many lowly section chiefs—just the representative of part of a village or one block of the township—who rushed to fill this gap. They became the representative of some RUF commander who wanted to exert himself on a neighborhood, and many section chiefs started calling themselves full chiefs! And they ran protection rackets, forcing people to give them food or cigarettes so the RUF guys would not cause them trouble, or they would just harass people. I did not do this, so I had the trust of the RUF and also the trust of the people."

Given his postinvasion position as civilian leader and RUF liaison, Michael was asked to attend a conference in Freetown. "From eight months after Makeni was invaded, the UN boss went around to the different towns and organized a nationwide consultative conference as to whether we as a nation were going to pursue war or peace against the rebels. She went everywhere to find delegates to get an idea of what all the leaders in Sierra Leone wanted to do about the rebels. It took a long time to organize this. So the representatives from the three provinces went to Freetown. And the northern region—all of us in Makeni and elsewhere—voted for a peace line, while the south, east, and the western area chose the war option. The war line meant we would continue fighting the RUF with arms, while the peace line meant that we were willing to bring them to the table to negotiate. We in the northern region voted for a peaceful resolution. We wanted peace because the rebels were occupying our homes and there was no way we could ask them to leave. Did we want the army coming in and setting fire to our homes to flush out the rebels? Of course we did not! We just wanted them to go and leave us, no more violence. But we were booed in Freetown! They started calling us rebels, and this is why we were against going to war. But it was the year 2000 and we had been occupied for two years! There was no way we could go to war; we could not advocate bombing in order to end the war, because this was our home! The government had just left us languishing for that time, doing nothing, and now they were attacking us for wanting peace."

This statement is a clear example of Michael setting up Makeni as a marginal place: attacked from all sides and able to depend only on itself. The "leaders" from the south and east who voted for war came from areas where RUF conscription had torn families apart, with people acting against their will to save their lives, and yet according to Michael they showed no sympathy for their occupied fellow citizens. He portrayed this conference as a harbinger of future politics. The crucial difference in the semantics is, again, a question of loyalty. A place that is occupied, forcibly and against its will, must be liberated in order for the nation to be whole. If people actively fought the rebels, this would be the case. A "rebel place"—with rebels as residents, belonging to that place—is not part of the nation. In order for the nation to save itself, that place and its people must be destroyed. Michael emphasized that Makeni was in danger, and this was the reason he approached Foday Sankoh to plead for peace. Viewed from the outside, Kamara approaching Sankoh after this conference would appear to be consorting with the enemy.

CONVINCING THE RUF TO SUPPORT PEACE

Though Michael appeared to be assisting the RUF, he insisted that his only loyalty was to the town, that he dealt with the RUF out of necessity. He stated that he believed that although some administrators in Makeni were reasonable, at its core, the RUF leadership was faulty, based on Foday Sankoh's illusion of being a big man through his access to diamonds, but lacking the substance of wisdom and care.

"The RUF had a good plan, if you sit and talk with them, but the leadership was wrong about the whole thing. Foday Sankoh, he was very much interested in me when he came to Makeni. We held two meetings, and the general public was impressed that we could have a civilized dialogue. But I never trusted him, and I never liked him. He was just pretending, he was all bluff and bluster. He was not educated, and he used force because he had money. He had diamonds, so he threw his weight around." Michael had appeared in public with Sankoh, and so qualified those interactions with his "true" feelings. A consistent thread in his narrative is his lack of respect for uneducated people, whom he feels have no right to determine the destiny of others, no right to be big in the modern world, in direct contrast to his own position.

"I remember when we were about to start disarmament in 2000, this was right before the seizure of the UNAMSIL team here in Makeni. Foday Sankoh called me to Freetown and asked me how I saw the situation. I told him outright, I said, 'Look, you said you want to hear from me. I want you to go into the Sierra Leone Broadcasting System and make a public announcement. You will say, "In the interest of peace for my people, I accept that the date proposed, the 16th of April, 2000, is the day for disarmament."' Disarmament in this country was supposed to be simultaneous, because they built the disarmament camps around the country. I said, 'If you go on the radio, make a statement, "In the interest of peace for my own people, I will accept this date that disarmament starts."' I said, 'I am not giving you the assurance that you will win the elections, but you will make a very formidable opposition to government if you are a man of your word.'

"He thought for some time, raised his head, bowed it, and then he called on the most illiterate officer in the room, Komba Bundama, who was later killed in a battle. He was a very wicked fellow. He had polio, but because he had a powerful command presence, he had a following, even though he was evil and had no education. Sankoh called on him and said, 'Commander Komba, you know Mr. Kamara?' He said, 'Yes Pa, I know him in Makeni. He is a good man.' Sankoh said, 'He has come with a suggestion that we should submit and accept the date for disarmament.' And Komba said, 'No, no, no, Pa! If we allow it, the government will just come and kill us!' Like that! Sankoh turned around, and said to me, 'Mr. Kamara,' to quote him exact, '*Yu don yeri, Ah only di lida, den dey di wan den dey fɛt.*' So he was saying that if the fighters say no, I will also say no, because they are the ones that fight. I shook my head, I said, 'Eh?' He said, 'Yes, this is a fact!' I said, 'It is not a fact! I don't want to argue because you are the leader. Because you are the leader, you have the power to tell them what to do!' He said, 'No, let's talk about other things.'"

Michael frames this conversation as his plea to Sankoh to end the war, for the nation, but especially for Makeni. Sankoh refusing to surrender was interpreted as a failure of true big man substance—wisdom and concern for people—rather than as emergent from an egalitarian ethos, which many RUF ex-combatants suggested that Sankoh possessed. As it turned out, Sankoh did accept the date for disarmament. Resonant with

Michael's suggestion that he was merely lusting for more resources as a route to power, Sankoh embraced a lavish settlement with the Lomé Accords, then abandoned his fighters. Only a few days after the conversation Michael reported, Gibril Massaquoi reacted to this breach of inter-RUF loyalty by assaulting the disarmament compound in Makeni. This was followed shortly by Kabbah's decision to bomb, which was a repeated theme in Michael's account. Often he moved to the subject of the gunship, letting it dominate the conversation so that I understood clearly, from the perspective of someone whose home is bombed by his own government, just what betrayal looks like.

"LOYALTY" MEANS DENOUNCING THE GOVERNMENT

"Life in Makeni came to the worst when the government used the helicopter gunship, which destroyed a lot of property and lives. Kabbah decided on the gunship after the RUF guys attacked all the peacekeepers. That was a way to scare the rebels, but to the amazement of all, almost all the people killed were civilians. Every time it came, it targeted another place where civilians gathered. The worst time was when it went straight to the lorry park and killed a pregnant lady there. She couldn't run away because her belly was heavy, and the gunship dropped a bomb straight on her. The pilot saw that she was pregnant. Was she a rebel threat? She was buying rice. And now she is buried right next to the lorry park."

Once again, Rugiatu Kanu was summoned into conversation as the icon of government betrayal. Michael used her death to make it clear that Kabbah was taking revenge on Makeni and, having obliterated the town, would take it back on his own terms. Michael framed himself as an ardent supporter of gunship withdrawal, which gained him more support among civilians in Makeni, among whom he had the reputation of caring only about the town's best interests. He brought his social resources to bear on convincing the president to stop the bombing, though he did not petition President Kabbah himself. Michael had contacts at the United Nations from the initial conference, and took his protests there.

"The UN finally intervened and said that the government cannot continue sending in the gunship because it destroys life. So the government was advised to withdraw the helicopter gunship forthwith! I also championed that cause, I left here June 9, 2000 and went to Freetown. I had many political reasons to go, and used the chance to make several contacts. I was very lucky to board a vehicle that was owned by an NGO. They let me on the vehicle because I had some important information for the British High Commission in Freetown. We had taken custody of one of their soldiers who had been seized by the RUF. They abandoned him in Makeni and my friend took him in, and we pled with the RUF that we should be allowed to take him to Freetown."

This part of Michael's narrative has no support in factual accounts, as there are no records of British captives in Makeni after the escape of Major Ashby and other UN observers in March 2000. It would not be otherwise clear how he established contacts at the British High Commission, and if this was information he did not want me to know, it was best to frame his narrative as, once again, a selfless act undertaken both because he was compassionate and because Makeni might benefit. The *truth* of Michael's narrative was his dedication to saving Makeni, which just happened to put him in contact with important, influential people. If a white man *did* stay in Makeni during the gunship bombings, that information has otherwise been lost.

"This man was very brave; in the weeks he was with us he wanted to confront the gunship himself! He thought that if they saw a white guy in Makeni they would think twice about whether or not it was just rebels living here. When he heard the helicopter, he came out of the house. The only problem was that the rebels also had a Ukrainian who was helping them. And we were afraid that maybe they would just send some bombs here thinking that this is the Ukrainian. And he said, no, no, this is not the case. Let me just come out. But already the information had been given to the pilot to search for this Ukrainian rebel, so he was unable to stop the bombings. But by then the commission knew their man was in Makeni, and they wanted him back.

"The RUF trusted me at this point because I had done everything they asked of me. They told me to go to the bush with a megaphone and I did it. They did not want to lose me, but they let me leave Makeni so I could negotiate with the British to get him back and make them look good. The RUF thought I was on their side! They did not know that after my conversation with Sankoh, after he decided to let these ragtag boys run the war, that I could not support anything they were doing. I could not do it even though they were fighting the government. I was going to fight my own battles for this town. But under their own belief they let me go and I could get the word out as to what was really happening in Makeni. So I spoke with a lady who was a reporter, I was interviewed in the vehicle and I gave her the information about what was happening in Makeni, especially how many civilians had already been killed by the gunship."

BEING A DOUBLE AGENT, BEING LOYAL TO YOUR TOWN

Michael arrived at the British High Commission in June 2000, and he convinced the British government to pay him to spy on the RUF leadership in Makeni. His greatest opportunity to influence events was the Abuja peace talks, which he attended officially as an RUF representative. The talks occurred in 2001 in Nigeria, and were a last-ditch effort by the United Nations to negotiate resolution with the RUF as the international community pushed more decisively—in the wake of Britain's successful raid on the West Side Boys—towards military resolution. Michael's comment on the RUF's official position was, "We had cause to support peace." His meaning was that the RUF had put itself in a precarious position, where its political respectability—and the vice presidency Foday Sankoh had been given under the Lomé Accords of 1999—was in dire jeopardy. The attack on UN peacekeepers in Makeni and Foday Sankoh's bodyguards firing on unarmed protestors in Freetown had forced the RUF into a weak negotiating position. The only way they could recoup these losses—at least, in a way that would assure the cadres amnesty—was by agreeing to more peace talks. The Makeni leadership, acting on its own, sent Michael as their representative. By agreeing to go, Michael officially presented an image of collaboration for the rest of the nation, while Issa Sesay was himself maneuvering into a position of power, reinforcing his image as that of legitimate political big man, as well as RUF big man.

"When we were about to go to the peace settlement in Abuja, the RUF leadership felt that Makeni should be represented by a civilian. I was chosen, and in June 2001 we went to Abuja to sign the peace accord. Just before that I had gained employment for one year and six months for the British High Commission. But it was purely under secret cover. Nobody knew that I was operating on a double standard, in a double role! The RUF, they trusted me so much when we went to Abuja, the way I was attacking the government. They had a feeling I was totally with them. I was very outspoken, attacking government, saying that they are not trying to bring peace to this country."

Michael's assault on the government was not disingenuous; even if he had not been representing the RUF in Makeni, he was being loyal to his hometown. Food and medicine were scarce and inhabitants blamed their plight on a vengeful government. Even as the government had the capability to use the helicopter to deliver supplies for civilians, it instead tried to kill them. Michael's passion on behalf of the citizens of Makeni was not dictated by the RUF presence. In his mind, the RUF occupation merely proved what he believed to be true already: the government hated Makeni, and wanted to cast it out of the nation. His loyalty to his home meant attacking the government. This was a tremendous gamble, as his position was open to multiple interpretations: rebel, collaborator, loyal son of Makeni, greedy would-be big man, or wicked opportunist.

"Finally we went to Abuja, and Kabbah's current vice president, Solomon Berewa, then Minister Berewa, he went as well. And the man who is now in the custody of the Special Court, Hinga Norman, went as the representative of the Kamajors. They picked me up as a civilian RUF representative, and two army officers went to represent the armed forces. These two were my friends. They were at Teko Barracks in Makeni in the 1970s when they were just junior officers. They knew me because I had taught their kids! Just after the fourth session at Abuja, they called me. They said, 'Hey, Mr. Kamara, come. Why did you stay in Makeni?' I said, 'Well, I had no means to run away because I don't have money. I don't want to go and suffer and die in the bush.'

"One of them took offense and challenged me, asking me why I was attacking the government. I said, 'If I am on the side of the RUF then I must definitely attack you, because we know that you are not doing the correct thing. If you allow the rebels to run around, it is your fault. The war started in Kailahun, so if you allow the rebels to stay in Makeni and declare Makeni as a headquarters, that is what annoys me the most.'" Michael paused in his story to explain further. "You cannot just declare Makeni the rebel headquarters when the place was only occupied seven years into the war. They came to settle here and suddenly declared Makeni as their headquarters. It was a pleasure for the government to change things around, to rewrite history so the war started here, just to punish us in the north. This was all because Makeni people were mostly for the APC. Kabbah took great offense that we did not like him, that we were not loyal, so he decided to punish us. And that is why he let the RUF stay, and that is why he sent the gunship."

Michael, like many people in Makeni, believes that Kabbah's hatred for Makeni did not originate with the RUF invasion of the place; rather the invasion and occupation were expressions of how much Kabbah already disliked the town and wanted to punish residents because they did not vote for his party. Makeni had been the seat of the APC party since the country's independence, and Kabbah came to power under the SLPP. Michael saw Kabbah rationalizing how he was owed love: because the APC watched over the deterioration of the country before the war, by leading the country through war, he could expect the support of every citizen.

Michael evoked a typical sentiment in Makeni: love is not given freely, and cannot be earned through fear, neglect, and punishment. Residents did not profess loyalty simply because Kabbah was president and vowed to end the war. Unfortunately for them, Kabbah was willing to exert his authority just as Siaka Stevens had done: those disloyal to the regime were punished to prevent them gaining the resources and adherents to challenge it. Kabbah refused to liberate an invaded town, turned a blind eye to the occupation, bombed the "rebel place," and rewrote the war to lay the blame on Makeni. Thus did he punish the town for not voting for his party and being ungrateful for his leadership. Michael harnessed these negative feelings to move himself into a position of power in Makeni by publicly attacking Kabbah and being openly APC.

"I was leaking the secrets of the RUF to the British High Commission. They wanted to know what was going on behind the scene, to know what the RUF leadership was really thinking. Because every time they had gone to peace talks in the past, the RUF had broken the accord. Would they tell the truth this time? The High Commission employed me to find out for them. I went to RUF meetings and then I passed information to the British. They wanted to know exactly what to talk about with the RUF, and I coordinated that. But this was secret, so I didn't tell my friends who had come to Abuja representing the army. I just explained everything to them that was already true: that the government, not the RUF, was killing Makeni, and it was my responsibility to speak for the people of Makeni and get the world to understand how we were experiencing the war. And these guys understood, they were northerners as well and they were satisfied. We were all frustrated: why did the government allow the RUF to stay here? Because when they attacked, the government merely withdrew all the surviving soldiers. And they sat idle for over a year, and nobody tried to do anything! They never tried to assist us before they sent the jets to bomb us. When the war reached the peak, when the rebels seized members of UNAMSIL, they sent the helicopter gunship, rather than sending in troops to liberate us.

"But the war was difficult to understand, because everyone was just reacting to what the other side was doing. The RUF had spies in Freetown, and the government also had spies in Makeni. The government got information from their spies, who were feeding them information on the developments in Makeni with the RUF. The RUF also had people who gathered information on when the gunship was being sent. They would radio RUF command in Makeni, 'Hey, the gunship will be here at this time!' And you found all the rebel commanders would disappear from their posts."

For residents, the fact that actual RUF members were never killed in the gunship attacks was emblematic of longstanding government hatred for the town; Kabbah was using the occupation as an excuse to kill his political enemies. They remembered that the RUF had "taught" them to run when they heard the gunship even as commanders received advanced warning about gunship attacks and could themselves be out of harm's way. The more civilians were killed, the more the surviving residents hated the government. Rage against Kabbah drove Michael's verbal attacks, even as he knew that the RUF, though seemingly buoyed by his stance, did not harbor humanitarian intentions towards residents. They preyed on Makeni's isolation by courting public opinion. Actions that occur underneath everyday activities are potentially powerful generators of big status; RUF commanders were not immune to underhanded activity in support of their quest for legitimacy as big men.[1]

KNOWING WHEN TO LAY LOW AND WHEN TO BECOME BIG

The first Abuja Peace Accord triggered a massive deployment of UN peacekeepers throughout the country, including Makeni. RUF authority was coming to an end. Not willing to jeopardize his wartime political and social gains, Michael consolidated relationships with the civilians he believed would lead the town once demobilization was complete. Michael was careful to remain cordial with Issa Sesay, as he knew the latter had democratic political ambitions, and he needed to maintain appearances as the RUF's man in Abuja. Otherwise, he made arrangements to look after his family in a postwar world, and assessed his options for future employment:

"Since the talks I just kept a low profile, came back to Makeni, reported the matter to Issa Sesay, the commander in Makeni. Issa was from Makeni and I taught him in form one for a few months before he decided to go to the government boys' school in Magburaka. But he still had a lot of respect for me, so when I came back to Makeni, he made sure that I had enough food. Only one child was staying with me, the rest of the family was still in Freetown. Things were becoming cool rapidly because the RUF had no choice but to accept the presence of the UN. Within a year they started paying the teachers again, and once in a while I went to Freetown to collect my salary. I would leave some with my wife, and then I came back. When the war finally ended in 2002, I came with two other boys, and at the end of 2002 my wife and the youngest decided to join me. She wanted to make sure we had total peace before she moved the family back completely."

Michael's work situation was not as peacefully resolved as his family life. He was still on his school's payroll, but through his covert position with the British High Commission he had met Dr. Francis Kai-Kai, who was directing the disarmament program. Dr. Kai-Kai offered him employment with NCDDR, which he accepted just as he finished his contract with the High Commission. His connections with powerful people who knew he was a spy, and not an RUF lackey, were paying off. Michael was suddenly doing too well compared to his compatriots, and this was stirring up jealousy. In his narrative, his ability to be big required he relinquish one job, lest he appear too wealthy.

"I resigned from teaching in 2001. It was not my own fault that I had to resign, the principal had given me flexibility because of my other commitments. Mr. Kai-Kai said, 'Mr. Kamara, you have done very well. We want to give you some compensation so you will also share part of the cake!' So I was made adjutant of one of the camps. After this I had a meeting with the principal. I said to him, 'For now, I have gained some employment with the DDR program. The government compensates me as a teacher, and Dr. Kai-Kai compensates me.' I explained to him that I had other commitments. I needed to know what he wanted me to do, now that the minister for education has announced that all teachers who have not appeared in their schools will receive their last salaries and be terminated. He said that wasn't a problem, and that I could go back on the roster and teach when I was not working at the camp. So I split my time."

Whatever the actual substance of the conversation, Michael had to be upfront about his varying commitments in order to stave off bad feelings that he was eating, which would put all of his success in danger as he could have been fired from both jobs, or have family and friends emerge to demand a share. Dr. Kai-Kai made no attempt to hide the fact that he was offering Michael employment with DDR because he was loyal, a rationale that was clear in his offer to share in the "cake" of international funding for disarmament. There were many sources of jealousy: those who felt they could compel Michael to share with them, and those who, because they had no stake in his success, would be content to pull him down, suffering no ill effects themselves. Michael's fellow teachers were in the latter category:

"My personal successes became a problem because when I came back to school, some saw me with a new bike, going up and down with the DDR. Some people took offense and became jealous. They complained to the board that some teachers in Makeni are receiving salaries without coming to school. So they passed a decision in a board meeting, that whoever does not show up in his or her own school every day will lose their salary. I said, 'Mr. Principal I have explained to you. I will not abandon this DDR job for a teaching job because I am making something far better than what the government is paying me in school. So if you say so then I shall resign.'

"He said, 'What about your benefits?' I said, 'I am not going in for benefits when the other teachers are not getting their own pay, so forget about me.' So I took my things and left. After the final disarmament, I got my final severance pay from DDR, and I decided that it was time to build a new house for my family. The other one had been spoiled during the war because there was no money to maintain it, and it was hard to have my family live there. I bought some land, and I had enough money for some materials. I raised one wall, which is standing. But I could not make enough money to complete it. Then I remembered that the British High Commission had not given me my final salary. So I traveled to Freetown and they paid me. While I was in Freetown I bought a power saw to do timber, and a grating machine to grate cassava. From this I am able to make a small income. But I thank God for it because it is consistent, there will always be a need for a saw and grater!"

With a small but reliable income, Michael steadied his family situation even as he knew that he might have made a mistake by choosing the large temporary salary over a smaller but constant teacher's salary. By using his DDR salary to purchase land and raise one wall, he was able to stave off demands from others, as the money had already been invested. The power tools provided only enough to feed and care for his family.

Having resigned from teaching and yet armed with the knowledge that his wartime relationships would soon cease to bear fruit, Michael decided to cement his wartime gains by putting himself forward for the town council. "In 2004 I was very close with Ernest Koroma, the leader of the APC, who was then just the opposition leader. People in town wanted to pay me back for all I had done for them. So they asked me if I was interested in running for town council. I said, 'I have never had an interest in politics, but since Ernest has served as the leader of the APC, I will follow him.' We in Makeni, we in the APC, are all in this together, brothers. We grew up in the same neighborhood on the west side of Makeni, just one street apart. So we were very close, although I am ahead of him in terms of age. That's how I came to politics, and I was very popular anyway. Even though there were many people running for seats in this ward, I was one of the favorites. So in May 2004 we emerged as victors in the election, and June 20th I was sworn into the council."

In spite of all that Michael had done for Makeni during the war, his decision to run for a position on the new town council could only occur with the support of Ernest Koroma, a support based on a long familial history of neighborliness and loyalty to the town. Michael would have risked losing his status if he had run for a council seat without support. Losing face by losing the election would have meant the end of his power play as a potential big man. However, campaigning with the APC—though it was the only logical route by which he could climb to potential big man status, having spent the entire war attacking the SLPP government—meant he could thrive only within the party's own fortunes. That is the essence of being a big man through love: it entails embracing the available nurturing, and achieving within those bounds.

AN APC COUNCIL IN AN SLPP WORLD

When Michael stated that people in Makeni wanted to repay him for his work during the occupation, this meant they would vote for him over everyone else. His vigorous defense of the town against Kabbah proved his loyalty to the town, and thus to the APC, no matter the questions about his RUF involvement. Indeed, he was the town's primary supporter against the conditional love of Kabbah's government. A vote for Michael was support not just for him and the APC, but also for the region's opposition to the SLPP and Tejan Kabbah, whom they still resented for the gunship. An all-APC council was elected, and they faced an uphill battle in an SLPP nation. Kabbah did not forgive the town, or the APC.

"Things are very difficult for us as a young council. We have the expectations of the town on us; they want to see results immediately! And the government does not back us because we were elected under the banner of the opposition. We are all opposition, as the north. They treat us badly even though, by the tenets they agreed with the international community, they were supposed to work hand-in-hand with us. The government wanted the UN to only channel money through them. The international community said that all support must be nonpartisan. This was because they wanted to assess the strength of the government as well as the opposition. They wanted to see how popular you are from 1996 till now, to get a trajectory of politics in the country. They wanted to see if other people were doing good work, if you had the support of the people even if you were not SLPP, and then they would give you money as well.

"And then look what happened: the SLPP lost the northern region headquarters and the capital city. And that is a big blow! Of the nineteen councils, you had only Makeni town council totally APC. And Freetown area city council gained a lot more APC but they have a few SLPP. But still the SLPP are not satisfied, they would like to have Freetown and Makeni. They had the rest of the seventeen councils headed by SLPP, but they wanted to get a foothold in Makeni and in Freetown. And of course most of the assessment of the government happens in the capital city, because that is where all the diplomats stay, and they are giving reports to their national governments. They are the ones who give advice about aid and where to channel it. So the fact that the capital city is not all SLPP was a real problem for the government."

As the nation's biggest big man, Kabbah did not see that the international community would appreciate political diversity as proof of a vibrant democracy; rather he saw himself losing face in front of his own people by failing to gain and retain support in the capital city. He was in power when the new army successfully repelled the RUF invasion in 1999, therefore those who voted for the opposition were deliberately rejecting his achievements. Like Makeni, residents were betraying him, and this made him angry. He used his control over international aid to punish Makeni.

"We know that the diplomats keep an eye on the government when they send their intelligence reports. And I am not talking about the government being corrupt and not doing enough to lift everyone out of poverty immediately. The country is difficult in terms of everyone gaining their livelihood. However, there are basic things government must do, and this is the fifth month that we as a council are going without an allowance. We knew we would not get full salaries; that this position was an honor and a sacrifice and we were expected to keep our old jobs. But there was the expectation that they would compensate us for this work, so that we are not impoverishing our families. At first the allowances came, but now they do not. So we are just barely alive, just merely existing. But we accept our fate right now . . ."

Michael trailed off and spared into space, lost in thought for several minutes. To seek out big man status was a double-edged sword, as the chance for resources, adulation, and permanence was matched by the risk of encountering the jealousy and competing desires of others, leaving one with the possibility of nothing. The rain had died down, leaving us alone with our thoughts, shifting in damp discomfort in the town council conference room, a room laden with humidity and overburdened with expectations. According to Michael, the councilors should have predicted their fate, once the euphoria of victory had passed and they faced reality. Their situation was different from the calculated embrace of members of the disgraced army at the war's end. To welcome soldiers back to barracks was a deliberate act that solidified loyalty where the government needed it most: amongst its fighting factions. Managing the anti-SLPP sentiment of a region that blamed the government for their suffering was quite another situation. Rather than love the region and earn their respect, Kabbah continued punishing them for disloyalty, attempting to force acquiescence through poverty and disaffection, including among the local big men.

The SLPP government used a divide-and-conquer strategy. Making life difficult for the council would slow any progress they could make, thus encouraging townspeople to lose their faith in the APC and vote differently in the next election. The councilors themselves would never find success after failing so miserably to meet expectations, and their bids to become big would have come to naught. I witnessed this situation as it unfolded; from my first weeks in Makeni, when jubilation engulfed the town upon electing their own council, to the joyous occasion of the inauguration, and on through the months of expectation and heartbreak, as the SLPP government turned off the financial taps, sat back, and waited.

Michael and I shared a memory of the council inauguration nearly a year earlier, which President Kabbah had attended. He had a throne on the stage, where his every motion and reaction could be observed. Throughout the inauguration, he acted bored and disinterested, occasionally fiddling with his cell phone, propping his head in his hand, rarely stirring to observe or participate in the proceedings. Kabbah's mood only changed when the program moved to the inauguration of the Bombali district council, which was housed in the same headquarters as the town council. Unlike the all-APC town council, some villages in the district had elected SLPP candidates to represent their interests. As each was called, Kabbah shot to his feet, smiled broadly and applauded wildly.

As Michael had mentioned, the president made no attempt to appear nonpartisan, or even pleased that the first council elections in almost thirty years had taken place, without a hitch, under his administration. What mattered was that everyone knew his displeasure at failing to sweep the elections, and his approbation of district sections loyal to the SLPP. He felt that the whole nation should be grateful to him for bringing the country through war, therefore anyone questioning his hand in this—let alone a whole township stating openly that they did not want him—caused a violent reaction. If the council wanted money, it had to pursue different avenues.

"Instead of just us grumbling about our lack of salaries, we went to the chairman to do something. But he cannot do something without anything. He sympathizes with us. He is a very cheerful young man, very understanding. He was one of my students. He has been working with NGOs, so he has the skills to talk to people and maneuver, convince people to accept the world as it is, to see the reality of the situation. If there were the means to change things around for us he would do it, because he doesn't like to see our people suffering. That you can read from his face and the way he talks to us. This is why he is the chair! He is a sympathetic man.

"And he was also very honest with us. The government was not just slighting us with the allowances. The corruption in the ministries meant that none of the councils were getting their allowances. So we should not feel offended because we are APC, apparently Kabbah could not even manage his funds to take care of his own councils! But he could do other things against us. Whenever the government would get a donation from overseas that was meant for all the councils, they would find a reason not to give us our share. The government received three garbage trucks for the three town councils, but they sent ours to Kono! Kono does not even have a council, but Kabbah's excuse was that we have the Catholic mission here working for us and so they should share the benefits around. Kabbah was punishing us for being APC, he wanted to add to his popularity in the diamond district. You see, Kono was not always for the SLPP; in the past they had their own party. So Kabbah knows he needs to give them enough to keep them with him."

Kabbah's big man status was being threatened by his own inner circle, as the plum cabinet positions he gave his cronies resulted in rampant high-level eating, to the point where the benefits failed to trickle down to his other loyal people on the town councils. Not being as astute at managing the shadow state as Siaka Stevens had been, Kabbah was reduced to telling the councils—all of them—to find their own money. He used the aid he did receive to attempt to consolidate his power in swing districts, as it would have been a waste of resources to attempt to turn Makeni residents.

When Michael and I ended our conversation, it was on a heavy yet hopeful note. Things in Makeni were bad, but they were infinitely better than they had been during the war. However begrudgingly, Kabbah had brought Makeni back into the nation, and stood back while Makeni residents defiantly elected a council of their own choosing. Though handicapped by being the opposition party, they garnered enough external support to keep the council limping along. Not all development money had to come through the national government; on the contrary, the ministry of finance had told the council that they had to receive their own development grants from donors.

When I returned to Makeni in 2006 after six months' absence, the council had received a large grant from an international donor. Within weeks of disbursing the grant, a scandal exploded: embezzlement in the town council. Michael Kamara suddenly found himself in a position to solidify his status, if he could prove that he was a trustworthy challenger to the disgraced town council chairman, his former friend, who now faced the town's wrath and the APC party's disgust.

THE PERMANENCE POWER PLAY: WHO IS MAKENI'S BIGGEST BIG MAN?

In his narrative of May 2005, Michael had nothing but praise for the town council chairman, but a year later everything had changed. The problems began when the council chairman left the grant disbursement in the hands of the deputy chairman and treasurer while he was traveling. The chairman had instructed his deputies to put the contracts for infrastructure improvements—bridges, drainage systems, garbage removal—out to bid to qualified contractors. When he returned, he found contacts awarded to unqualified contractors, bids accepted at extraordinarily high prices, minimal work accomplished, and millions of leones unaccounted for. The town was in an uproar, the APC was howling for his resignation, and the rest of the council obstinately refused to support him. Michael Kamara was leading the charge to remove the chairman. These events were clear manifestations of big man politics, and the importance of lavishing care on constituents.

With limited resources, one who aspires to be big must be willing to pull down the person who stands in their way. Though cohesive and friendly at first, after two years of no allowances, impoverished councilors were squabbling and bitter. Councilors were jostling to put themselves in the best possible position to take advantage of the scandal, and Michael Kamara, as the oldest councilor, was socially in the best position to do so. However, because he was keeping a low profile, I did not seek another interview. In an attempt to sort through the bewildering flood of rumors and conflicting accounts of the scandal, I gathered my research assistants and friends for a conversation.

"It is all about this big man business!" said my neighbor Abu, laughing derisively as he crossed his long legs and rested his chin thoughtfully in his palm. "The chairman thought he could be a big man in this town by following the rules and developing the town honestly. But he thought he could do this without being concerned about how the rest of the councilors were doing. He was not getting his salary and he struggled on his own, but for the rest of the council, they looked up to him to take care of them, because they had elected him to this position. So he was supposed to take care of them like his family. But he would never open the council purse to help them out. It was always, 'No, no, this money is for the operating budget and not for you.' Some of the council members became angry. They were leaning on the treasurer to open the coffers, and he wouldn't do this while the chairman was around. But the treasurer got his own opportunity when the big grant came and the chairman left on a trip."

By the rules of Sierra Leonean sociality, the chairman was failing miserably in his duty to look after his inner circle of loyalty: the other councilors. He was venturing into socially dangerous territory by treating donor money as a public good alone; indeed, how could he think about garbage collection contracts when the other councilors, who elected him as chair, needed food for their families? His own people were struggling to make ends meet. There was no doubt that the chairman had earned his position: he was the most educated councilor, a former program manager for international NGOs who had negotiated with the RUF to bring food convoys to the malnourished town. However he had to work continually to retain his status, which involved ensuring a steady flow of resources to his loyal people. And here he was, thwarting his closest—and most powerful—associates by ignoring their needs. He was failing in his social duties, thus they were within their rights to take what they needed. However, anger and need were also clouded by greed; merely sustaining life was overcome by the temptation to eat, and this is where the councilors overstepped the bounds of proper sociality.

Governance in Sierra Leone is corrupt by Western standards, and in spite of this Sierra Leoneans still believe in the democratic process. It should not be the case in a democracy that elected officials think about helping themselves to the operating budget. However, the councilors had been forced into this position by the exercise of eating that pushed the country to war to begin with. Once reelected, Tejan Kabbah owed his key supporters rewards for years of loyalty, and his supporters—as Stevens' supporters had done before—treated their ministry positions as personal food troughs. They distributed resources to those they *loved* or whose support they themselves needed, and the coffers were emptied. This left the local councils vulnerable.

The councilors had no choice, if they wanted to feed their families, but to pressure the chair to support them where the national government failed. And the chair, as big man, had the duty of love to respond. If he could not or would not, his thwarted councilors had the right to pull him down. The country is poor because high-level consumption has bankrupted the ministries and paralyzed development and social services, but the effects trickle down. Local big men, to maintain their positions in an uncertain economy where salaries fail to arrive, must tap into earmarked funds. And as the local councils flounder on their disappearing budgets, people lean more heavily on their relationships to survive where the government cannot or will not nourish them. The three council members took millions of leones, but whether to feed their families or to become big themselves was never revealed.

The disgraced councilors resigned their positions and melted into the landscape of the town. In spite of his protestations of innocence, the council chairman was not allowed to go quietly. The townspeople were angry. Their council had betrayed them, and youth started spreading rumors that the chairman allowed the embezzlement. Ernest Koroma proclaimed the chairman's guilt, and demanded his resignation from the council and the APC party. As Abu narrated the scandal, it became clear that no matter the chairman's actual guilt or innocence, it was the job of the big man to take the fall:

"They had to make an example of him. The APC had a real problem with their image because Siaka Stevens was corrupt and he just passed it around the party. The international community is suspicious that these bad elements are still around, and also the people are suspicious! The APC will always have support here, but how would they ever make room in the rest of the country with this kind of scandal? So they had to make sure they swept the council clean, and they had to take down the person most responsible. Though he did not take a single leone from the treasury, he was away at the time and could not have done anything wrong . . . well . . . at the end of the day, the chairman is the chairman, right? The conduct of the council is his responsibility."

Traditional big man politics and democracy-driven big man politics collided unhappily in this scandal, as, with limited resources, there was no possibility of being able to satisfy all needy and deserving parties. Voters and councilors had treated the election as a performance of love, rather than political will, and the scandal was a predictable outcome of a financially starved council in an impoverished town. There were simply not enough resources to go around, and many people were going to be neglected, disappointed, bitter, and angry. The chairman's fall was as much vengeance as it was democratic process.

In the end, only four members of the council, including the chairman, were fired. Standing safely on the sidelines was Michael Kamara, the most senior councilor. According to Abu, Michael spent the previous months, as the scandal slowly leaked, quietly maneuvering himself into the best possible position. He made public his independent income, absolving himself of any possibility that he needed the money, or wanted to *eat*. From this distance, he denounced the council officers, attacking their brazen abuse of power, criticizing their bids to be politically big when they had no economic foundation, and calling for their removal. Abu believed that Michael himself started the rumors among the youth about the chairman's role in the embezzlement to add emphasis to his own bid to become chairman. But Abu was not certain about Michael's future on the council: "There are many people who think he is also taking advantage, and some of the councilors are these same people. Perhaps they will pull him down too."

Michael's future as a big man was in question. He had maneuvered himself into a powerful position by playing the RUF and government off each other, launching himself into Sierra Leone's tumultuous, problematic political elite. In his narrative he portrayed it as almost an accident that his earnest concern for the security of his home had turned into a multi-year quest to rescue his hometown from certain destruction. Throughout this process Michael promoted his own interests by building relationships with outsiders, relationships he used to bolster his political ambitions. But why did he harbor these ambitions at all? Why take the risks of being big? One clue is in the case of Sierra Leone's most famous big woman, Mende chief Mammy Yoko, who nurtured and consolidated her power, though she was unable to have children, by adopting dozens of female wards from prominent families in her chiefdom. Michael, invoking Mammy Yoko, had always wanted a daughter:

"As I am talking now, I have four boys. The first one will complete his education soon, he is at the vocational school in Lunsar. The second is in his first year of secondary school, the third is in middle school, the last is in his second year of primary school. I have four boys. I was longing to have a girl, and I never had one. I know what daughters are capable of doing for their parents. Girls are extremely loyal, especially if you are good to them. As we were running from the war, many people in this town survived because their daughters overseas took care of them. Normally boys, except if their parents are very lucky, tend to pay more attention to their wives' parents than their own. This is because the girls have the option of leaving if their husbands are bad! So boys must take good care with their in-laws. But because I never had a girl, I had to put all my effort into these boys, and I am caring for them. I have never sent them to any brother, sister, or uncle to look after them. I am raising them, and I do everything for them. And I hope at the end of the day they will realize that their father has done something for them, and they will give back. I have that hope. I have that hope."

Though he has taken immaculate care of his sons, Michael was uncertain about whether they would appreciate his sacrifices and express their gratitude. He believed girls were more likely show gratitude and tend to aging parents, because they needed a safety net in case of a bad marriage. It was possible in the bleak economic atmosphere of postwar Sierra Leone that his sons would concentrate on satisfying their in-laws once they married. Had he had a daughter, he would have retained her love and gained the loyalty of her husband as well. Michael did not have a son like Alimamy, who in narrative and deed actively performed his love for his mother. Without a girl, a girl like Adama's daughter, the risk of being abandoned in Michael's advancing years was all too frightening a possibility, so he sought other ways to secure a comfortable old age. Becoming big, with resources and a large circle of people, was a possible substitute. Michael's quest for bigness was laid bare in this conversation. His concern about whether his own family relationships were strong enough to ensure that he would be cared for in his old age was the biggest influence in every decision he made. As he was never certain of success, he continued to pour resources into his sons and hope for gratitude, if nothing else.

Makeni, May 2010

I arrived back in Makeni seven years after my first visit to the dusty, beleaguered northern capital. The country had undergone a peaceful transfer of executive power in 2007, and the new president, Ernest Koroma, was a Makeni native. Residents were hopeful that his tenure would mean improvement in the town's infrastructure, even as he promised to apply development money fairly. Some things had changed. Smooth paved roads had replaced the potholed arterial routes through town, and the new commercial buildings flanking them rose smartly from the pockmarked landscape. According to one resident, the SLPP made a last-ditch preelection effort to convince Makeni that it cared by paving the roads, and Makeni people were not fooled. Some things—unemployed youth chatting idly on corners, garbage piled up in ditches—had not changed at all. The town had achieved "city" status by surpassing a population of three hundred thousand in 2009, and the new city council building had governance admonishments painted on the walls: *If you pay your taxes you will see development.* The council had sent the police out to collect a "head tax," which was, according to my former neighbor Abu, "a tax just on being alive! People want to see development first before they are taxed for breathing the air." It was a familiar impasse: residents demanding the government love them first, investing their own resources before squeezing their citizens.

I attempted to reconnect with all those whose stories are in this book, and was more successful with some than others. Time had not been kind to everyone.

Captain Mansaray accepted redundancy in an army drawdown in 2006, and was unsuccessful in finding civilian work. Under pressure to support his aging parents, he applied for security jobs through foreign contractors working in the Middle East. At the time of writing, he was employed as a private security contractor—a gate guard—at a foreign military base in Iraq.

David remained unemployed, prompting him to accept a deal from Special Court prosecutors to testify against RUF commander Issa Sesay. According to a former friend, "he and the other guys who took this deal lost their friends when they returned from Freetown, so they just had to go!" It was widely known in Sierra Leone that the prosecution offered attractive incentives to entice former RUF combatants to serve as prosecution witnesses, but it was unacceptable to his circle in Makeni that David would betray the RUF—even though he had been kidnapped—for money, and thus betray, by association, his friends. He returned to Makeni for a few days in 2009, and had not been seen in town since that time.

Alimamy's family suffered a tragedy when a younger brother died of a mysterious illness in 2006. In his inimitable way, Alimamy had pushed on, deciding after his graduation from secondary school to enroll at the town's polytechnic university. Though his father had maintained his civil service position, the salary money was not enough both to secure Alimamy a place at Fourah Bay College in Freetown, which he dreamed of attending, and also to move the family out of their tiny rented home. At the time of my visit, his family was completing construction on a new house, a handsome structure with large windows. Alimamy commented somewhat resignedly that he accepted that his parents would secure a home before contributing more to his future. Upon my marveling at the house, he brightened, "It is big enough that you can stay the next time you come!"

Kadiatu had moved her business to a larger stall with more storage room. She greeted me warmly, saying that business was still good, as was her family. Her only complaint was the battle she was fighting with a microfinance organization. She had contributed money to a rotating credit account, and had received nothing when her time to collect came. She had taken her case to the anticorruption commission, where it was pending. Ever the businesswoman, she lamented only the fact that, had she kept her money, she could have purchased more stock when prices were low.

Adama lived alone and hosted traveling preachers until she contracted a serious illness in 2008. According to her neighbors, Adama's daughter arranged for her to travel to the United States for treatment, and she never returned. They assumed that she died and was buried in America. Squatters now occupy the house.

Musa lost his NGO job in the aid drawdown in 2006. He worked as a casual laborer for a mobile phone company until a takeover by a rival company resulted in mass layoffs. When I visited him at home he had been unemployed for a year, and was depressed about his prospects. Elizabeth had taken up the burden of paying their daughters' school fees by trading small items in the market. Both girls were healthy and doing well in school.

Michael remained in politics for the rest of his five-year term. He served out his time quietly, and did not stand for reelection in 2009. I visited his home—a stately, fortified building with a large porch and tiled entry—and spent a short time visiting with his son. We phoned Michael, who had been in his natal village for several months. He was rebuilding his ancestral home, and regretted that he would not be able to return before my departure date. We did not have a chance to meet again, but his pilgrimage to the ancestral village implied that he had managed to gain some of the security that he so craved during his political career. The treasured village home marks the ability of a big man to return to his roots, and to meet old age surrounded by extended family.

NARRATIVE, LOVE, AND CHALLENGES TO THE SOCIAL WORLD

Eloquence is a valued skill in Sierra Leone, where it is often said that, "A story only becomes a *good* story if you add something to it." Narrative is the art not just of telling the past, but of doing so in a compelling and socially relevant manner. Michael Jackson describes it as "a vital human strategy for sustaining a sense of agency in the face of disempowering circumstances."[1] The narratives in this book addressed a struggling present as well as a devastating past; indeed the past helps make sense of the present and reinforces the rightness of people's survival. The narrators emphasized qualities that resonated with their ideas of a functioning social world: love for family, sacrifice for others, one's own survival always dependent on relationships, whether with God, rebels, or terrified civilians. Every person emphasized that the government had a duty to act in care of its citizens as its primary responsibility, and that the war would never have persisted—nor the aftermath been so difficult—had politicians loved their fellow Sierra Leoneans as much as they loved themselves. It was government that forced people into other relationships, big men who abandoned their people and compelled them to look for sustenance elsewhere.

At the same time, each narrator emphasized his or her own righteous position within the social world, that each one's choices secured their own survival, from which point they could build a positive world. Captain Mansaray risked his own life defending the actions of his soldiers, and returned to the government that betrayed him, just as Kadiatu traded in looted food to save her own children, and restarted a functioning market for all residents in Makeni. By framing these decisions in a rubric of love, all the narrators emphasized that they were exemplary members of this world, and were defending the *truth* of the world. Narrative became a part of truth-telling, thus a part of world-making, just as it was an explicit political project of demanding the government set the "collaboration" record straight.

Everyone spoke about loyalty as an intrinsic condition of love; however the problem with loyalty is loyal*ties,* the uncomfortable friction that occurs when relationships conflict. People never chose between relationships freely; there were always consequences to prioritizing one relationship over another. There are no perfect loyalties; there is no way to successfully nest one's priorities to satisfy everyone. This was where individuals used narrative to create their social selves in the present. There were many insistent clarifications, individuals emphasizing what they wanted me to see: Michael Kamara was a humble servant of the people, Alimamy *joined* the rebels rather than becoming a rebel, and Adama went to the RUF hospital not because of isolation and fear, but because she had been called to give Jesus to the dying. No one apologized for thinking of the nation second: in doing so they issued a direct challenge to President Kabbah for failing to care for his people first.

In instances where they ostensibly betrayed the nation, narrators made that fact irrelevant compared to their continual validation of the social world by loving, faithfully, in circumstances so dire they defied the cultivation of material relationships. This was a refutation of the accusation of collaboration for material gain—eating—but also a refusal of "bare life." These individuals insisted that they never allowed their situation or their government to strip them of their citizenship or their humanity. They continued to demand their rights as humans by acting as full members of their social world, acting in love and care even when it seemed counterintuitive to do so. Everyone was still Sierra Leonean, and it was therefore unfair of the government to convince the rest of the nation that they were dealing with traitors. Part of telling is being heard: I was listening, which reinforced the rightness of their positions even as there was no possibility of gaining the president's ear.

The turbulent recent history of Makeni was predicated on a disagreement about the answer to a single question: who must take the risk of giving love first, and hope for future return? Do ordinary individuals, from soldiers to farmers to the citizenry of an impoverished town, offer unmitigated loyalty to their president before he nurtures them, or should the big man, the president, embrace his people first? The inherent problem with relationships based on loyalty is that participants must have qualities that make them worth having. Makeni, throughout its history, had no material resources, nothing to offer save each president's pride in possessing the love of the entire nation. Indeed, David also had nothing to make him worth having, except when he picked up a gun. Mohamed was stripped of his ability to contribute because he earned his position through the love of a deposed big man, throwing his loyalty into question. Through the vagaries of fortune, the marginal emerge as those without the recognized ability to contribute, those unworthy of love. The will of people to live harmoniously was the only factor preventing war erupting twenty years earlier. This is itself commentary on the tremendous power of this social world.

The occupation brought issues of marginalization and investment to a head as it clarified how individuals understand their relationships. Residents wanted Kabbah to fight for them by expending resources to liberate the town. Kabbah wanted residents to prove their desire to be part of his nation: fighting for *him* by resisting the occupation, and even sacrificing themselves to the nation by offering their martyrdom. He wanted soldiers, as soldiers are worth having. In an understandable reaction, residents did not want to be part of Kabbah's nation on his terms as much as they wanted to survive the war themselves, to bring their families through safely, to support their friends, and to create small livable spaces out of a hell imposed on them by their president. They refused to be soldiers. From Kadiatu's insistence that the government destroyed the town before the occupation to Musa's narration of the gentlemanly victim, residents demanded recognition as citizens; they insisted that being Sierra Leonean made them worth having, even if they had nothing tangible to give.

With the occupation, Makeni residents were issuing the same challenge to the government as were the young, disaffected members of the RUF: the desire to alter the foundations on which love is offered. From residents steadfastly caring for their families in an occupied town, to the yearnings of RUF members to "belong" to the nation—to have the president call them out of the bush, as one rebel phrased it—each challenged the government to love the people of Sierra Leone first, even as the government was not their own primary concern. In essence, the government's love for its people must be "naked." The president must accept nested loyalties and resist feeling betrayed when citizens prioritize their intimate relationships. This requires a shift in perceptions of bigness as well; it demands that a big man not require constant affirmation from below, that he trust his people, and by extension the nation, with the resources he gives, without demanding they cling to him and punishing them when they do not. This would be an end of eating, an acknowledgement that, though it is more difficult to become big through consensus than through resource monopoly, it is worthwhile to do so. Above all else, a big man should want people to sing his praises.

These are not easy things to petition from a social world; however they are reassuringly nested within that world. No one is asking for an end to love. The RUF certainly did not demand it; Foday Sankoh himself recognized the need to inculcate love within the ranks, to position himself as *pa*. Every individual in this book navigated and interpreted the war through the rubric of love, and they are recreating their worlds in the aftermath on that very same foundation. What they ask for is an end to the systematic inequalities that continually threaten that world even as those same inequalities force everyone to conform to it. They want their very same world, only better.

Notes

INTRODUCTION

1. See articles on gang culture in South Africa by Kate Mooney (1998) and on loyalists in the first Kenyan election by Daniel Branch (2006).

2. See Das's book *Life and Words* (2007, 7). For another example from West Africa of the "event" being always attached to the ordinary, see Mary Moran's book *Liberia: The Violence of Democracy,* where she argues that in Liberia, violence and democracy are mutually constituting forces, so that in "ordinary" life one is always part of the other.

3. See Nordstrom's monograph *A Different Kind of War Story.*

4. See Sverker Finnström's monograph *Living with Bad Surroundings.*

5. See Henrik Vigh's monograph *Navigating Terrains of War.*

6. See Andrew Oldenquist's article "Loyalties," 178.

7. Anthropologist Catherine Lutz, in *Unnatural Emotions,* seeks to deconstruct the Western notion of emotion, arguing that it is a practice that emerges within cultures, not a psychobiological structure that is preexisting and just waiting to be discovered (1988, 4).

8. There is a small but growing literature on resentment—a brooding lack of forgiveness when someone has transgressed—as a moral call to restore a fair world where rights are respected. Rather than sullying the world by harping on the past, resentment instead refuses to accept a diminished world in which transgressions are acceptable (Brudholm 2009; J. Murphy 2003.)

9. In her work with Sierra Leonean Muslims in Washington DC, Joann D'Alisera discovered that the diaspora clung to an image of the cotton tree as representing Sierra Leone. They saw the Freetown cotton tree as a symbol of endurance, cooperation and unity (2004, 42).

10. Ibid., 42.

11. A particularly poignant episode of accusations of witchcraft is discussed in Michael Jackson's book, *Life within Limits* (2011, 138–41).

12. Christopher Webersik makes this argument with respect to violence between sub-clans in Somalia: clans were a way of making claims to resources in a corrupt state. As access to resources shifted with capitalism, clans were perceived as unnecessary for access and loyalty, and therefore fragmented, even at the level of the family (2004, 530). In Sierra Leone, Rosalind Shaw writes that politicians often turn to diviners to help them "consume power" or *eat* resources in ways hidden from ordinary view (1996).

13. See Susan Shepler's 2005 article, "The Rites of the Child."

14. See Hannah Arendt's 1970 book, *On Violence*, 41.

15. Other examples appear in Ashforth (1998, 231) in South Africa, where people use witchcraft to limit the good fortune of their neighbors; and Sanders in rural Tanzania (2003, 164), where witchcraft is part of a social economy of "nightmare egalitarianism." In Guinea-Bissau wealth is kept hidden to avoid jealousy and accusations of witchcraft that would result in leveling (Gable 1997, 213).

16. See the work of Marilyn Strathern on "dividuals" in *The Gender of the Gift*, which concerns the giving of the self through gifts to others, thus making persons dividable among those they nurture.

17. See the work of Gberie (2005), Olonisakin (2008), Abdullah (2004a), Peters (2006); and Richards (1996) respectively. See also Gershoni (1997) and Hoffman (2006).

18. Jean-François Bayart explores expertly the idea of *eating* resources as an expression of power and bigness in *The State in Africa: The Politics of the Belly*. The rush for spoils is the goal of all people, in Bayart's analysis, and some are merely more successful than others.

19. A more erudite discussion of this phenomenon can be found in William Reno's book *Corruption and State Politics in Sierra Leone*. Reno coined the term "the shadow state."

20. Journalist Aminatta Forna wrote her memoir *The Devil That Danced on the Water* about her childhood memories of her father, Mohamed Forna, who was a founding member of the UDP.

21. See Lansa Gberie's 2003 book *A Dirty War in West Africa*.

22. Mariane Ferme argues quite convincingly that Stevens manipulated the Mende political ethos of the importance of unity in politics to push the ideology of a dictatorship (1998, 567).

23. See Alie (1991, 250).

24. This army officer was stationed in a border outpost, and spoke of the "lack of security consciousness" among people in his area of operation who longed for war. As he was a well-paid agent of the APC, they would not hear his pleas in favor of patience.

25. See Kpundeh (2004, 93–94).

26. Keke's experience of the shadow state is echoed in Hannah Arendt's comment on the inherent violence of bureaucracy: "The rule of Nobody is the most tyrannical of all" (2004, 237).

27. See Gberie (2005, 58).

28. See Abdullah (2004a), Gberie (2005, 60), and Olonisakin (2008, 13).

29. These are Alison Des Forges's conclusions, from her report to *Human Rights Watch*, entitled *Leave None to Tell the Story*.

30. See Agamben's book *Homo Sacer: Sovereign Power and Bare Life*, 138.

31. See Richards (1996, 9–10).

32. I found many former student revolutionaries in Freetown who participated by helping Strasser plan the coup. Even qualified students could not penetrate the inner circle of the APC, and many hoped a coup would provide an opening for a return to democracy, from which they as the intelligentsia could benefit (Bolten, 2009).

33. Bai Bureh is a legendary figure in Sierra Leonean history. His arrest by colonial officials sparked the Hut Tax War in 1898. Many RUF commanders took on nicknames to increase their reputations as fearsome warriors. The most common nickname was "Rambo."

34. See Shepler (2005, 199).

35. For a range of children's experiences as members of fighting factions during the war, see Peters and Richards, "Why We Fight" (1998).

36. See W. Murphy (2003, 62).

37. Reintegration was especially problematic for children who were powerful within the RUF. Coulter notes that Sankoh's interest in altering a gerontocratic power structure extended to giving command to children who "proved themselves" on the battlefield.

38. This discussion occurs in more lengthy and erudite fashion in A. Douglass and T. Vogler's introduction to their edited text, *Witness and Memory: The Discourse of Trauma* (2003).

39. See Johannes Fabian's article, "Forgetful Remembering: A Colonial Life in the Congo" (2003).

40. Augé (2004, 17).

41. Ana Douglass recounts the trouble with testimony brilliantly in "The Menchú Effect" (2003).

CHAPTER 1

1. For a description of the material dimension of intimacy, see Cole (2009, 115).

2. Oldenquist (1982, 178).

3. In political economic terms, punishment for disloyalty is called *negative externalities*. See Reno (1995).

4. For concise overviews of the history of Sierra Leone, see C. Magbaily Fyle's *The History of Sierra Leone* and Joe Alie's *A New History of Sierra Leone*. These conclusions are also based on the month of archival research I conducted in the National Archives of the United Kingdom in Kew Gardens, which contains colonial archives of Sierra Leone.

5. Captain Stanley, the commissioner for the northern province, gave the report on the failure of the rice crop for the year 1925. National Archives, Box CO 267 610.

6. In the archive boxes containing official correspondence between administrators and MPs in London were also the "Blue Books," the official yearly reports on the public works expenditures of each province. From the 1920s, when Blue Books began, until independence, Makeni consistently received an average of one public works project for every three that Bo and Kenema received.

7. This was revealed in a Savingram from the governor of Sierra Leone to the secretary of state for the colonies, dated June 21, 1949 (Box CO 267 652).

8. From "Annual Report on the Provinces, 1930" (Box CO 267 634).

9. From "Protectorate Highway Tolls Ordinance, 1936" (Box CO 267 652).

10. See "Public Apology to Dr. Stevens," in *We Yone,* March 20, 1977.

11. The full report can be found in Frank Kposowa's 1986 article, "Wusum Kinsmen Honor Minister."

12. The skirmishes over the local administrator's refusal to grant Makeni a civil militia came to a head in a demonstration in 1994, with soldiers firing into a crowd and killing several people. The administrator was replaced, and the situation returned to what I would call the "tense ordinary" of a nation that is at war, but has not yet seen fighting. The event and aftermath were documented heavily in Freetown newspapers.

13. Responses include Karwigoko Roy Stevens's article "Riding a Tiger"; the anonymously penned letter "Why Should the North Apologize?"; Sorie Fofanah's "Kabbah: An Unfortunate Northerner!"; Ourmar Farouk Sesay's "Who Said These Words?"; and Mustapha Sesay's "Why the Fuss about Kabbah's Makeni Speech?"

14. See "Minister Assures North" in *For Di People* from March 25, 1999.

15. See "Rebels Demand Money from Upline Escapees" in *For Di People* from May 18, 1999.

16. See "ECOMOG Must Leave Makeni" in *Awoko* from November 20, 1999, and "Makeni Feels Unwanted" in *The New Citizen* from November 25, 1999.

17. See "No Funds for Northern Province" in *For Di People* from December 22, 1999.

18. See "Disastrous Exodus from Makeni to Nowhere" and "Thousands Flee or Perish" in *The New Citizen.*

19. The received wisdom in Freetown was that ex-combatants remained in Makeni because they were too afraid to return home, having committed atrocities in their home areas, and also because they were welcomed by Makeni resident/collaborators. See Bolten (2008) for counterarguments.

CHAPTER 2

1. The earliest archival mention of Njala University is from 1924 (British Archives, Box CO 267 629), when it rose to prominence as the colony's premier agricultural research station.

2. This headdress is the small, decorated round cap known in West Africa as the *kufi,* meaning crown. Elders wear it to denote their wisdom and status as leaders. The fact that Strasser, aged thirty, wore the *kufi* is perhaps one indication of why he was no longer appropriate as chairman.

3. Lansana Gberie believes that the *sobel* phenomenon started in 1994, when soldiers loyal to officer Yayah Kanu, who was executed for refusing to join the NPRC coup, joined the RUF after losing their commander (2005, 81).

4. This comment refers to the fact that Siaka Stevens had purged the army of Mende officers and inserted only Limbas into positions of power. In the intervening five years of war, most young officers were recruited, as Valentine Strasser himself had been, from the "militariat" elements of undereducated, otherwise unemployed working youth in Freetown (Kandeh 1996, 388).

5. Gberie (2005, 84).

6. Zack-Williams (1997, 375).

7. Hoffman (2006, 5).

8. Cannibalism permeates stories of ritual in Sierra Leone, especially the rituals of "witches," whose consumption of human flesh brings them power and wealth in the invisible "witch city" (Shaw 2002, 207–8). It is handmaiden to deeply unsocial practices, such as secretiveness and eating alone, but creates emotional and ideological impasses when one depends on these same people for protection.

9. Shepler (2004, 20).

10. I interviewed one officer who was stripped, beaten, and locked in the trunk of a car for two days before being released. Because he was a quartermaster, responsible for soldiers' rations and welfare, he bore the brunt of the blame for his soldiers' neglect under both the decadent NPRC and during the Kamajors' rise. He was widely despised for his openly lavish lifestyle. According to one lance corporal, even an honest soldier would be tempted to go after such an officer.

11. Gberie (2005, 113).

12. Gberie (2005, 115).

13. See Just (2001).

14. Uvin (2009).

15. Lewis (2005) and Fowler (2007) have covered this event in the popular press.

16. See Brudholm (2009), Cole (2010), and Wilson (2001) for examinations of the role of resentment in victims' refusal to forgive, the TRC as a theatric performance of transition to a post-apartheid state, and the TRC as vehicle legitimizing the post-apartheid state by attaching it to human rights discourse.

17. See Besteman (2008).

CHAPTER 3

1. See Bledsoe (1990 and 1992).

2. In her work in Belfast, Begona Aretxaga (1997) described the decisions made by young people to engage in IRA activities as "choiceless decisions": the prospect of bodily death in IRA activities was countered by the guarantee of social death if one refused to participate.

3. Peters notes that using punishment to prevent escape will initially enhance cohesion, but if it is used excessively "recruits" will look for more opportunities to escape (2006, 62). For Peters, the RUF's cohesion was promoted by the

institution of a "people's court" to adjudicate matters of punishment. Cadres were thereby invested in the process of internal "justice," and had a framework from which to invest in being a rebel.

4. See Jackson (1994).

5. Fabian notes that when people speak of past events, silence, perhaps the active will to forget the past as part of memory construction, must necessarily speak louder than words as an acknowledgement that the unspoken can still be understood (2003, 493). I argue here that the unspoken can be acknowledged, if not necessarily understood implicitly.

6. See Peters (2006, 67) and Richards (2001, 79).

7. Human Rights Watch (2003, 21, 41).

8. Relationships of exchanging coerced sex for protection are a common feature of war. Women in Berlin were forced into similar situations with occupying Russian forces during the Second World War, and were often better nourished than their noncompliant counterparts. Despite its commonness, the topic is still so stigmatized that even the most famous journalistic account of war-coerced sexual relations in Berlin continues to be published anonymously, several years after the author's death (*A Woman in Berlin, A Diary* 2000).

9. Chris Coulter (2009) argues that the actions people tolerate in war are shaped by what they tolerate in peace. The treatment of women in the RUF was merely an extension of the servitude and docility women were meant to display in ordinary times.

10. This was caught on camera by Sierra Leonean filmmaker Sorious Samura in his movie *Cry Freetown*.

11. Gberie (2005, 257).

12. Ashby (2000, 189).

13. See Hanlon (2005, 461), Peters (2006, 129), and Nilsson (2008).

14. "Issa Sesay Dismantles the RUF in Makeni" in *Awoko* from May 21, 2002.

15. Peters (2006, 122).

16. Peters is kinder to the ex-combatants, arguing that because the United Nations farmed out skills training to many different organizations, it was impossible to standardize the quality of training.

17. Coulter (2009) documents how relationships of love circulated resources into impoverished households. Ex-combatants married local women, who channeled money and food to their families. Ex-combatants were appreciated by local people for their good faith effort to be loving people.

18. See Ginifer (2003, 46).

19. In her work with demobilized women, Coulter found that some women were denied the opportunity to marry their bush husbands legally because their families objected. Some remained as shunned members of their natal families, others remained with their husbands (2009, 10).

20. Michael Jackson wrote about the central paradox of life: "We must both open ourselves up to and, to some extent, seal ourselves off from the surrounding world if we are to survive. While complete closure and fixity hastens entropy, absolute openness also increases the likelihood that life will be lost" (2011, 95).

CHAPTER 4

Chapter epigraph is from Jackson (2002, 22).

1. See also Appadurai (1986).

2. See Jensen (2008), Sen (2007), and Trawick (2007).

3. See Jackson (2004) for a corroborating story of the children of the RUF taking the lead in the attack.

4. See Busbandt (2008), Nkpa (1977), and Pandey (2002) for articulations of the power of rumor.

5. As much as people invoked *love* during the war, they often complained about it during peace, as one is more likely to get a job with "family" connections, even if one is not qualified for that work. See Cohen (1981).

CHAPTER 5

1. See Bledsoe (1990) and Shepler (2004).

2. See Akanji and Famuwiya (1993).

3. For a parallel situation in another cultural context, see *A Woman in Berlin* (2000).

4. Daniel Goldstein writes about a similar attitude among shanty communities in Bolivia who practice vigilante justice. He argues that vigilantism doesn't occur outside the state, rather it presupposes the existence of the state, and demands that the state act as legitimate as it claims to be, by upholding its duties towards all citizens (2003, 24).

5. Journalist Daniel Bergner wrote about his time with Ellis in his book *In the Land of Magic Soldiers: A Story of White and Black in West Africa* (2003).

6. Clark describes traders in Kumasi, Ghana, having a relationship with the state that is mutually dependent and constantly negotiated, as each side attempts to extract more resources from the other (1994, 392).

CHAPTER 6

1. Among Mayan widows in Guatemala, evangelical Protestant sects, locally called *cultos,* drew worshipers away from the Catholic faith (Green 1999). That the *cultos* were social was the source of their popularity: the services were personalized and pleasant, pastors were community members, and prayer addressed everyday problems such as alcoholic husbands and unemployed sons.

2. Michael Jackson documented an entire community in northeastern Sierra Leone participating in the killing of a witch in the 1990s. Twenty years later, the community stood behind the killing as socially correct, because a witch is not human (2011, 138–40).

CHAPTER 7

1. See Human Rights Watch (2003), Hoffman (2003), Rosen (2007).

2. Susan Shepler argues it was inimical to social healing when children in Sierra Leone were not held accountable for their crimes during the war. In times

of peace, Sierra Leonean children exercise an extensive agency denied to the "protected" Western childhood; the responsibility accompanying this agency stems from the fact that a child who does not work and obey elders is a bad child (2004 and 2005).

3. RUF commanders distinguished between camp helpers and members of the Small Boys Units. Everyone used the domestic services provided by children in the camps, whose jobs ranged from drawing water to cooking meals, but to take charge of a combat unit of small children was another matter entirely.

4. See Ashby (2002).

5. The program Musa worked for was not the United Nations' DDR, which was responsible for the sub-par training that left so many ex-combatants with no option but to sell their toolkits. He worked for a private NGO that trained all "war-affected youth" in literacy, numeracy, and basic artisanal skills.

CHAPTER 8

1. See Ferme (2001).

EPILOGUE

1. Jackson (2002, 15).

Bibliography

SUGGESTED READING

Forna, A. 2002. *The Devil That Danced on the Water: A Daughter's Quest.* New York: Atlantic Monthly Press.

Mahmood, C. 1996. *Fighting for Faith and Nation: Dialogues with Sikh Militants.* Philadelphia: University of Pennsylvania Press.

Olonisakin, 'F. 2008. *Peacekeeping in Sierra Leone: The Story of UNAMSIL.* Boulder: Lynne Reinner.

Weigert, K.M. 2008. "Structural Violence." In *The Encyclopedia of Violence, Peace and Conflict,* vol. 3, edited by L. Kurtz. Oxford: Elsevier.

FREETOWN NEWSPAPER ARTICLES

Conteh, S. 1994. "Trouble in Makeni." *The New Globe.* April 20–24.

"Disastrous Exodus from Makeni to Nowhere." 2000. *The New Citizen.* June 8.

"ECOMOG Must Leave Makeni." 1999. *Awoko.* November 20.

Fofanah, S. 1996. "Kabbah: An Unfortunate Northerner!" *The Vision.* November 28.

"Government Sends Peace Mission to Makeni." 1994. *The New Citizen.* April 25.

"How Makeni Exploded into Violence and Death." 1994. *The New Citizen.* April 25.

"Issa Sesay Dismantles the RUF in Makeni." 2002. *Awoko.* May 21.

Kposowa, F., with F.J. 1986. "Wusum Kinsmen Honor Minister." *The New Citizen.* January 16.

"Makeni Feels Unwanted." 1999. *The New Citizen.* November 25.

"Makeni Now Calm." 1994. *The Weekly Echo.* April 26–30.

"Minister Assures North." 1999. *For Di People*. March 25.

"No Funds for Northern Province." 1999. *For Di People*. December 22.

"People's Defense Force Formed." 1994. *The New Citizen*. April 25.

"Public Apology to Dr. Stevens." 1977. *We Yone*. March 20.

"Rebels Demand Money from Upline Escapees." 1999. *For Di People*. May 18.

Sesay, M. 1996. "Why the Fuss about Kabbah's Makeni Speech?" *The Standard Times: Plein Tok*. December 2.

Sesay, O. M. 1996. "Who Said These Words?" *For Di People*. November 30.

Stevens, K. R. 1996. "Riding a Tiger." *The Daily Mail*. November 21.

"Thousands Flee or Perish." 2000. *The New Citizen*. June 12.

"Why Should the North Apologize?" 1996. *The New Citizen*. November 28.

SECONDARY SOURCES

Abdullah, I. 2004a. "Bush Path to Destruction: The Origin and Character of the Revolutionary United Front (RUF/SL)." In *Between Democracy and Terror: The Sierra Leone Civil War*, edited by I. Abdullah. Dakar: CODESRIA.

———. 2004b. "Introduction: Between Democracy and Terror." In *Between Democracy and Terror: The Sierra Leone Civil War*, edited by I. Abdullah. Dakar: CODESRIA.

Abraham, A. 2004. "The Elusive Quest for Peace: From Abidjan to Lome." In *Between Democracy and Terror: The Sierra Leone Civil War*, edited by I. Abdullah. Dakar: CODESRIA.

Agabmen, G. 1998. *Homo Sacer: Sovereign Power and Bare Life*. Palo Alto: Stanford University Press.

Akanji, A., and O. Famuyiwa. 1993. "The Effects of Chronic Cassava Consumption, Cyanide Intoxication and Protein Malnutrition on Glucose Tolerance in Growing Rats." *British Journal of Nutrition* 69: 269–76.

Alie, J. 1991. *A New History of Sierra Leone*. London: Macmillan Africa.

Appadurai, A. 1986. "Introduction." In *The Social Life of Things: Commodities in Cultural Perspective*. Cambridge: Cambridge University Press.

Arendt, H. 1970. *On Violence*. Orlando: Harvest Books.

Aretxaga, B. 1997. *Shattering Silence: Women and Political Subjectivity in Northern Ireland*. Princeton: Princeton University Press.

Ashby, P. 2002. *Unscathed*. London: Macmillan.

Ashforth, A. 1998. "Witchcraft, Violence, and Democracy in the New South Africa." *Cahiers d'Études Africaines* 38(150–52): 505–32.

Augé, M. 2004. *Oblivion*. Translated by M. de Jager. Minneapolis: University of Minnesota Press.

A Woman in Berlin, A Diary: Eight Weeks in the Conquered City. 2000. New York: Metropolitan Books.

Bayart, J.-F. 2009. *The State in Africa: The Politics of the Belly*. Malden, MA: Polity Press.

Beah, I. 2007. *A Long Way Gone: The True Story of a Child Soldier*. New York: Harper Collins.

Berdal, M., and D. Malone. 2000. *Greed and Grievance: Economic Agenda in Civil War*. Boulder: Lynne Reiner.

Bergner, D. 2003. *In the Land of Magic Soldiers: A Story of White and Black in West Africa*. New York: Farrar, Strauss, and Giroux.

Besteman, C. 2008. *Transforming Cape Town*. Berkeley: University of California Press.

Bledsoe, C. 1990. "No Success without Struggle: Social Mobility and Hardship for Foster Children in Sierra Leone." *Man* 25(1): 70–88.

———. 1992. "The Cultural Transformation of Western Education in Sierra Leone." *Africa: The Journal of the International Africa Institute* 62(2): 182–202.

Bolten, C. 2008. "'The Place Is So Backward': Durable Morality and Creative Development in Northern Sierra Leone." PhD diss., University of Michigan, Ann Arbor.

———. 2009. "Rethinking Burgeoning Political Consciousness: Student Activists, the Class of '99 and Political Intent in Sierra Leone." *The Journal of Modern African Studies* 47(3): 349–69.

Branch, D. 2006. "Loyalists, Mau Mau, and the Elections in Kenya: The First Triumph of the System, 1957–1958." *Africa Today* 53(2): 27–50.

Brudholm, T. 2009. *Resentment's Virtue: Jean Amery and the Refusal to Forgive*. Philadelphia: Temple University Press.

Burchell, G. 1991. *The Foucault Effect: Essays in Governmentality*. Chicago: University of Chicago Press.

Busbandt, N. 2008. "Rumors, Pamphlets, and the Politics of Paranoia in Indonesia." *The Journal of Asian Studies* 67(3): 789–817.

Clark, G. 1994. *Onions Are My Husband: Survival and Accumulation by West African Market Women*. Chicago: University of Chicago Press.

Cohen, A. 1981. *The Politics of Elite Culture: Explorations in the Dramaturgy of Power in a Modern African Society*. Berkeley: University of California Press.

Cole, C. 2010. *Performing South Africa's Truth Commission: Stages of Transition*. Bloomington: Indiana University Press.

Cole, J. 2009. "Love, Money, and Economies of Intimacy in Tamatave, Madagascar." In *Love in Africa*, edited by J. Cole and L. Thomas. Chicago: University of Chicago Press.

Coulter, C. 2009. *Bush Wives and Girl Soldiers: Women's Lives through War and Peace in Sierra Leone*. Ithaca: Cornell University Press.

D'Alisera, J. 2004. *An Imagined Geography: Sierra Leonean Muslims in America*. Philadelphia: University of Pennsylvania Press.

Das, V. 2007. *Life and Words: Violence and the Descent into the Ordinary*. Berkeley: University of California Press.

Des Forges, A. 1999. *Leave None to Tell the Story: Genocide in Rwanda*. New York: Human Rights Watch.

Douglass, A. 2003. "The Menchú Effect: Strategic Lies and Approximate Truths in Texts of Witnessing." In *Witness and Memory: The Discourse of Trauma*, edited by A. Douglass and T. Vogler. New York: Routledge.

Douglass, A., and T. Vogler. 2003. "Introduction." In *Witness and Memory: The Discourse of Trauma*, edited by A. Douglass and T. Vogler. New York: Routledge.

Fabian, J. 2003. "Forgetful Remembering: A Colonial Life in the Congo." *Africa: Journal of the International African Institute* 73(4): 489–504.

Fermé, M. 1998. "The Violence of Numbers: Consensus, Competition, and the Negotiation of Disputes in Sierra Leone." *Cahiers d'Études Africaines* 38(150–52): 555–80.

———. 2001. *The Underneath of Things: Violence, History, and the Everyday in Sierra Leone.* California: University of California Press.

Finnström, S. 2008. *Living with Bad Surroundings: War, History, and Everyday Moments in Northern Uganda.* Durham: Duke University Press.

Fowler, W. 2007. *Operation Barras: The SAS Rescue Mission, Sierra Leone 2000.* London: Cassell Military Paperbacks.

Fyle, C.M. 1981. *The History of Sierra Leone.* London: Evans Brothers.

Gable, E. 1997. "A Secret Shared: Fieldwork and the Sinister in a West African Village." *Cultural Anthropology* 12(2): 213–33.

Gberie, L. 2005. *A Dirty War in West Africa: The RUF and the Destruction of Sierra Leone.* Bloomington: Indiana University Press.

Gershoni, Y. 1997. "War without End and an End to War: The Prolonged Wars in Liberia and Sierra Leone." *African Studies Review* 40(3): 55–76.

Ginifer, J. 2003. "Reintegration of Ex-combatants." In *Peacekeeping in Sierra Leone: UNAMSIL Hits the Home Straight,* edited by M. Malan, P. Rakate, and A. McIntyre. Pretoria: Institute for Security Studies.

Goldstein, D. 2003. "In Our Own Hands: Lynching, Justice and the Law in Bolivia." *American Ethnologist* 30(1): 22–43.

Green, L. 1999. *Fear as a Way of Life: Mayan Widows in Rural Guatemala.* New York: Columbia University Press.

Hanlon, J. 2005. "Is the International Community Helping to Recreate the Preconditions for War in Sierra Leone?" *The Round Table* 94(381): 459–72.

Hoffman, D. 2003. "Like Beasts in the Bush: Synonyms of Childhood and Youth in Sierra Leone." *Postcolonial Studies* 6(3): 295–308.

———. 2006. "Disagreement: Dissent Politics and War in Sierra Leone." *Africa Today* 52(3): 3–22.

Human Rights Watch. 2003. *We'll Kill You If You Cry: Sexual Violence in the Sierra Leone Conflict.* 15(1).

Humphrey, C. 1997. "Exemplars and Rules: Aspects of the Discourse of Moralities in Mongolia." In *The Ethnography of Moralities,* edited by S. Howell. Routledge: London and New York.

Jackson, J. 1994. "Chronic Pain and the Tension between Body as Subject and Object." In *Embodiment and Experience: The Existential Ground between Culture and Self,* edited by T. Csordas. Cambridge: Cambridge University Press.

Jackson, M. 2002. *The Politics of Storytelling: Violence, Transgression and Intersubjectivity.* Copenhagen: Museum Tuscalanum Press.

———. 2004. *In Sierra Leone.* Durham: Duke University Press.

———. 2011. *Life within Limits: Well-Being in a World of Want.* Durham: Duke University Press.

Jensen, S. 2008. *Gangs, Politics, and Dignity in Cape Town.* Chicago: University of Chicago Press.

Just, P. 2001. *Dou Donggo Justice.* New York: Rowman and Littlefield.

Kandeh, J. 1996. "What Does the 'Militariat' Do When It Rules? Military Regimes: The Gambia, Sierra Leone, and Liberia." *Review of African Political Economy* 23(69): 387–404.

———. 2003. "Sierra Leone's Post-conflict Elections of 2002." *The Journal of Modern African Studies* 41(2): 189–216.

Kpundeh, S. 2004. "Corruption and Political Insurgency in Sierra Leone." In *Between Democracy and Terror: The Sierra Leone Civil War*, edited by I. Abdullah. Dakar: CODESRIA.

Lewis, D. 2005. *Operation Certain Death*. London: Arrow.

Lutz, C. 1988. *Unnatural Emotions: Everyday Sentiments on a Micronesian Atoll and Their Challenge to Western Theory*. Chicago: University of Chicago Press.

———. 1999. "Ethnography at the War Century's End." *The Journal of Contemporary Ethnography* 28(6): 610–19.

MacLeod, J. 2009. *Ain't No Makin' It: Aspirations and Attainment in a Low-Income Neighborhood*. 3rd ed. New York: Westview Press.

Mooney, K. 1998. "'Ducktails, Flick-Knives, and Pugnacity': Subcultural and Hegemonic Masculinities in South Africa, 1948–1960." *The Journal of Southern African Studies* 24(4): 753–74.

Moran, M. 2006. *Liberia: The Violence of Democracy*. Philadelphia: University of Pennsylvania Press.

Muana, P. 1997. "The Kamajoi Militia in Sierra Leone: Civil War, Internal Displacement, and the Politics of Counter-Insurgency." *Africa Development* 22(3–4): 77–100.

Murphy, J. 2003. *Getting Even: Forgiveness and Its Limits*. Oxford: Oxford University Press.

Murphy, W. 2003. "Military Patrimonialism and Child Soldier Clientalism in the Liberian and Sierra Leonean Civil Wars." *African Studies Review* 46(2): 61–87.

Nilsson, R. A. 2008. *Dangerous Liaisons: Why Ex-Combatants Return to Violence, Cases From the Republic of Congo and Sierra Leone*. Uppsala: Department of Peace and Conflict Research, Uppsala University.

Nkpa, N. K. 1977. "Rumors of Mass Poisoning in Biafra." *The Public Opinion Quarterly* 41(3): 332–46.

Nordstrom, C. 1997. *A Different Kind of War Story*. Philadelphia: University of Pennsylvania Press.

Oldenquist, A. 1982. "Loyalties." *The Journal of Philosophy* 79(4): 173–93.

Opala, J. 1998. "Sierra Leone: The Politics of State Collapse." An essay prepared for the SAIC Conference on Irregular Warfare in Liberia and Sierra Leone, Denver, July 30 to August 1, 1998.

Pandey, G. 2002. "The Long Life of Rumor." *Alternatives: Global, Local, Political* 27(2): 165–91.

Peters, K. 2006. "Footpaths to Reintegration: Armed Conflict, Youth, and the Rural Crisis in Sierra Leone." PhD diss., Wageningen University, Netherlands.

Peters, K., and P. Richards. 1998. "Why We Fight: Voices of Youth Combatants in Sierra Leone." *Africa: Journal of the International African Institute* 68(2): 183–210.

Reno, W. 1995. *Corruption and State Politics in Sierra Leone.* Cambridge: Cambridge University Press.

Richards, P. 1996. *Fighting for the Rain Forest: War, Youth, and Resources in Sierra Leone.* Oxford: James Currey.

———. 2001. "Are Forest Wars Resource Conflicts? The Case of Sierra Leone." In *Violent Environments,* edited by N. Peluso and M. Watts. Ithaca: Cornell University Press.

Rosen, L. 2007. "Child Soldiers, International Humanitarian Law, and the Globalization of Childhood." *American Anthropologist* 109(2): 296–306.

Sanders, T. 2003. "Invisible Hands and Visible Goods: Revealed and Concealed Economies in Millenial Tanzania." In *Transparency and Conspiracy: Ethnographies of Suspicion in the New World Order,* edited by T. Sanders and H. West. Durham: Duke University Press.

Scarry, E. 1988. *The Body in Pain: The Making and Unmaking of the World.* Oxford: Oxford University Press.

Sen, A. 2007. *Shiv Sena Women: Violence and Communalism in a Bombay Slum.* Bloomington: University of Indiana Press.

Shaw, R. 1996. "The Politician and the Diviner: Divination and the Consumption of Power in Sierra Leone." *Journal of Religion in Africa* 26(1): 30–55.

———. 2002. *Memories of the Slave Trade: Ritual and the Historical Imagination in Sierra Leone.* Chicago: University of Chicago Press.

Shepler, S. 2004. "The Social and Cultural Context of Child Soldiering in Sierra Leone." Paper for the PRIO-sponsored workshop on Techniques of Violence in Civil War. Oslo, August 21–24, 2004.

———. 2005. "The Rites of the Child: Global Discourses of Youth and Reintegrating Child Soldiers in Sierra Leone." *The Journal of Human Rights* 4(2): 197–211.

Strathern, M. 1990. *The Gender of the Gift: Problems with Women and Problems with Society in Melanesia.* Berkeley: University of California Press.

Trawick, M. 2007. *Enemy Lines: War, Childhood, and Play in Batticaloa.* Berkeley: University Of California Press.

Uvin, P. 2009. *Life after Violence: A People's Story of Burundi.* London: Zed Books.

Vigh, H. 2006. *Navigating Terrains of War: Youth and Soldiering in Guinea-Bissau.* New York: Berghahn Books.

Webersik, C. 2004. "Differences That Matter: The Struggle of the Marginalised in Somalia." *Africa: Journal of the International African Institute* 74(4): 516–33.

Wilson, R. 2001. *The Politics of Truth and Reconciliation in South Africa: Legitimizing the Post-Apartheid State.* Cambridge: Cambridge University Press.

Zack-Williams, A. B. 1997. "Kamajors, 'Sobel,' and the Militariat: Civil Society and the Return of the Military in Sierra Leonean Politics." *Review of African Political Economy* 24(73): 373–80.

Index